METHADONE TREATMENT IN NARCOTIC ADDICTION

Program Management, Findings, and Prospects for the Future

METHADONE TREATMENT IN NARCOTIC ADDICTION

Program Management, Findings, and Prospects for the Future

ROBERT G. NEWMAN, M.D., M.P.H.
Beth Israel Medical Center
and
Mount Sinai School of Medicine
New York, New York

In collaboration with
MARGOT S. CATES
New York City Department of Health
New York, New York

ACADEMIC PRESS New York San Francisco London 1977
A Subsidiary of Harcourt Brace Jovanovich, Publishers

ACADEMIC PRESS, INC.
111 Fifth Avenue, New York, New York 10003

United Kingdom Edition published by
ACADEMIC PRESS, INC. (LONDON) LTD.
24/28 Oval Road, London NW1

Library of Congress Cataloging in Publication Data

Newman, Robert G
Methadone treatment in narcotic addiction.

Bibliography: p.
Includes index.
1. Narcotic habit–Treatment. 2. Methadone Irydrochloride. I. Cates, Margot S., joint author. II. Title. [DNLM: 1. Methadone–Therapeutic use. 2. Heroin addiction–Rehabilitation. WM288 N554m]
RC566.N48 362.2′93′097471 77-74059
ISBN 0–12–517050–5

PRINTED IN THE UNITED STATES OF AMERICA

Contents

Preface

This book discusses the history, policies, procedures, and experiences of the two largest addiction treatment programs in the country: the Methadone Maintenance Treatment Program and the Ambulatory Detoxification Program of the New York City Department of Health. In the four years following its inception in November, 1970, the New York City Methadone Maintenance Treatment Program admitted over 20,000 individuals, and by December, 1974, had an active patient census of 11,469. The New York City Ambulatory Detoxification Program, which began in July, 1971, had 63,500 admissions through December, 1974, representing 38,000 different individuals.

In Part I, the rationale for these programs, their planning and implementation, and selected policy issues are discussed. This section deals with several issues that are not unique to the field of addiction treatment: the problems encountered in the rapid development of a wide network of service units, administered locally but adhering to procedures established and monitored by a central office, are relevant to any large-scale social program; the difficulties of reconciling the perceived self-interest of the general community with that of a special, narrowly defined target population occur in any program with high visibility, serving individuals identified as antisocial; the rationale for ensuring strict confidentiality of client records and the difficulties inherent in implementing such safeguards involve conflicts that arise in any discussion of the "right to privacy"; and the ethical questions associated with coercing individuals to enter a "treatment" program on the grounds that it is in their own interests arise with respect to all forms of deviant behavior.

Part II is prefaced by a summary of the major conclusions drawn from the comprehensive analyses of program data. In the chapters which follow, the experience of the New York City Methadone Maintenance and Ambulatory Detoxification Programs, from their inception to 1975, is described in detail with respect to intake of applicants, the characteristics of those applicants, and their course during treatment and following discharge.

These programs are a product of the cooperative efforts of the New York City Department of Health and numerous other City agencies, voluntary and municipal hospitals, community service organizations, and countless individuals who contributed their time, interest, and knowledge. To the degree that the programs have achieved their objectives, however, the primary credit belongs to the patients themselves.

ROBERT G. NEWMAN, M.D., M.P.H.

Acknowledgments

This book was made possible through the support of the Drug Abuse Council, Inc., of Washington, D.C. Alex Tytun and Sylvia Bashkow, of the New York City Department of Health, played a key role in the editing of the manuscript. The computer systems which permitted the detailed analyses presented in the second part of this book were developed by Bent Werbell, Project Manager of the New York City Health Services Administration Electronic Data Processing Center.

Robert DuPont, Director of the National Institute on Drug Abuse, Peter Bourne and Methea Falco, of the Drug Abuse Council, Inc., Vincent Dole and Marie Nyswander, of The Rockefeller University, James Kagen, formerly First Deputy Commissioner of the New York City Addiction Services Agency, and Herbert Singer, member of the Board of Trustees of the Beth Israel Medical Center, reviewed the manuscript and provided constant support and encouragement.

The annual budget of the Methadone Maintenance Program (fiscal year 1975) was $20 million, of which $3.6 million came from the State Drug Abuse Control Commission (contract #77634); $6.7 million from City tax-levy funds; and the remainder from Medicaid reimbursement for eligible patients. The Detoxification Program budget was $1.3 million: $250,000 from the Model Cities Administration (contract #CBE 19); $370,000 from the National Institute on Drug Abuse (contract #1-H80-DA-01577-01); and the balance from City funds.

Margot Sands Cates

No one has been more instrumental in the writing of this book or in the operation of the programs which it describes than Margot Sands Cates. She was directly responsible for the design, implementation, and operation of the management information systems of the New York City Ambulatory Detoxification and Methadone Maintenance Programs. In addition to permitting the comprehensive analyses presented in Part II of this book, these systems have continued to serve as the foundation upon which rest the ongoing monitoring, evaluation, and control of the programs. Ms. Cates also directed the New York City Narcotics Register from 1972 to 1975; during this time she created a unique, fully computerized resource for addiction research from what had previously been an unwieldy, out-of-date, incomplete, and duplicative manual directory. Some of the cooperative studies in which the Register has participated are reported in Chapters 15, 18, and 20.

Beyond these operational responsibilities, however, Ms. Cates played an even more critical role in determining the philosophy, policies, and procedures of the two treatment programs. In fact, for almost four years, every decision of any consequence was reached only after her input had been obtained.

On March 10, 1977, two months after this manuscript had been submitted for publication, Ms. Cates died of carcinoma. She was 31 years old. As a token of my gratitude and devotion, this book is dedicated to her memory, to her husband Jim, and to their son Alexander.

ROBERT G. NEWMAN, M.D., M.P.H.

Introduction

THE PAST AND THE PRESENT

The most recent wave of concern regarding narcotic addiction in the United States culminated in early 1972 when drug abuse was proclaimed the major domestic crisis facing the nation (1). The alleged changes in the century-old problem of drug addiction which gave rise to this intense concern were as follows:

The increase in the 1960's of the absolute number of addicted individuals
The spread of the problem from urban ghettos to smaller communities and the middle and upper classes
The rise in narcotic use among adolescent and preadolescent youths
The increase of crime, attributed in large part to the growing addict population
The reports of widespread narcotic use by American military forces and a growing concern over the impact of thousands of addicted soldiers returning to this country

In fact, each of these developments had played a similar role fifty years earlier in precipitating public alarm over addiction. In 1916, ". . . an estimate purported to establish that there were 200,000 highly dangerous drug fiends roaming the streets of New York City . . ." and within a few years this figure had increased to 300,000. The New York City Commissioner of Health in 1919 told the press that drug addiction ". . . is born in the underworld and is the twin brother of every crime in the great categories of violence." By 1920 it was reported that ". . . there were 1.5 million 'victims of the drug habit' in the United States, that no part of the country was without its quota of addicts, and that the problem was ballooning everywhere. . . . It was authoritatively reported and widely believed that drug abuse had shifted its point of incidence and overnight had become a great threat to young people; 70% of known addicts were discovered to be under twenty-five years of age; children in the New York public school system were allegedly turning up in their classrooms completely stoned." The problem was no longer confined to "criminal classes," but extended to all levels of society. Simultaneously, "... it was revealed that drug peddlers were concentrating their efforts on military camps, ... that new addicts were being found in alarming numbers among young soldiers," and there were "press rumors about addicts in the armed forces and 'dope fiends' coming home from overseas to menace the community" (2).

Although the focus of public concern was identical in both eras, the response of the government was markedly different. Beginning in the early 1920's, drug addiction was, for all practical purposes, removed from the purview of the medical profession and delegated to the law enforcement agencies. In 1922, a Congressman described Federal policy in managing drug dependence:

> It seems to me that the untutored narcotics agents of this great Government... might have been better employed than in taking sides in a medical controversy involving the broad subject of what will or will not constitute the proper medication in the treatment of addiction. Yet this was done, and I am sorry to say is now being done by our Government, and will continue to be done until the end of time unless some protesting voice is raised against undue interference by lawyers, policemen and detectives in the practice of medicine, and furtherance of its research and study (3).

Since the government felt that addiction could be eliminated through vigorous law enforcement measures, and that addicts could be "cured" if simply cut off from their supply of drugs, the prescribing of narcotics for addiction treatment and research was effectively outlawed. The medical profession, in general, appears to have shared the government's orientation: in 1921, a member of the American Medical Association's Committee on Narcotic Drugs attacked the notion that "... drug addiction is a disease which the specialist must be allowed to treat, which pretended treatment consists in supplying its victims with the drug which has caused their physical and moral debauchery ..." (4).

When narcotic addiction once again emerged as a major national concern in the early 1960's, a policy of "more of the same" promised little political advantage; the public, given to demanding quick and easy solutions even to the most complex problems, would hardly have been likely to endorse continued reliance on the law enforcement approach which, after all, had failed to prevent the resurgence of addiction in the first place. It was precisely at this time of maximum receptivity for change that Dr. Vincent Dole and Dr. Marie Nyswander reported their encouraging initial experience with methadone maintenance treatment. Although the conclusions drawn by those involved in the early research were restrained, the media immediately heralded it as the long-awaited "medical breakthrough," labeling methadone a "Cinderella drug" (5) which could be economically applied to hundreds of thousands of addicts and, in short order, solve the narcotic addiction problem. Balancing the enthusiasm of the press, however, was the severe criticism of maintenance treatment voiced by the medical establishment and law enforcement advocates who clung to the notion that administering narcotics to addicts was unethical, immoral, and ineffective.

The response at the Federal and local levels of government was to cater to both parties in the controversy. Thus, most governmental agencies involved in funding addiction treatment programs encouraged a "balanced approach," carefully expanding drug-free modalities to at least the same extent as chemotherapeutic programs. Nationally, it was repeatedly emphasized that ". . . the effort to make maintenance programs available should not obscure the need to expand other approaches" (6), and the Special Action Office for Drug Abuse Prevention presented data to confirm its multimodality orientation: ". . . between June 1971, and March 1973, the number of Federally funded patients in methadone treatment doubled. During that same period the number of patients in non-methadone programs increased five-fold" (7). At the State level, the New York Drug Abuse Control Commission in 1973–1974 allocated 2600 "slots" for methadone maintenance out of a total capacity of 13,741 (8). And in New York City, where the total number of patients in addiction programs increased by more than 400% between 1970 and 1972, the proportion of patients in methadone maintenance facilities remained unchanged at approximately 55–60% (9).

Not even the most enthusiastic advocates of methadone maintenance could take issue with the premise that exclusive reliance on a particular modality would be inappropriate. From the outset, however, numerous conditions were imposed on methadone maintenance as the price of even limited endorsement by those agencies concerned with funding and regulating addiction treatment programs. By the end of 1974, restrictions on methadone dosage, the duration of treatment, and other aspects of the treatment regimen had markedly altered not only the procedures of methadone programs, but their underlying philosophical orientation as well. Although the label "methadone maintenance" has continued to be applied, the programs today bear more similarity to their drug-free counterparts than to the early programs which employed the Dole–Nyswander model.

Beyond the modifications imposed on methadone maintenance programs, there has been a more fundamental change in the role of all addiction treatment programs. As a result of the widespread publicity given the massive "war on addiction," and the implication that the tremendous investment of money and personnel would eradicate the problem, the expectations of the general public were unrealistic from the outset. Later claims that "the corner has been turned," made by national and local leaders as early as 1973, seemed to justify these high hopes. Thus, when it became necessary to concede that these pronouncements of success were premature and that, nationwide, ". . . conditions [with respect to heroin addiction] have been gradually worsening since early 1974" (10), cynicism replaced confidence. By this time the state of the economy had overshadowed crime and addiction as the major focus of public concern, and hastened a return to the punitive approach which, though more costly in financial as well as human terms, appeared simpler and less controversial than medical management.

In retrospect, treatment advocates have mostly themselves to blame for the rapid swing of the pendulum back to a law-enforcement emphasis. Proponents of specific treatment approaches rarely missed an opportunity to make exaggerated claims for their own modality and to vilify publicly other therapeutic efforts. To preserve their own dwindling credibility, public methadone programs joined in the attack on private facilities. Drug-free program staff members were vocal participants in community efforts to keep out (or drive out) maintenance clinics, and program directors spent more time trying to discredit the evaluation studies of others than in assessing candidly their own effectiveness. Clinical experience was ignored, and philosophical principles were sacrificed to accommodate the rapidly changing priorities of funding agencies: drug-free programs which had vociferously damned methadone maintenance agreed to provide "temporary" maintenance when "methadone money" was all that was available; maintenance programs readily acceded to the wishes of regulatory agencies and adopted detoxification as a universally applicable objective of treatment; and both drug-free and chemotherapeutic programs, which were designed to treat narcotic addicts, hastened to redefine their mission when attention (and dollars) began to concentrate on the "soft-drug" user and the alcoholic, even though there remain ". . . several hundred thousand daily chronic users of heroin not currently in treatment" (11).

THE FUTURE

Although addiction and the response to addiction are dynamic processes greatly influenced by complex and unpredictable societal factors, two "truths" exist: heroin addiction will continue to be a major medical and social problem in this country for many years to come, and there will be a persistent polarization of views regarding how best to deal with it. The intent of this book is not to achieve consensus regarding the many difficult issues which exist, but rather to facilitate a reasoned debate by bringing into focus fundamental, substantive questions. At the same time, it provides one perspective of the issues, and describes the results when this perspective is translated into program policies and procedures in the large-scale treatment of addicts.

ROBERT G. NEWMAN, M.D., M.P.H.

Part I

PROGRAM RATIONALE, PLANNING, AND IMPLEMENTATION

The New York City Methadone Maintenance Treatment Program
Chapters 1–10

The New York City Ambulatory Detoxification Program
Chapters 11–13

1

Background

Initially, the conceptual impetus as well as the financial support for methadone research came from the Administration of the City of New York. As early as 1959, Mayor Robert Wagner announced that the City would provide funds to major medical centers in New York for addiction treatment research efforts (12). A year later, the Mayor's Advisory Council on Narcotic Addiction recommended that the highest research priority be given to the development of ". . . a pharmaceutical substitute for heroin which would enable addicts to function" (13). This recommendation was accepted, and in 1962 the New York City Health Research Council* actively began to solicit proposals for finding ". . . a chemical compound that would relieve the need for drugs in addicted persons" (14).

At that time, however, there was little interest in addiction among the academic medical community, and ultimately the Health Research Council invited Dr. Vincent Dole of The Rockefeller University to undertake the research.† The initial grant to Dr. Dole was for $100,000. He was joined in this project by Dr. Marie Nyswander, a psychiatrist with many years of frustrating experience trying to rehabilitate narcotic addicts through the use of conventional psychotherapy.

In the course of their early work, Dole and Nyswander prepared to wean two addicts from morphine dependence by transferring them to equivalent, high doses of methadone in a hospital setting. They observed a remarkable transformation: the patients lost their preoccupation with drugs, stopped demanding ever-increasing doses of narcotics, and expressed an interest in leaving the hospital during the day in order to seek employment and school-

*The Health Research Council was established by Mayor Wagner in 1958 to stimulate research dealing with critical health problems.

†Dr. Dole, a physician specializing in metabolic disease research, was at the time a temporary member of the Council, filling in for a colleague who was on sabbatical.

ing opportunities. A similar change was noted among the next four addict-patients placed on methadone. Furthermore, Dole and Nyswander demonstrated that with the administration of methadone, the patients developed an exceedingly high tolerance not only to methadone, but to all other narcotics as well.* As a result, the "maintained" patients experienced no euphoria or other central nervous system effects of the medication, and were shown to be pharmacologically unable to achieve a "high" through supplemental use of heroin, morphine, or other drugs of this class.

THEORETICAL BASIS FOR METHADONE MAINTENANCE TREATMENT

In an attempt to explain the therapeutic effectiveness of methadone treatment in their initial patients, Dole and Nyswander hypothesized that, in addition to possible psychological dependence, repeated opiate use induces a "metabolic change" which is reflected in the physical craving for narcotics. While this craving, or "heroin hunger," can be controlled by the administration of methadone, the underlying metabolic change might be irreversible; therefore, methadone maintenance may be indicated indefinitely for many patients, regardless of their successful social rehabilitation. It is this assumption which has created the most controversy.

Although definitive cellular aberration attributable to narcotic addiction has not been demonstrated, there is much experimental evidence supporting the theory of lasting physical effects:

> After withdrawal of narcotic drugs, addicted animals and men continue to show physiological abnormalities that distinguish them from normal controls. Regulation of temperature, metabolism, vasomotor reactions, and other homeostatic functions are abnormal for months after drug withdrawal. Responses to challenge doses of a narcotic drug continue to be abnormal for months, perhaps indefinitely; a specific tolerance to narcotic effects and the addict-type of brain waves can be demonstrated when a narcotic is injected into an animal after a long period of abstinence. To be sure, these findings merely reveal persistent physiological consequences of drug addiction and do not go directly to the problem of what generates the abnormal drive for narcotics in abstinent animals, but the question as to whether an animal or man is restored to physiological normality after withdrawal of the drug can now be answered decisively. The post-addict is not normal. Narcotic drugs leave an imprint on the nervous system, and the abnormal drug-seeking behavior that follows may well have a neurochemical cause" (16).

*Tolerance is "the ability to endure, without ill effects, the continued or increasing use of a drug" (15). It is a frustrating reality to any physician who has attempted to ease the pain of a victim of terminal cancer, only to see the patient become totally unresponsive to the analgesic effects of narcotics after repeated, frequent use. With respect to methadone itself, it can be readily confirmed that tolerance develops universally to the miotic effect in maintenance patients. What is true of the pain-killing and pupillary actions of narcotics is also true of other properties, including the ability to produce euphoria.

The experimental findings are supported by subjective as well as clinical experience. Addicts report that even after prolonged abstinence they do not respond to narcotics as they did prior to becoming addicted. Tolerance to certain effects (such as nausea) is not extinguished regardless of the duration of the drug-free interval before reexposure, and tolerance to the analgesic, euphoric, and depressant effects develops more rapidly after each successive episode of abstinence.

There are, of course, many factors which determine recidivism. The fact that some ex-addicts remain abstinent without methadone maintenance treatment is not surprising, and is not a persuasive argument negating the theory of a lasting metabolic change.* The hypothesis used to explain the effectiveness of treatment, however, is irrelevant to the more fundamental question: Is the therapeutic regimen successful in the treatment of addiction?

THE POSITION OF THE NEW YORK CITY ADMINISTRATION REGARDING METHADONE MAINTENANCE (1965–1969)

Based on their encouraging initial results, Dole and Nyswander obtained a grant of $1,400,000 in City funds from Dr. Ray Trussell, who at the time was Commissioner of Hospitals. Trussell also arranged to provide them with in-patient beds at the Manhattan General Hospital, a municipal institution which later became part of the Beth Israel Medical Center.

The first report of methadone maintenance to appear in the medical literature was an article by Dole and Nyswander published in 1965 in the Journal of the American Medical Association (18). Although based on only 22 patients, it had an immediate impact in the political as well as medical arenas. In the mayoral campaign that same year, John Lindsay's platform regarding addiction included support for ". . . further experimentation with methadone maintenance" (19). Shortly after his election, however, for reasons which were not specified, Lindsay abruptly discontinued financial support of the controversial new methadone programs,† and recruited Dr. Efren Ramirez, who had developed a network of therapeutic communities in Puerto Rico, to become the City's Narcotics Coordinator. Soon after his arrival in New York, Ramirez was appointed Commissioner of the newly created Addiction Services Agency in a step heralding the ". . . refocusing of [the City's] priorities

*Critics of the metabolic theory have noted that in therapeutic communities, ". . . these victims of a supposed metabolic defect ably carry out socially responsible and often creative social and interpersonal activities without drugs . . ." (17).

†The methadone maintenance programs which had been started at Beth Israel Medical Center, Harlem Hospital, and Bronx State Hospital were kept alive with funds provided by the New York State Narcotic Addiction Control Commission, established in the same year.

toward the therapeutic community and a commitment to establish more drug-free centers" (20).

A swing back toward methadone maintenance began in 1968: "Lindsay had every reason to assume that his Democratic Party opponent in the mayoralty election in November, 1969, would propose the methadone maintenance approach as an alternative to the City's program. Moreover, the proponents of the methadone approach continued to expand. Initially, the support had come from within the large medical centers of the City. However, the 'success' of the program had attracted 'good government' people and even some leading members of the black and Puerto Rican communities*—which previously had been almost unanimous in opposition to the program" (21).

The Mayor's renewed interest in methadone treatment was not shared by his top-level administrators: both the Health Services Administrator and the Commissioner of the Addiction Services Agency "... rejected incorporation of a methadone maintenance program into their respective agencies..." (22). Rather than demand the compliance of unwilling City agencies, the Mayor asked the Vera Institute of Justice, a private foundation, to prepare a protocol for a methadone program which would be City-sponsored, but independently operated. The resulting program was the Addiction Research and Treatment Corporation (A.R.T.C.).†

When A.R.T.C. began operations in October, 1969, there were approximately 2000 patients enrolled in existing methadone maintenance programs, and several thousand applicants awaiting admission. The A.R.T.C., however, differed significantly from the early Beth Israel program and others patterned on the Dole–Nyswander protocol in emphasizing maintenance on low dosages of methadone and eventual abstinence. It "... was guided by a strong commitment to a multi-modality approach" (24), and its primary objectives were geared more to research than to treatment. With its emphasis on experimental modifications, the new program represented an attempt to resolve some of the conflicts and controversies generated by the original model, rather than an endorsement by the City Administration of methadone maintenance treatment. The situation was to change radically in the ensuing months.

*A "Committee for Expanded Methadone Treatment" was established in 1968, and included in its ranks Roy Innis, the Associate National Director of the Congress of Racial Equality; Congressmen Charles Rangel and Herman Badillo; State Senator Basil Paterson; Manhattan Borough President Percy Sutton; the co-owner of the Amsterdam News, Clarence Jones; Joseph Monserrat of the Board of Education; and rent-strike leader Jesse Gray.

†Although the City's share of the funding was never more than 10% of the program's total budget, with the remainder coming from the National Institute of Mental Health, A.R.T.C. was portrayed as "the City methadone program" (23).

2

Planning and Organization

THE INITIATIVE OF THE HEALTH SERVICES ADMINISTRATION

Almost immediately after his appointment as Health Services Administrator in January, 1970, Gordon Chase began to plan for a City-operated methadone maintenance treatment program. He considered issues such as dosage, duration of treatment, and the optimal "mix" of supportive services to be of secondary importance while there remained thousands of heroin addicts who wanted treatment but had to wait many months for admission to existing facilities. In March, 1970, I was recruited by Chase to oversee the preparation of a substantive proposal for a methadone program which would admit between 20,000 and 50,000 patients within one year.*

Initially, Chase's unrealistic program projections created considerable anxiety. There was a widespread fear that quality of care would be sacrificed to achieve the short-term political objectives of the "numbers game." Realizing that methadone maintenance treatment, already under severe attack and close scrutiny, could be irreparably damaged by a large-scale fiasco and the attendant publicity which would be associated with a program operated by the City of New York, proponents of methadone treatment offered the most insistent arguments against expanding too rapidly. Chase, however, considered "maximum effort" and "realistic goals" to be inherently contradictory concepts, subsequently acknowledging: "When I wrote that memo [indicating a target of 20,000 admissions within one year], everybody got a lot of laughs. 'Wow! Look at that nut.' But the point I wanted to get across was that *that* was the magnitude of what had to be done. It was important that we

*At the time, I was the Director of the National Nutrition Survey in New York City, and had no prior experience in the field of addiction treatment.

recognize it as that kind of magnitude and start going in that direction, even if it took longer than a year" (25).

By the middle of April, 1970, a proposal was drafted by the Health Services Administration (H.S.A.) and submitted to the Mayor's Narcotic Control Council, an advisory group established earlier that year to formulate policy and coordinate the Administration's efforts in the area of drug abuse.* Criticism of the proposal came, not unexpectedly, from the Addiction Services Agency (A.S.A.), and reflected the basic conflicts between the chemotherapeutic and drug-free philosophies. Thus, the A.S.A. voiced concern that there was insufficient emphasis in the protocol on psychiatric services, and urged that more stringent admission criteria be employed to ensure that methadone maintenance be limited to those addicts who had previously failed in other forms of treatment. The A.S.A. also urged that the program be experimental in orientation, that special attention be given to the utilization of low dosages of methadone and, above all, that eventual withdrawal be the ultimate therapeutic goal. In response, the H.S.A. noted that the proposed program was patterned closely on the Dole–Nyswander model, which had successfully demonstrated an ability to attract and retain large numbers of heroin addicts, and to assist in their rehabilitation.

No significant modifications in the proposal were made, and it was submitted to the State Narcotic Addiction Control Commission in June, 1970.

OPERATIONAL RESPONSIBILITY: H.S.A. VERSUS A.S.A.

At its inception in 1967 under the leadership of Dr. Ramirez, the New York City Addiction Services Agency was firmly and outspokenly committed to an approach which was ". . . generally anti-drug, anti-methadone, anti-intellectual, and pro-drug-free treatment on the Synanon model" (26). The appointment of Larry Alan Bear to succeed Ramirez in 1969 did not change the Agency's orientation. Nevertheless, once the concept of a large-scale methadone program was accepted by the Mayor and the Narcotic Control Council, Bear insisted that ultimate operational authority rest with the A.S.A. On the surface, it seemed reasonable that a program designed to provide the largest addiction treatment capability in the City should be under the control of the agency which had the mandate to coordinate,

*At my insistence, the projected number of admissions during the first program year had been reduced to 3500. Even this goal represented an increase of more than 100% in the methadone maintenance capacity of all the existing programs combined. Although the State ultimately approved a first-year budget based on a capacity of 2000 patients, supplemental City funds were available, and in its first twelve months of operation the Program admitted 3715 patients.

monitor, and direct the City's efforts in the field of drug abuse. On the other hand, there were substantive arguments in favor of giving the responsibility for operating the new program to the Health Services Administration.*

H.S.A. emphasized its organizational and contractual ties to municipal and voluntary hospitals and District Health Centers, which could provide space as well as backup medical services for the program clinics. Additionally, there was an obvious need to coordinate with the other methadone programs in the City; the polarization which had developed between the A.S.A. and those programs did not portend a good working relationship.

The undisguised ideological hostility of the A.S.A. toward chemotherapy in general, and methadone maintenance treatment in particular, would inevitably have an impact on the implementation of the program and the nature of the services provided. In rationalizing its insistence for control over a treatment modality which it emphatically rejected, the A.S.A. argued that its skepticism would ensure a diversified, experimental approach to methadone treatment, and pointed to the many unanswered questions relating to optimal staffing patterns, dosage levels and ultimate detoxification. The H.S.A. did not refute the need for additional clinical research into these and other aspects of methadone treatment, but maintained that a major research design within the framework of the overall operation of the program would not be practical.†

*It is interesting to note that Chase sought responsibility for this large and extremely controversial undertaking. His appointment as the first nonphysician Health Services Administrator had been severely criticized by the medical establishment (27) and by numerous minority community leaders (28). He had his hands full even without venturing into the area of addiction treatment, which logically could have been left to the A.S.A. As the head of the H.S.A. he was ultimately responsible for the Department of Health, the Office of the Chief Medical Examiner, the Department of Mental Health and Mental Retardation, and all health care provided in the City's schools and correctional facilities. The combined annual budget of these agencies amounted to almost one billion dollars. In addition, he had the simultaneous role of Chairman of the Board of the new Health and Hospitals Corporation, which within six months of his appointment was scheduled to assume responsibility for operating the 18 municipal hospitals. In retrospect, Chase explained his desire to operate the methadone program by pointing out that he considered addiction the major health problem facing the City, and the need to expand methadone treatment capacity the top priority of the Administration. He was convinced that the H.S.A. could implement a large-scale program more quickly and effectively than any other agency, and consequently felt an obligation and a challenge to do so (29).

†Others have reached the same conclusion: "Programs focused primarily on experimentation and research such as dosage level manipulation, random termination, use of placebo substitution and the like might best do this on a small pilot basis rather than in the context of a broad treatment program in the community" (30). This position was subsequently adopted by the A.S.A. as well, which in its 1972 *Comprehensive Plan for the Control of Drug Abuse and Addiction* stated: "In the interest of both treatment and research we recognize that these functions must be kept distinct. Our approach is to foster and help develop small and carefully controlled research programs while simultaneously continuing to expand the large treatment-oriented programs which must meet the existing demand..." (31).

Perhaps the most persuasive argument in the eyes of City Hall was Chase's "track record for mounting new programs rapidly," while the Addiction Services Agency was generally viewed as "incompetent to mount and manage the proposed large-scale methadone maintenance treatment program" (32). The fact that Chase and his staff had taken the initiative and had a final proposal ready for immediate submission to the State for funding, while the A.S.A. had only lengthy memos criticizing the suggested "Beth Israel model," further enhanced the credibility of the H.S.A.*

On June 10, 1970, Mayor Lindsay announced a "compromise" solution. The Addiction Services Agency would submit the proposal to the State and be the recipient of the anticipated funding; these funds would then be turned over to the Health Services Administration, which would have sole responsibility for operating the program. While this "fragmentation" of addiction treatment services has been conscientiously avoided in most localities, in retrospect it has had many advantages in New York City. Since the staffs of the chemotherapeutic and drug-free programs have been organizationally distinct, internal philosophical conflicts, and pressures for programmatic compromises, have been kept at a minimum. Equally important, the City Administration's commitment to expand rapidly methadone maintenance treatment capacity did not detract from the simultaneous effort of the Addiction Services Agency to expand and improve drug-free treatment and prevention programs; competition for personnel and other resources, which would have been inevitable had the City's programs all been under the aegis of a single agency, were avoided. At the same time, it was found that communication between the two agencies could be maintained, and a satisfactory working relationship developed.

"FISCAL INTERMEDIARY"

The consensus among the planners of the New York City Methadone Maintenance Treatment Program (NYC MMTP) was that a large-scale program could not be launched within the City bureaucracy, given the complex and time-consuming civil service and budgetary restrictions for hiring staff, purchasing supplies, renting equipment, and leasing and renovating facilities. Thus, a "fiscal intermediary" was sought with which the City would contract to operate the program. Under such an arrangement the City could retain complete control over the program's operation, but without the usual

*Even before the organizational dispute had been resolved, the H.S.A. had tentatively identified space and backup facilities for the first 12 clinics, worked out arrangements for urine toxicology to be performed by the Bureau of Public Health Laboratories, and obtained commitments from other programs to assist in the recruitment and training of staff.

bureaucratic red tape.* In June, 1970, the H.S.A. urged the City Budget Director to approve the operation of the program "entirely outside of the City line-item system by using a fiscal intermediary" (33). The following arguments were presented:

Salary levels under civil service would not be competitive. Physicians' pay scales were cited as an example: the Department of Health could pay a maximum of $16,800 for a full-time clinician, while all existing methadone programs in New York paid at least $30,000.

Acquisition and alteration of space through the Department of Real Estate routinely took at least 18 months. The H.S.A. goal of opening 20 clinics within 12 months would obviously be out of the question.

Many hospitals, which were counted on for backup medical services, would refuse to participate in a program forced to operate under the severe restrictions and delays inherent in the City's bureaucratic procedures.

In early 1970, however, the Lindsay Administration had come under strong public criticism for its allegedly lavish use of outside consultants to perform tasks which, it was claimed, could have been carried out by the City itself at considerably less cost. Consequently, City Hall was reluctant to use an approach clearly intended to circumvent the civil service system, especially with such a highly visible program, and refused to approve the use of a fiscal intermediary. Ultimately the Program was given the option of contracting with individual hospitals for the administration of the clinical units, but the Central Office staff, which would determine the direction and monitor the quality of the Program, would have to operate within the framework of the civil service system. Under this plan, I had serious misgivings that I would be able to exercise authority and maintain direct supervisory responsibility. In addition, contracting with hospitals would conflict with the practices of other large methadone programs, which also relied on hospitals for backup services, but hired all personnel on their own budget lines.

In retrospect, the anticipated difficulties were largely overcome by strong and consistent support from the Mayor's office. Throughout the Lindsay Administration the Program was given highest priority by all of the many City agencies upon which it had to rely, including the Purchase and Personnel Departments, the Department of Real Estate, the Budget Bureau, and even the Department of Marine and Aviation (which, for over a year, placed a ferry boat at the Program's disposal for use as a temporary clinical facility serving almost 1000 patients).

*This mechanism had been used previously to operate other projects carried out by the Department of Health and other City agencies.

DEGREE OF CENTRALIZED RESPONSIBILITY FOR PROGRAM OPERATIONS

The one organizational option which neither Chase nor I ever considered was that the H.S.A. serve as a funding agency, providing grants to hospitals and other institutions to run separate, autonomous programs, with accountability to the City limited primarily to fiscal matters. From a strictly political perspective, it would have sufficed to obtain funds and make them available through subcontracts to outside agencies, which would be responsible for meeting whatever program objectives were specified. The demands on the H.S.A. for staff and other resources would be minimal, since its role would be limited to carrying out periodic audits and determining, at the end of each contract year, whether funding should be renewed (this is the primary mode of operation of the Addiction Services Agency). In addition to being the easiest and least expensive way in which to establish a wide network of facilities addressing a particular problem, this approach would also have ensured the greatest flexibility and individuality among the various facilities, and might have been expected to increase the speed with which the program could be launched and expanded. Finding satisfactory space in the neighborhood, gaining the support of the local community,* hiring staff and developing procedural guidelines could, theoretically, be accomplished more expeditiously by numerous individual contract agencies than by a central Bureau operating within the New York City Department of Health.† However, the price associated with these potential advantages—loss of control over the development and operation of the Program—was totally unacceptable both to Chase and me, for somewhat different reasons.

Chase refused to relinquish direct control over the speed and the scale of program implementation. Obtaining maximum effort from his own staff was clearly easier than dealing with several dozen hospital administrators over whom his only hold would be contract termination. With a centralized operation, directly responsible to him, Chase could constantly monitor the Program's status and apply immediate pressure to achieve greater results.

I had a different concern. My personal commitment lay in providing a specific form of treatment to all those who wanted and needed it. Simply overseeing the disbursement of funds to contract agencies would make it

*The Board of Estimate, which must approve all contracts entered into by the City, insisted that each proposed clinic have the written endorsement of the local Community Planning Board.

†The experience of the Addiction Services Agency in establishing its Methadone-to-Abstinence Program in 1972–1973 demonstrated that this advantage is more imaginary than real. The A.S.A. left implementation to the hospitals with which it contracted, and almost 18 months elapsed before the first clinic was opened.

impossible to determine Program policy, and to ensure compliance on a day-to-day basis with procedures which would be established and the philosophy upon which they would be based. As it was, there was considerable skepticism that programmatic control could be maintained by City employees over clinic staff working for the contract hospitals.

3

Management Information System

INTRODUCTION

The New York City Methadone Maintenance Treatment Program (NYC MMTP) comprises more than 40 clinical units located throughout the five boroughs, and staffed by employees of over a dozen contract agencies. Two factors have been instrumental in maintaining centralized control over this widespread network of facilities, and ensuring compliance with uniform policies and procedures. The first is the Program's organizational structure, in which one individual is assigned total responsibility for monitoring the on-going activities of several clinics (see "Management Analyst," Appendix I). The second factor is the comprehensive data system, which evolved from a cumbersome, manual operation to an efficient, computer-based system designed to facilitate clinical as well as management functions.

OBJECTIVES OF THE NYC MMTP DATA SYSTEM

From a management standpoint, prompt, accurate, and comprehensive information regarding the Program's operation was indispensable. In the early years of the Program, it was necessary to know the demand for treatment, i.e., the number of applicants and their geographical distribution, in order to determine the need for expansion. Admissions from the waiting list (which at one time numbered over 8000) had to be scheduled in the order that applications were received, and the rate of admissions to the Program's treatment units had to be controlled on a day-by-day basis. While a few clinics accepted patients almost as quickly as they could be screened by the counseling and medical staff (as many as 50 clinic admissions weekly), the staff of most treatment units had to be pushed to admit 10–15 patients per week until the census approximated the facility's capacity.

Since the capacity of each component clinic is a function of terminations as well as admissions, it was important for the Central Office to monitor attendance at each clinic and identify inactive patients who should be terminated. Optimal utilization of resources also required information regarding the pattern of scheduled visits in each treatment unit, to avoid an excessive patient load on any given day of the week (patients in the NYC MMTP are scheduled to attend the clinic from 2 to 6 days per week, depending upon length of time in treatment and demonstrated progress toward rehabilitation).

As the "Program Sponsor" of each of the NYC MMTP clinics, I was responsible for the accurate accounting of all methadone used by the Program. Consequently, the data system had to provide a reliable means for ensuring that only those individuals who were actively enrolled received medication, and for documenting the precise amount administered and dispensed to each. It also had to enable Central Office to identify any deviation from Program guidelines and Federal and State regulations governing methadone dosages and take-home medication.

Program evaluation was another critical function of the information system which was developed. Since the NYC MMTP is publicly funded and operated, there has always been an obligation to document the Program's experience in treating heroin addicts.

METHADONE ACCOUNTING: THE FOUNDATION FOR CONTROL

The ultimate control over all aspects of the NYC MMTP data system stems from the methadone accounting procedures which have been established. Physicians and nurses recognize that strict compliance with these procedures is a legal and professional obligation, as well as a programmatic requirement. For this reason, it has been possible to demand, and obtain, an accurate, day-by-day record of every patient visit to each clinic, and the amount of medication administered and dispensed to each individual.

A computer-printed "Medication Dosage and Pickup Schedule" (MDPS, Appendix II), based on orders written by the clinic physicians, is updated weekly*; for each clinic, the schedule lists every active patient, and indicates the dose of methadone which is to be given each day of the following week. Any dosage order submitted by a clinic for an individual who is not an active patient (i.e., whose admission has not been processed by Central Office, or who has been terminated) will not appear on the MDPS.

*The turnaround time is 36 hours; medication orders received from the clinics each Wednesday are reflected in the computer printouts delivered to each clinic on Friday, for use during the following week.

In addition to its function as a prospective attendance and dosage schedule, the MDPS also serves as the primary methadone accounting document, providing Central Office with an historical record of actual clinic visits and dosages received by each patient. As each patient reports to the clinic, the precise amount of methadone administered and dispensed is recorded directly on the form, which is returned to Central Office at the end of the week for key-punching and analysis. Dosage and attendance information on patients admitted during the week, who were not included on the computer-printed MDPS, is entered by hand. Since the data system rejects hand-written entries for individuals who have not been cleared by the Central Office, the clinics are unable to account for medication given to anyone who is not an active patient.

This methadone accounting system is integrally related to all other components of the data system, and is the basis for ensuring compliance with the Program's admission, termination, and patient-evaluation procedures. Before a patient can be admitted (i.e., administered the first dose of methadone), the clinic must telephone the central staff, which immediately verifies that the individual's application has been received and that he (she) has been notified to report for admission screening to that particular clinic. Preadmission clearing with the Central Office prevents a patient from simultaneously enrolling in more than one NYC MMTP facility. It also allows central monitoring to ensure that applicants are scheduled for admission to the clinic nearest their home, in chronological order of application. In addition, the Central Office is able to follow up in the case of applicants who are not admitted, and determine the reason for clinic rejection of those who appear to meet the basic requirements of age, duration of addiction, and residence. Above all, the system guarantees that the Central Office knows at all times the precise census of every clinic. This accuracy, which is built into the daily operation at the clinic level, in turn permits the other components of the data system to operate more effectively.*

Since an admission can be accomplished only if the Application Form (Appendix III) is processed by Central Office, all applicant information is available for analysis.

Central Office is able to identify every new patient for whom an Admission Screening Form (Appendix IV), with demographic, social, and drug-use history information, has not been submitted.

Computer-generated billing of Medicaid for every clinic visit by eligible

*An alternative means of achieving the benefits of centralization involves the establishment of "central intake units." The advantage of the NYC MMTP approach is that papers, and not patients, are processed centrally; applicants have contact only with staff directly involved in the delivery of treatment services.

patients is based on the historical record of attendance contained on the MDPS.

Bimonthly Patient Progress Reports (Appendix V) indicating current medical or psychiatric problems, drug abuse, legal problems, employment, schooling, welfare status, and other information relevant to patient assessment are the basis for Program evaluation. Reports are initiated centrally for every patient on the active census, providing computer-printed dosage and attendance history, and the results of all urinalyses performed during the two-month reporting period.* These forms are sent to the treatment units for completion by the counseling staff, and are then returned to Central Office for keypunching and analysis of the clinical information. By correlating the number of reports sent to each clinic with the number returned, it is possible to achieve a degree of completeness approaching 100%.

Before the Patient Progress Reports are sent to the clinics, the dosage and attendance records printed on the forms are reviewed by the central staff to identify patients who have received no methadone for the entire 2-month period. The appropriate clinics are contacted, and terminations are instituted when indicated. This process prevents patients remaining "active" when they are no longer receiving medication.

By processing all terminations centrally, uniform definitions of the reasons for discharge from the Program can be applied, based on a thorough review of the patient's clinical record. The last date of methadone administration is known for all patients, and can be used as an objective date of termination, in order to eliminate the distortion in retention data associated with delays in initiating and completing the processing of terminations.

THE INTEGRATION OF ADMINISTRATIVE AND CLINICAL FUNCTIONS OF THE NYC MMTP DATA SYSTEM

Although the NYC MMTP data system was developed by the Program's managerial staff primarily to meet management needs, it was designed to be an integral component of patient care. Every data form serves a critical clinical function, in addition to providing data relevant to the administration of the Program. The Admission Screening Form, for example, contains questions which identify potential problem areas of new patients, and which are important in the planning of appropriate treatment services. The Patient

*Urinalysis results are entered into each patient's computerized file on a weekly basis, from reports submitted to Central Office directly by the laboratory.

Progress Report, in addition to permitting assessment of clinic and Program performance, ensures that the narrative record in every patient's chart is complemented by a concise, readily accessible, bimonthly summary of progress and problems, as well as a record of the patient's attendance and dosage history and urinalysis results. The weekly medication schedule, which serves ultimately to control and monitor the entire operation of the Program, also guides the nursing staff in the accurate administration and dispensing of methadone, and is simultaneously the primary methadone accounting document.

This integration of management and clinical objectives has proved the key to obtaining consistently accurate and timely data. Providing information intended solely for Program administration and evaluation, without direct and immediate relevance to the treatment services, would inevitably have received low priority by those who must collect the data. By addressing the needs of clinic staff, the data system of the NYC MMTP has, at the same time, made it possible for the Program to develop as a single organizational entity, operating according to uniform policies and procedures, with central accountability.

4

Relationship with the Community

INTRODUCTION

"Maximum feasible participation" of the community in the planning and delivery of services is usually a requirement for government-sponsored health projects. Such an approach, however, is not possible in the case of addiction treatment. Addicts themselves are hardly in a position to serve in an advisory capacity to program planners. They can only "vote with their feet," by accepting or rejecting services once they are made available. As for the nonaddict community, it is unrealistic to believe that it can identify with, and represent the interests of, the addict population. The all-encompassing involvement with the pursuit of drugs results in the isolation and disfranchisement of most addicts. Local support for individuals and agencies purporting to speak for "the community" is unlikely to come from that specific segment of the population which an addiction treatment program is designed to attract.

Politically, however, a narcotic addiction treatment program must seek to benefit the nonaddict, tax-paying public as well as the patients who are being treated. In the case of the New York City Methadone Maintenance Treatment Program (NYC MMTP), the City's Board of Estimate must approve all proposed leases and contracts, and their renewal on an annual basis. Such approval generally can not be obtained in the face of opposition from local organizations.* Consequently, the relationship with the community has been of critical importance to the expansion and ongoing operation of the NYC MMTP.

*Methadone programs not operated under the aegis of the City have similar constraints imposed by Federal funding sources, and by State regulatory agencies which consider the "suitability" of proposed locations in the decision to license clinics and approve them for Medicaid reimbursement.

COMMUNITY OPPOSITION TO THE OPENING OF NYC MMTP CLINICS

Initially, I assumed that any community opposition to the establishment of NYC MMTP treatment units would focus on issues related to the use of methadone. The approach which I thought would overcome anticipated resistance was to explain the rationale for methadone maintenance treatment, and point out the positive results to date in enabling the majority of patients to give up heroin abuse and lead socially productive lives. I believed that such a presentation would make it clear that the community shares in the benefits when methadone maintenance is provided to former heroin addicts.

The experience of the NYC MMTP demonstrated that this simplistic analysis of community opposition to addiction programs was wrong. Criticism of the treatment modality itself was surprisingly rare. To the extent that opponents of proposed clinic sites believed such myths as methadone "gets in the bones," leads to senility and sterility, and is a covert plot to commit genocide, these issues did not seem to concern them. Whether the community was primarily Black, Hispanic, Italian, Jewish, or any other demographic group, there was an almost total disinterest in what methadone maintenance does, as long as it does it on some other street.

In retrospect, the resistance encountered by the NYC MMTP was essentially the same as that which met efforts to establish addiction treatment facilities, employing widely disparate therapeutic approaches, for more than 50 years. The following account is typical.

> On August 5, 1919, the *New York Times* reported: "About 500 residents of The Bronx in the vicinity of Pelham Bay Park held a mass meeting... last night and protested against the proposal [of the New York City Department of Health] to have the City use the buildings of the Pelham Bay Naval Training Station as a hospital for drug addicts.... Resolutions were adopted condemning the proposal. A petition containing about 1,000 signatures will be presented at today's meeting of the Board of Estimate asking City officials not to vote for the project" (34).
>
> The effectiveness of the community opposition was headlined the following day: "No Addict Hospital in Pelham Bay Park—Patients Will Be Housed at Tuberculosis Institution on Staten Island." According to the news release, the Mayor's decision to choose an alternate site "... met with the unmistakable approval of a large delegation of residents of The Bronx, who had appeared to protest against the establishment of a drug addict hospital in their borough" (35).
>
> The Mayor quickly discovered that his constituents in Staten Island were no more willing to accept addict-patients than were those in the Bronx. On August 10, the *New York Times* continued the story: "Drug Addicts Undesired—Staten Island Residents against Housing Them in Sea View. Staten Island commenced yesterday to organize for an aggressive campaign to prevent Health Commissioner Dr. Royal E. Copeland from bringing drug addicts to the Sea View Hospital now used for tuberculosis patients.... A vigilance committee of 150 members has been formed who threaten to picket the ferries in the effort to prevent drug addicts from being

brought to Sea View. A former Assemblyman, who led the successful fight to prevent the City from locating a garbage disposal plant on Staten Island, has volunteered to lead the fight" (36). Once again, the community prevailed and the City was forced to abandon its plan (37). [Almost 50 years later, the City tried again to utilize the Sea View Hospital for the treatment of addicts; as in 1919, community opposition defeated the plan (38).]

Virtually all of the 44 clinics established by the NYC MMTP were opened after a protracted, uphill struggle to overcome neighborhood opposition. Arguments which stressed the need for services, the voluntary nature of the Program, and the strongly positive conclusions regarding the outcome of methadone treatment reached by independent evaluators after several years of study, all fell on deaf ears. As a rule, community meetings began with the local residents emphatically declaring their support for methadone maintenance treatment; there was generally an impatience with attempts to describe the therapeutic regimen and its impact on the lives of patients. The response was the following: "We know all that, and agree that methadone maintenance is worthwhile; we hope you open dozens of clinics to treat all the addicts in the City. But not here!"

Efforts by the Program to select locations which would not be objectionable were futile, since the rationale for rejecting proposed sites could be adapted to any circumstance. It was based on the proximity of a site to a school, or a church, or a playground, or a bar, or an Off Track Betting Office. Where public transportation was not accessible within a block or two, inconvenience to the patients was the reason for insisting on an alternate location; where a subway or bus stop was directly adjacent, the argument was that patient flow in and out of the clinic would compound an existing problem of congestion. In one case the community rejected a building which was across the street from a police station, on the grounds that patients should not be obliged to risk surveillance as they came to the clinic; where there was no nearby police station, concern over security was the basis for disapproval. In residential areas, it was vehemently stated that a drug treatment program would destroy the neighborhood and lower property values; in commercial districts, business leaders argued that customers would be frightened away and their stores plagued by thefts. A common goal of communities was to have clinics located within hospitals, an alternative generally rejected by the physicians, union representatives, and administrators of the many hospitals contacted by the Program.

The fundamental obstacle to overcoming community resistance was the widely held view that addiction treatment facilities were a part of the addiction *problem,* rather than a response to this problem. This orientation was frequently expressed in terms such as the following: "We've got enough to deal with in this neighborhood. We're already overwhelmed with junkies, prostitutes, panhandlers, loiterers, and thieves. The last thing we need is to compound all these troubles by allowing a methadone maintenance clinic to open up." Even in areas with a particularly high prevalence of narcotic addiction, and where the residents were willing to admit to such prevalence, there was a fear that hordes of heroin addicts from all over the City would descend on the neighborhood to seek admission to the new clinic. The implication seemed to be that methadone patients from outside the local community were a greater potential threat than were the existing heroin addicts.

Another factor which played a role in the opposition to proposed clinics was the tangible target which a treatment center offered for the enormous frustration which pervaded many neighborhoods. The "plague of addiction," and innumerable related and unrelated urban ills, generated fear, anxiety, and resentment, but were too amorphous to be attacked directly. A request by a City agency for approval of a methadone maintenance facility permitted the community's frustration, borne of a long-standing sense of hopelessness and impotence, to be focused on a concrete, attainable objective. "Success" was defined as thwarting the bureaucracy's efforts to open a clinic, and was worth pursuing for its own sake, regardless of the ultimate consequences of denying treatment services to addicts.

That the communities approached by the NYC MMTP were responding to issues far removed from drug abuse per se was repeatedly made apparent. At one meeting, following my lengthy presentation concerning the Program, and the advantages to the neighborhood of providing methadone treatment to heroin addicts, a local resident demanded to know, "Why haven't you picked up my garbage in the last week?" My attempt to explain that the NYC MMTP had no connection with the Sanitation Department was greeted by cries of "buck passing!" The consensus was that since the City refused to provide adequate garbage pickup, the community should refuse to allow the establishment of a City-sponsored addiction treatment clinic. Other seemingly extraneous issues which were raised included school busing, excessive welfare payments to the indolent, inadequate and unsafe public transportation, and poor medical care for the elderly. Resentment of the hospitals with which the Program planned to contract for backup services was also directed at proposed clinics; in more than one case, approval was denied based on the allegation that the hospital was seeking to drive out its neighbors to facilitate institutional expansion.

In the initial stages of Program development, NYC MMTP staff attended three or four community meetings each week.* As many as ten possible

*Initially, a special community relations unit was planned as part of the NYC MMTP Central Office. Instead, however, the functions envisaged for such a unit were assumed by treatment staff and Central Office personnel directly responsible for establishing clinics and monitoring

clinic sites were located and presented to neighborhood groups before one was ultimately approved. In some areas, such as the west side of Manhattan (home of the notorious "Needle Park"), approval was *never* obtained. Meanwhile, the gap between demand for treatment and availability of services continued to widen, until at one point over 8000 applicants were on the Program's waiting list. It was not until the end of 1972, 2 years after the NYC MMTP began, that the City-wide methadone maintenance capacity was sufficient to accommodate all those who sought admission.

COMMUNITY RESPONSE TO OPERATING CLINICS OF THE NYC MMTP

Resistance to the establishment of new clinics is only half the story of the Program's relations with the community. Once a clinic was opened, local opposition generally was minimal, regardless of the site which had been chosen: some clinics were in residential areas, others in commercial districts; one treatment unit was established on an unused floor of a hospital nurses' dormitory; another in a Wall Street office building; one clinic shared a City-owned building with a parochial elementary school, which had been displaced from its original location by fire. While there were a number of complaints from local residents regarding loitering, drug trafficking and crime which were allegedly associated with some of the clinics, community pressure was not so great as to seriously threaten the operation of any treatment unit of the NYC MMTP.*

By far the most common complaints received by the Program have been with regard to loitering in the vicinity of treatment units. The Program has developed several responses to this problem. Whenever possible, scheduling is arranged to minimize patient flow; for example, instead of having all patients who come to the clinic 3 days a week report on Monday, Wednesday, and Friday, some are scheduled for Tuesday, Thursday, and Saturday. In addition, many clinics reserve special hours for working patients. When complaints of loitering persist, staff members walk through the areas in-

*This has not been true of the private methadone programs in New York City, many of which have been forced to close. Here, too, the criticism has been based largely on the premise that the clinics properly belonged in some other neighborhood. Extraneous issues, such as the amount of income generated by private methadone clinics, also have received prominence. To date, however, attempts by the City Council to pass legislation eliminating all private methadone clinics have not been successful (39).

---

their operation. This organization has ensured that those who are most knowledgeable about a specific facility relate to the local community, and has been considered more effective than relying upon a special community relations staff.

volved and ask patients to disperse. Of course, none of these measures has an impact on loitering by nonpatients. Rather than simply disclaim responsibility in such cases, the Program has frequently requested New York City Police Department support; increased police visibility has generally been effective, both in terms of discouraging loitering and in reassuring local residents.

The fear that an increase in crime would be associated with the establishment of a methadone maintenance clinic was almost always expressed in the community meetings which preceded clinic openings. In order to confirm the Program's impression that such fears were not warranted, a questionnaire was distributed in the summer of 1972 to each police precinct in which a NYC MMTP clinic had been established. Commanding officers were asked to compare arrest rates, in the immediate vicinity of the clinic and in the precinct at large, during the 6 months after the clinic opened with the corresponding 6 months of the previous year. All 22 precincts responded, and with only one exception, the arrest rate was reported to have remained the same or decreased after services were initiated.

In those instances where an increase in crime was attributed by the community to a Program clinic, however, Police Department data were rarely persuasive. The most widely publicized example involved Greenwich Village residents who in August, 1972, protested the temporary use of a ferry boat, moored at a Hudson River pier adjacent to the Village, as a NYC MMTP clinic: "Greenwich Village merchants, block associations, political and special interest groups say the center, which has been used to treat drug addicts from throughout the City, has been responsible for large increases in both major and minor crimes throughout the West Village area. . . . [Merchants] complained that panhandling, muggings, shoplifting, and apartment break-ins had multiplied since the arrival of the ferry." The newspaper account of the protest included a direct reference to the before-and-after arrest study described above: "The Commanding Officer of the Charles Street Precinct . . . quoted a study comparing the first six months of this year with the same period last year [before the boat-clinic was established]. According to the study, serious crimes in the 6th precinct, which covers the West Village, decreased by 25.9% during this period" (40).

It is significant that the protest march to close the ferry boat operation occurred after community leaders had been informed that a permanent facility outside the Village had been obtained, and that relocation was imminent. One reporter rhetorically asked: "If the boat is moving, why was a march needed demanding its move?" He went on to provide the answer: ". . . the march gave many Villagers the opportunity to make their rage over what has happened to the neighborhood known. For Villagers are not fed up just with the boat. They are sick of the hustlers, derelicts, winos, and junkies who have taken over 8th Street, Sheridan Square, Washington Square Park, and Christopher Street. . . . There was also some politicking going on. . . . Some residents associated with the Community Planning Board feel the march was organized so that a handful of people could take credit for the boat moving. So when it sets sail the Village will be left with two problems—the crime not caused by the clinic's patients and the neighborhood's never-ending power plays" (41).

CONCLUSION

The difficulties encountered by the NYC MMTP in gaining community acceptance have been experienced by all treatment modalities, and are essentially the same today as those experienced more than a half-century ago. The basic problem is that since "treatment" is viewed with great skepticism, communities generally perceive the same threat from patients enrolled in treatment programs as they do from street addicts. As far as most neighborhood residents are concerned, the only acceptable approach is *first* to get rid of the addicts and then, in another locale, to provide them with therapeutic services. Since each community has precisely the same sentiment, however, this is hardly a practical solution.

While there have been enormous difficulties in establishing addiction treatment facilities in the past, the prospect for the immediate future appears to be even worse. Cynicism toward treatment efforts, which has always been widespread, has been greatly heightened in the last decade by the exaggerated promises of politicians and advocates of specific modalities, by premature and unwarranted claims of "success," and by the endless public attacks of one program upon another. In New York City, where the *untreated* addict population is estimated to be twice as great as the total capacity of all treatment programs, the future looks grim indeed.

Selected Policy Issues

Initially, the appropriate course of action with respect to many important issues was determined on a case-by-case basis. It was impossible to predict the complexity of situations which had no precedent, and attempts to rely on preconceived Program guidelines would have necessitated fitting artificially each new set of circumstances into a specific category. On the other hand, the need to make impromptu decisions under pressure, in response to existing crises which demanded immediate resolution, clearly had its drawbacks.

In the chapters which follow, the evolution of the NYC MMTP policies and procedures will be discussed with respect to

voluntarism
confidentiality of patient records
dosage levels and duration of treatment
ancillary services

5

Voluntarism as a Criterion for Admission

INTRODUCTION

In discussing the encouraging results of the first 750 patients treated with methadone maintenance, Dole and his co-workers stressed that "A notable feature of the treatment program has been the absence of compulsion" (42). From the outset, admission criteria stipulated that only voluntary applicants be accepted, and explicitly excluded those for whom methadone treatment had been made a condition of probation or parole (43).

Although the moral, ethical, and pragmatic issues associated with involuntary treatment of addiction are equally relevant to all treatment modalities, the coercive application of methadone maintenance has stimulated the most controversy. Proponents of compulsory treatment were attracted by the relative effectiveness and economy of the early methadone programs; others viewed with alarm the spectre of hundreds of thousands of addicts, mostly black and Puerto Rican, and poor, being forced to remain physically dependent upon narcotic drugs dispensed by government-controlled programs. These fears were not limited to those who rejected the fundamental concept of chemotherapy; one of the most emphatic critics of involuntary treatment with methadone was Dole: "I would object to the imposition of methadone maintenance treatment just as strongly as I have objected in the past to its unavailability when the needs of motivated volunteers could not be met" (44).

As long as thousands of applicants remained on waiting lists for existing treatment programs, involuntary treatment was largely an academic issue. By 1972, however, the expansion of programs in New York City had closed the gap between availability of services and spontaneous demand, and interest in the use of coercion increased. This chapter discusses the rationale for the NYC MMTP's consistent opposition to involuntary treatment.

SEMANTIC CONSIDERATIONS

As with many other controversies in the field of addiction, polarization regarding voluntarism has been compounded by semantic ambiguity. Therefore, a careful consideration of precisely what is meant by "voluntary treatment" is a prerequisite to any meaningful discussion of the principles involved in forcing people to accept therapy against their will.

An act is defined as "voluntary" if it is the result of ". . . the exercise of one's free choice or will . . . whether or not external influences are at work" (45). The difficulty, of course, is in determining what constitutes "free choice." Providing several options does not, per se, necessarily set the stage for voluntary decision-making. To the contrary, coercion *requires* that the subject choose between two or more courses of action, one of which is somewhat less abhorrent than the others. In the case of compulsory treatment of addiction, the addict always retains the alternative of imprisonment, the sanction associated with not entering a treatment program, and one might theoretically maintain that there are consequently only voluntary patients and others who are punished for not volunteering—but no involuntary patients. An operational definition of voluntarism will serve to avoid such abstract arguments.

Voluntary treatment describes a therapeutic relationship in which the primary responsibility of the clinician is to the patient. In an involuntary treatment setting, the clinician's primary responsibility is to some third party. An obligation to report patient attendance, progress, or termination to an outside individual or agency defines the relationship as involuntary, even if patients are forced to sign, in advance, authorizations for such reports.*

The physical environment and the nature of the treatment which is forced on addicts are totally irrelevant to the debate concerning involuntary treatment. In practice, decisions regarding the specific treatment program the addict must enter are based primarily on the subjective bias of the physician,

*Federal regulations governing confidentiality of addiction treatment program records endorse the concept of requiring open-ended consent to disclosure as a prerequisite to "diversion" from the criminal justice system (see page 35). The paradox of labeling consent "voluntary" in these cases is highlighted by the fact that these clients are forbidden to change their mind: "An individual whose release from confinement, probation, or parole is conditioned upon his participation in a treatment program may not revoke consent [for future release of information] . . . until there has been a formal and effective termination or revocation of such release from confinement, probation or parole" (46).

the judge, the district attorney, and others involved in the commitment process. Whether a facility is behind bars, in a locked residential setting, or in a neighborhood store-front serving ambulatory patients, whether the form of treatment provided is out-patient methadone maintenance, a drug-free encounter group, or a religious community, enforced enrollment raises precisely the same issues. It is impossible, therefore, to advocate selectively compulsory treatment with one modality without simultaneously endorsing the imposition of any and all other treatment approaches.

THE RATIONALE FOR INVOLUNTARY TREATMENT

When laws designed to protect society are violated, the Constitution requires that punishment be imposed equally, and only after conclusive determination of guilt. There is no provision for deviating from the usual standards of due process because the defendant is a "drug abuser"; or because the punishment is euphemistically labeled "treatment"; or because the setting in which the punishment is applied is a hospital or ambulatory facility instead of a traditional penal institution. Legal decisions upholding the constitutionality of involuntary treatment of addicts, therefore, have been based on the premise that the addict is "sick," and not a criminal; by this logic, the due process safeguards do not apply, since the objective is to serve the medical needs of the individual, rather than the self-interest of the community at large.*

The addict, understandably, is not impressed with the rationale that he is being deprived of his liberty for his own good. He generally perceives "treatment" as simply another form of punishment. Proponents of compulsory treatment acknowledge this, and cite it as an argument for, rather than against, depriving the addict of free choice.

> C. You say that we are using a euphemism when we call that secured setting a rehabilitation center, while you opt for the label of a jail, prison or correctional facility. Now there is quite a difference between the structured environment of a civil facility and that of a jail or state prison.
>
> N. . . . [Y]ou said earlier that the person who has the most at stake in the decision is the addict who is about to be committed. He is the most concerned about the

*Although altruism forms the basis for the legal rationalization, it is nevertheless clear that societal self-interest is the major factor in the involuntary treatment of addicts: "Danger to self has never *by itself* been made grounds for commitment or compulsory treatment. If it were, participants in every hazardous occupation or sport would be liable to commitment, and Charles Lindberg could have been permanently institutionalized for his intention to fly the Atlantic. Similarly, no law provides for compulsory treatment of cancer or heart disease or any other noncontagious physiological ailment. . . . If addiction is truly a 'disease,' what could possibly justify its unique legal status in relation to civil commitment and compulsory treatment?" (47).

differences, and yet the addict himself puts these aside and evaluates the options by one criterion: where will I spend the least time? If he could spend two years in one of those very nice rehabilitation treatment facilities, and only one year in one of those disgusting jails, my impression and experience is that 95% will take the one year. So whatever the differences, they are not that impressive to the addict.*

C. They might not be impressive to the addict, but he has certain ends in mind which, as enunciated by the legislature, happen to be contrary to the will of society.

N. Freedom is the end in his mind.

C. No, the end in his mind is to be irresponsible (49).

The premise underlying the imposition of "treatment," and the denial of due process, is that drug use (but, significantly, only *illicit* drug use) is a sickness. Since no universally applicable physical ailment can be attributed to drug abusers, the condition which is purportedly treated is defined as mental.† The conclusions drawn from labeling addicts mentally ill have been summarized as follows: "In recent years, professionals, non-professionals, and groups best designated unprofessionals, have taken to viewing drug abuse as a symptom of psychopathology—necessitating verbal and/or chemotherapeutic intervention. . . . Once we view the drug abuser as being sick, we automatically fall into the trap of assuming and recommending 'treatment' for him" (51). Physicians who operate on the premise that all addicts are psychologically ill are at no loss for specific diagnoses to apply to individual patients. One study of 91 women addicts, for instance, concluded that every one suffered from either "chronic brain syndrome," "psychotic disorder," "psychoneurotic disorder," "personality pattern disorder," "personality trait disorder," or "sociopathic personality disorder" (52). Labels such as these presumably define the "diseases" which involuntary treatment aims to cure.

SUCCESS: POTENTIALLY MORE OMINOUS THAN FAILURE

The only condition which the courts have imposed on compulsory treatment is that it be "effective." As stated in a recent New York judicial decision: "The extended period of deprivation of liberty which the [New York State Narcotic Control Act] statute mandates can only be justified as neces-

*The same conclusion was reached by other critics, who observed that addicts ". . . would prefer to spend six, nine or twelve months in jail, where there is no rehabilitation, rather than risk commitment [to the State Narcotic Addiction Control Commission] for three years" (48).

†According to the American Medical Association Council of Mental Health, "There is a general agreement among all students of addiction that addicts have personality aberrations and that these psychiatric conditions preceded and played an important role in the genesis of addiction, its maintenance, and the high relapse rate after treatment. . ." (50).

sary to fulfill the purpose of the program. . . . If compulsory commitment turns out in fact to be a veneer for an extended jail term and is not a fully-developed, comprehensive and effective scheme, it will have lost its claim to be a project devoted solely to curative ends . . . and the constitutional guarantees applicable to criminal proceedings will apply in full measure" (53). Unfortunately, however, evaluation of treatment effectiveness is one of the most controversial and ill-defined aspects of addiction treatment; to the extent that evaluation is carried out at all, it is generally done by those who are responsible for program operations. This is a weak foundation indeed upon which to permit and encourage the "extended period of deprivation of liberty" of tens or hundreds of thousands of individuals.

To dwell on the evidence suggesting that involuntary addiction treatment fails to meet the legally required test of effectiveness would mask the more basic criticism—that "success" is a potentially far worse consequence for the unwilling subject. By definition, the involuntary patient enters the enforced therapeutic relationship rejecting the clinician's objectives. "Cure" and "rehabilitation," therefore, represent goals which the addict has not chosen, and can be achieved only by changing values and attitudes as well as behavior. Acting for society, the all-powerful clinical director is the sole judge of what is healthy and appropriate: He defines the disease and makes the diagnosis; he decides on the therapeutic goals and implements the procedures he hopes will achieve these goals, even though they are openly rejected by the patient; and it is he who measures the effectiveness of treatment.* "Failure" is attributed to the patient rather than to the program, and it is the patient who pays the price for failing to meet the clinician's expectations, either by continued imposition of unwanted therapy, or by incarceration.

Although drug abuse is the behavior which, by being labeled an illness, forms the medicolegal rationale for permitting treatment to be forced on the addict, the scope of the clinician's objectives will almost invariably be broader than simply eliminating the illicit use of drugs. All other forms of behavior which the clinican believes to be pathological, on the basis of his own and society's prejudices, will also be dealt with. Thus, the addict who is a homosexual may well find his sexual preference a focus of the therapeutic effort. The same is true of the involuntarily committed addict who belongs to a bizarre religious sect; or who is a member of a radical

*As the following candid statement reveals, addict-patients are considered "successful" when they are finally willing to accept whatever grim reality others consider appropriate: "From the addict's point of view, he properly perceives that the therapist is, in fact, trying to engage him in a conventional life, which will often mean low pay and prestige, continued insecurity, and poor access to the goals of our affluent society. This conformity, which society demands of the addict, is neither respected nor valued when it is achieved" (54).

political group; or who engages in any other activity which is classified as deviant and therefore viewed as an additional component of the "symptom complex." As a prerequisite to discharge and freedom, the involuntary patient has no choice but to acquiesce to these "rehabilitative" goals.

THE MEDICAL ETHICS OF TREATING THE INVOLUNTARY ADDICT

Legal experts may argue over the constitutionality of involuntary treatment of addicts. Politicians and the lay public may weigh the effectiveness of such treatment. Economists may enter into heated debates over its absolute and relative cost–benefit. But the clinician who accepts patients rendered powerless to refuse his services assumes the role of persecutor. Rationalizations can not obfuscate the issue: In dealing with an unwilling subject, a doctor is by definition striving to bring about a change in behavior which the patient does not wish; he accepts payment from society in order to work against the perceived self-interest of the patient, and in so doing violates the most basic canons of professional ethics.

There are legal restraints against an internist who, in his professional wisdom, may be tempted to imprison a diabetic who refuses to adhere to a prescribed diet. A surgeon, recognizing the inevitable consequences of ignoring a malignancy, is nevertheless restrained from operating on a cancer patient without informed consent. Similar ethical and legal sanctions, however, do not apply to coercive psychotherapy; this is particularly ironic in view of the wide gap which commonly separates the psychiatrist and the patient. "Evidence is accumulating that psychiatric patients and the professionals who serve them are worlds apart. This is especially true for patients of the lower social classes who constitute the major caseload of many hospital clinics and community mental health centers [and drug addiction programs]. These patients frequently have goals and expectations of treatment that differ from those of the therapists who treat them. . . . The dropout rates of up to 60% after the first interview have been attributed to these discrepancies" (55). Nowhere are these discrepancies more apparent than in the field of addiction treatment, as the following assessment of a methadone program in Pennsylvania illustrates: "[The patient] wants anything that will help him in his habit—either to overcome it or to help him live with it—but the therapist wants to lay hands on his psyche. . . . [Patients] considered themselves to be mentally and emotionally sound. . . . Nevertheless, 95% of the staff at the Program believed themselves to be basically involved in the treatment and rehabilitation of mentally disturbed persons. . . . As the patient sees it, he is being treated for an ailment that he does not have by a staff member employing techniques which he finds irrelevant or frightening or both" (56).*

INVOLUNTARY TREATMENT AS AN ALTERNATIVE TO CRIMINAL JUSTICE

"Diversion" of addicts from the criminal justice system to a treatment program has become a common practice throughout the country in recent years.† This approach, which purports to deal with addict-offenders as "patients" rather than as criminals, has been heralded as an enlightened, humane alternative to an expensive and ineffective prison stay. While the rationale is that the addict's alleged crime was due to his medical affliction, the period of compulsory treatment is determined less on clinical grounds than by the nature of the criminal offense which brought the addict before the court. Generally, addicts convicted of misdemeanors are committed to treatment for shorter periods of time than those convicted of felonies, ". . . a differential which smacks of penal rather than therapeutic aims" (59).

There are several mechanisms by which the criminal justice system forces addicts into treatment. In some cases, the court may impose a sentence on the convicted addict specifically mandating a term in a treatment facility in lieu of prison; such terms can extend either for an indefinite period of time, depending upon the "progress" perceived by the clinician, or for a minimum duration which frequently exceeds the longest sentence possible for the criminal act itself (60).

The other commonly used diversion technique offers a "choice" to the addict: either stay in prison, or "voluntarily" enter and remain in a specified treatment program. This practice is particularly invidious when applied (as is increasingly the case) to the pretrial addict-prisoner whose alleged offense is compounded by his inability to obtain bail money; frequently, the prosecutor's agreement to release a defendant is reserved for those persons whose charges are relatively minor (i.e., misdemeanors and low-degree, drug-related felonies). The composite, therefore, amounts to primarily poor people, arrested on charges of which they are presumably innocent under the law, and which even upon conviction would carry comparatively short

*The authors conclude that patients "lack the cultural background necessary to understand the nature of—or need for—psychiatric treatment" (57).

†"Increasingly, the major source of funds and the aegis for the expansion of treatment programs throughout the United States are programs closely integrated with the Criminal Justice System in various court-diversion schemes. These come primarily from the U.S. Department of Justice, and their primary focus is clear: expand treatment in order to contribute to the reduction of crime" (58).

sentences, being "offered the opportunity" to enter a treatment program they may or may not want or need, and which will in any event provide society with the means of observing and controlling their activities for an extended period of time. Ironically, it is in precisely these cases that advocates embrace diversion as an especially humane expedient.

Superficially, diversion seems to offer advantages to all the parties involved. Those who work in the criminal justice system are plagued by the knowledge that prisons do not as a rule "correct" anybody, and yet simply releasing criminals without punishment is not feasible. With addict-defendants, there is a third alternative: to force them, under threat of imprisonment, to enter a treatment facility with the assurance that the clinical staff will promptly report absconders. This option addresses the problem of ineffective and overcrowded jails; the judge and prosecutor are reasonably secure in the belief that the treatment facility staff will closely monitor the addict's behavior; the addict has been permitted to escape, at least temporarily, prison confinement for a more subtle punishment; and the treatment center frequently welcomes the added "business" and often believes that it will be more successful in dealing with a captive population. The means of achieving these alleged benefits, however, lead to other disturbing problems:

The judge and the prosecutor engage in inequitable justice by providing different punishment to different people charged with the identical offense, merely because one happens to be an addict and is deemed "treatable." In addition, they fail in their role as protectors of society by imposing as the primary condition of continued release from custody attendance at a treatment facility, based on the naive assumption that such enrollment, in and of itself, is beneficial to the individual and to the community. Finally, they are often left with the task of deciding which type of treatment program should be imposed, a decision for which they are rarely qualified.

The addict-defendant is obliged to accept treatment which he generally does not want for an illness which he more often than not believes to be nonexistent. Further, the addict who has not yet been tried and convicted forfeits the opportunity to prove his innocence by accepting treatment in lieu of prosecution.

The clinic staff, in agreeing to share the responsibilities of the criminal justice system, is faced with the conflict inherent in trying to meet a commitment to both the patient and the community. Clinical judgment must inevitably be compromised since medical decisions (for instance, to terminate treatment) are made with the knowledge that criminal sanctions will be imposed on the patient as a result.

CONSEQUENCES OF ABANDONING INVOLUNTARY TREATMENT

None of the arguments against involuntary treatment of addiction detracts from the necessity of continuing to provide *voluntary* services. Nor do the arguments against coercive diversion from the criminal justice system to addiction treatment programs imply the need for the continued ineffective and inhumane incarceration of addicts. The number and type of people imprisoned merely reflect the philosophy and practices of enforcement agencies. Rounding up drug users and imposing long jail terms for charges of possession of "dangerous drugs and paraphernalia" is no more rational or productive than sentencing such individuals to therapy. In addition, criticism of compulsory treatment in no way undermines the concept that the criminal justice system must retain alternatives to incarceration, such as parole and probation; these and other means of circumventing the futile and self-defeating practice of imprisonment, however, should not be used to impose "treatment" on individuals against their will.

If compulsory treatment as a form of punishment were to be eliminated, the addict-defendant would be unable to plead illness as a justification for crime, or as a rationale for avoiding the usual penalties imposed on nonaddicts for similar offenses. Equal severity of the law is no less important a principle than the corollary equal protection.*

In contemplating the impact of eliminating involuntary treatment of addicts, it is important to consider the insignificant role it has played in two countries where addiction seems to have been contained.

England, though reputedly dealing with addiction as a medical rather than criminal problem, does not compel anyone to enter treatment. Nor is the addict offered a "choice" of therapy in lieu of pretrial detention, or as a condition of release from jail after conviction.

In the case of Japan, the 1963 Narcotics Control Law did provide for compulsory hospitalization. At the same time, however, this statute ushered in a massive enforcement effort against narcotics importation and trafficking, which was launched by a police department with a reputation for efficiency and absolute incorruptibility. These and other factors in the ensuing 6 years resulted in a decline in the esti-

*The inconsistency and illogic of current policy in this regard are clear: "No existing law makes it a condition of commitment that a relation between the addiction and crime charged be shown. The addict is not even required to establish that his addiction existed at the time of the alleged crime. Thus an addict may be relieved of his obligation to answer a criminal charge even though his addiction was entirely unrelated to that charge" (61).

mated number of heroin addicts from 40,000 to a few hundred (62).* The role of involuntary hospitalization in this achievement was negligible: during the 6-year period, only 593 people were forced to accept treatment. It is also noteworthy that Japan never permits treatment to be substituted for prosecution or incarceration.

THE NYC MMTP POSITION

The arguments outlined in this chapter were offered by the NYC MMTP in defense of its position on voluntarism. Although few advocates of compulsory treatment were persuaded to change their views, fortuitous circumstance permitted the Program's original orientation to prevail without significant compromise.

Civil commitment of addicts in New York has always been a function of the New York State Narcotic Addiction Control Commission; the inability of the Commission to maintain the census in its own facilities at or near capacity precluded any pressure on local programs to share in this role. Rather, the difficulty faced by the NYC MMTP was generated at the City level by the implementation in 1972 of a federally funded "court diversion project" by the Addiction Services Agency. The A.S.A. viewed NYC MMTP's large network of clinics as a logical resource for the referral of addict-defendants. Since such clients were not voluntary, I argued that they could not be accepted. A high-level meeting was arranged to resolve the impasse, and despite my strong opposition, I was directed to accept referrals arranged by the new A.S.A. program from the criminal justice system.

At precisely the time the court diversion project began, however, waiting lists for methadone treatment in New York City started to decline. Within a matter of months many other program directors were anxiously seeking referrals from any source in order to maintain their census, and after accepting less than 100 clients, the NYC MMTP received no further referrals from the A.S.A. Project staff. The *de facto* resolution of this problem, however, is obviously impermanent. Renewed demands will inevitably be made ". . . for a crackdown on violent crime by interning hard-core addicts in treatment camps—if that's what they need" (63), and for more subtle but equally undesirable variations on the theme of compulsory treatment.

The analogy is frequently made between drug addiction and contagious disease. In that context, it should be noted that even where a readily defined illness, with a recognized etiology, exists (which is not the case with addic-

*Not to be overlooked is the fact that during this same period of time Japan experienced the most extraordinary economic growth in world history.

tion), and even where that illness can be universally cured by appropriate treatment (which also is not the case with addiction), elimination of the problem from a community generally requires far broader measures. Thus, tuberculosis was brought under control not by the introduction of chemotherapeutic agents, but by a substantial improvement in living conditions; in areas where that improvement has not occurred, the disease persists despite the availability of medication. Venereal disease is widespread throughout the world, even though each individual patient can be readily diagnosed and cured.

It must be recognized that addiction is a social problem which will never be eliminated by measures which are imposed on the addicts themselves. Until this is understood, our effectiveness in dealing with drug abuse will remain severely limited. In the meantime, there is an obligation to continue providing the optimal treatment services to those who voluntarily seek help.

6

Confidentiality: The Case of *People vs. Newman**

At stake in this litigation is the power of a local grand jury, intent on bringing before the bar of justice one suspect thought to have committed a crime involving one other person, to require a public official to act in a manner that jeopardizes and threatens irreparable damage to drug abuse treatment programs involving tens of thousands of patients throughout the country, for if the principle of absolute confidentiality is breached in New York, it will be virtually impossible to give addicts anywhere any meaningful assurance (65).

On June 7, 1972, Talmadge Berry was shot and killed in front of 1787 Amsterdam Avenue in New York City. Several days later a Police Department detective appeared at one of the NYC MMTP clinics, stated that he was investigating a homicide, and requested access to patient photographs to show to an alleged witness who believed she had seen the perpetrator being treated at the clinic on a prior occasion. After consulting me, the clinic refused. Approximately one week later, the Manhattan District Attorney served a subpoena *duces tecum* on the supervisor of the clinic involved, requiring that he appear before the Grand Jury and produce "photographs of all male Negro patients between the ages of 21 and 35 in the Methadone Maintenance Treatment Program."

At that time there were no Program guidelines to follow in responding to this unprecedented situation. The first decision which had to be made was whether to fight the subpoena or comply and produce the photographs. It was assumed that since this case involved murder, both the courts and the general public would be hostile to the Program's refusal to cooperate with the police. Furthermore, no Federal regulations then existed to interpret the laws governing confidentiality of addiction treatment records, or to support noncompliance. Finally, there had as yet been no court test of the

*See reference (64).

general policy of the NYC MMTP to refuse disclosure of patient information without written consent, and it was feared that pursuing this particular case might prove not only futile, but decidedly counterproductive; a negative court ruling could serve as a precedent to vitiate the Program's confidentiality provisions in far less dramatic cases. Despite these apprehensions, there was a consensus among the administrative staff that the challenge should be resisted, and the City's Corporation Counsel, reluctantly, agreed to attempt to quash the subpoena.

Once this decision had been made, it became imperative to remove the responsibility from the clinic supervisor. It was successfully argued that only the Program Director had ultimate authority to release confidential patient records, and the District Attorney agreed to reissue the subpoena in my name.* Accordingly, on June 30, 1972, an identical subpoena demanding the production of the photographs was served on me.

In the "Memorandum of Law" submitted by the Corporation Counsel to the New York Supreme Court in support of its motion to quash the subpoena, the following arguments were made.

Strict confidentiality is critical to ensure the success of methadone maintenance programs. "If such confidentiality is not maintained, the trust of the patients will be lost and many will not remain in treatment. . . . Those who do continue in treatment will have lost the trust in the clinic staff which is indispensable to successful patient management" (67).

Reference was made to federal confidentiality regulations which had been proposed in the Federal Register on April 6, 1972: "Information that would identify the patient will be kept confidential pursuant to section 303 of the Public Health Service Act and will not be divulged in any civil, criminal, administrative or other proceedings conducted by Federal, State or local authorities" (68).

Disclosure of the subpoenaed photographs would violate State law governing medical treatment in general: "Unless the patient waives the privilege [of confidentiality], a person authorized to practice medicine . . . shall not be allowed to disclose any information which he acquired in attending a patient in a professional capacity, and which was necessary to enable him to act in that capacity" (69). Since

*The revised federal confidentiality regulations promulgated in July, 1975, incorporated the NYC MMTP recommendation in this regard: ". . . a single member of the program staff should be designated to process inquiries and requests for patient information . . ." (66). It is critical that a specified individual, preferrably the director, be responsible for release of information to ensure that a program's responses will be consistent, and that the consequence of failing to comply with subpoenas and other requests fall squarely on the individual with ultimate responsibility for the program's operation.

the photographs were considered by the Program to be indispensable to the safe and effective management of its patients, they fell into the category of information which is a prerequisite to treatment, and therefore were protected against disclosure.

In a last-minute effort to resolve the issue through negotiation, a meeting was convened on June 30, 1972, by the Regional Office of the Department of Health, Education, and Welfare (H.E.W.). In the presence of a representative of the Corporation Counsel, the Assistant District Attorney and myself, an H.E.W. attorney suggested the following "compromise": if the Program promptly produced the photographs, the District Attorney would agree to tear up the subpoena and, in the future, the District Attorney would demand confidential information "only in particularly important cases." I did not feel that this proposal was satisfactory, and the court case proceeded.

The motion of the City to quash the subpoena was denied by the New York Supreme Court on July 14, 1972. At this point, indicating that it considered the case hopeless, the Corporation Counsel refused to support the NYC MMTP in further litigation. It was also made clear that there was no sympathy within the Corporation Counsel's office for the Program's position.† Consequently, if efforts to withhold the records were to continue, it would be necessary to obtain outside legal counsel.

Although the City Charter ordinarily requires that City employees be represented in such proceedings by the Corporation Counsel, an exception is permitted in cases where an official is personally threatened with a contempt of court citation (73). My brother, Thomas Newman, a partner in the firm of Siff and Newman which specializes in appellate law, was willing to take over the litigation without compensation.

On Tuesday, July 25, 1972, the motion to quash the subpoena having been denied, I appeared before the Grand Jury and once again refused to comply with the demand to produce the photographs. Accompanied by my brother, who was now serving as my attorney, I was taken before Supreme Court Justice Sydney Fine and found in contempt of court; the judge ruled that ". . . for the said Contempt of Court, the said Robert Newman be committed to the custody of the Warden of the Civil Jail of the City of New York for a

*I later learned that Corporation Counsel had urged City Hall to fire me if at this point I refused to drop the case and supply the photographs to the District Attorney. The press coverage in the early stages of the case undoubtedly played a role in the Administration's decision to ignore Corporation Counsel's advice: reports of the lower court proceedings in the Daily News (70) and the New York Times (71) were objective, subdued, and nonjudgmental. The only editorial comment in the New York City newspapers appeared in the Post, which applauded the refusal of the NYC MMTP to comply with the subpoena (72).

term of 30 days." In order to permit my counsel time to request a stay of sentence pending appeal, incarceration was delayed for two days.

Considerable outside support had been received for the Program's stance in the week prior to the contempt ruling. On Saturday evening, July 22, the Deputy Director of the Special Action Office for Drug Abuse Prevention (S.A.O.D.A.P.) had flown to New York from Washington and hand-delivered a letter signed by the S.A.O.D.A.P. General Counsel. The letter underscored the importance of assuring addicts that treatment records would be maintained in confidence: "Because a high proportion of heroin addicts are involved in a life style which puts them in fear of criminal prosecution, any effort to modify that life style through participation in a treatment program is bound to be compromised if the addict believes that such participation will generate records which increase the risks he already feels. Stated more positively, all the operators of treatment programs with whom we have talked believe that it is important for them to give assurance of confidentiality to persons entering treatment, and we share this view" (74).

On the same day I received a letter from the Steering Committee of the National Association of Methadone Program Directors, which stated: "The issue of confidentiality involved [in the current court case] bears directly and substantively on our ability to deliver effective services to drug dependent persons. The rupture of trust between patients and physicians which may result from this legal action will have serious and destructive effects on rehabilitation services not only in the City of New York, but also in major urban areas throughout the United States. The expectation of confidentiality is a necessary precondition for treatment, and we have noted that the concern of prospective patients in this regard is so great as to inhibit many of them from accepting services" (75). Additional letters of support were received from Dr. Vincent Dole of The Rockefeller University, from the Subcommittee on Confidentiality of the Health Data Committee of the New York City Comprehensive Health Planning Agency, and from the New York Civil Liberties Union.

Probably the most significant correspondence of all came from the Food and Drug Administration in response to the Program's request for an opinion regarding the relevance of the confidentiality regulations which were then still in the "proposed" state. On July 25, 1972, I received a telegram from the Assistant General Counsel of the F.D.A.: "After consultation with the President's Special Action Office for Drug Abuse Prevention and the National Institute of Mental Health, the Commissioner of Food and Drugs has concluded pursuant to Section 3 of the Comprehensive Drug Abuse Prevention and Control Act of 1970 that the confidentiality provisions of the Federal Register Notice on Methadone published April 6, 1972, shall be effective immediately pending promulgation of final regulations in this matter" (76). In essence, although the Program had only requested an opinion regarding the intent of the government expressed in proposed regulations, the F.D.A. responded by implementing the relevant regulation.

Late in the afternoon of July 26, the day before the jail sentence was to begin, a stay was granted by the Appellate Court over the strenuous objection of the District Attorney. This afforded the Program's counsel time to prepare an appeal, and in the subsequent months, as word of the case spread, dozens of letters of support were received from across the country.

Oral argument before the New York Appellate Division took place in September, 1972. In its decision, announced on October 2, the Court upheld the subpoena but at the same time modified and restricted the conditions under which disclosure was ordered: "... that the witness view the photos under supervision of defendent Commissioner or someone designated by him, and that none of the pictures may be exhibited to the police or prosecutor except that one which she may identify as the person sought..." (77). Since this modification still rejected the principle of absolute confidentiality, I decided to pursue the case and appeal to the highest New York State court, the Court of Appeals. Some individuals previously in support of the Program's position did not agree with this decision, fearing that the case would ultimately be lost anyway, and that the "partial victory" gained in the Appellate Division would be jeopardized in the process.

A number of developments in late 1972, however, seemed to enhance the Program's chances of having the lower court ruling overturned. In response to a request submitted in October, the NYC MMTP received a special "Grant of Confidentiality" from the Director of the Bureau of Narcotics and Dangerous Drugs, acting for the United States Attorney General. The Grant, based on a provision of the 1970 Comprehensive Drug Abuse Prevention and Treatment Act,* read as follows:

> ... I hereby authorize you to withhold the names and other identifying characteristics of persons who are the subject of research conducted pursuant to and in conformity with this research project [the NYC MMTP]. You may not be compelled in any Federal, State or local civil, criminal, administrative, legislative or other proceeding to identify the subjects of such research (78).

In the same month, S.A.O.D.A.P. published regulations interpreting the relationship of the 1970 Act, which was the basis for the Grant of Confidentiality, to the Drug Abuse Office and Treatment Act of 1972, which provided

*Under this Act, directors of research projects studying the effect of drugs could apply to the Attorney General for special, absolute privileges against enforced disclosure of patient information. It was subsequently learned that the NYC MMTP was the first addiction treatment program to request and receive such a Grant of Confidentiality.

that courts could authorize the release of confidential patient information after applying the "balancing test".* If, as the District Attorney argued, the earlier statute was repealed by the 1972 law, then it would be necessary to conclude that "the Attorney General's 'Grant' of Confidentiality is a nullity" (80). According to S.A.O.D.A.P., however, the 1970 Act was *not* superseded: "Nothing in either the language or the legislative history of the provisions of the [1972] Act indicates any intent on the part of Congress to amend the provisions of the 1970 Act or to reduce the protection which can be afforded under them" (81). The same opinion was stated in the *amicus curiae* brief supporting the Program's position which was submitted by the Federal Government to the Court of Appeals.

The case was argued before the Court of Appeals on March 23, 1973. On May 31 the Court decided in favor of the Program, ruling that ". . . the order of the Appellate Division of the Supreme Court appealed from . . . is reversed, . . . the adjudication of contempt vacated and the motion to quash the subpoena granted" (82). The decision was reached by a majority of four to three. In elaborating on its ruling, the Court stated that the critical factor had been its determination that the 1970 legislation was still in effect, and that consequently the Program's Grant of Confidentiality was valid and protected the NYC MMTP against forced disclosure. At the same time, the Court rejected the other arguments upon which the appeal was based, specifically the confidentiality afforded by State law to the patient–physician relationship.

The final chapter in this case did not come until January 21, 1974, 18 months after the proceedings began, when the United States Supreme Court denied the petition of the Manhattan District Attorney for a *writ of certiorari* (review of the decision). The vote of the Court was 7 to 2 to let stand the New York State Court of Appeals decision. The case was then closed, and the NYC MMTP had succeeded in maintaining confidentiality of its patients' records.

Initially, the Program had somewhat naively hoped that this legal victory would discourage further demands for confidential information. Actual experience proved otherwise, and subpoenas and other attempts to gain access to patient records continued unabated. In light of the precedent which was established, however, it has been consistently possible for the subpoenas to be quashed in the lower courts.

The difficulties associated with a case of this type go far beyond the legal

*The balancing test was designed to guide the courts in determining whether a program should be permitted to release patient information without consent: "In assessing good cause the court shall weigh the public interest and the need for disclosure against the injury to the patient, to the physician–patient relationship, and to the treatment services" (79).

arguments raised by the opposition. There is an almost irresistable temptation to justify yielding to the pressures which are created, and a limitless capacity for rationalization. This case, after all, involved a murder, so perhaps an exception to the usual Program policies would be warranted; the request was limited to some photographs and addresses, and the bulk of the patient records would be kept secret; adverse publicity could do far more harm to the Program than yielding in this one instance; chances were good that the witness would not be able to identify any of the photographs anyway; the general policy of preserving confidentiality was endangered, and it would be better to at least salvage some vestige of Program policy than risk total defeat; the case would detract from the many other obligations attendant to directing a huge, still expanding, treatment program; etc.

In retrospect, the single most indispensable element in the ultimate outcome of this case was the availability of competent and dedicated legal counsel, willing to contribute time and talent to achieve a highly significant victory against staggering odds. Had the defense of the Program's position been left to the City Corporation Counsel, the initial ruling by the lower court would never have been appealed, let alone reversed.* Giving up without exhausting all legal recourse, simply because the chances of success were small, would have destroyed the program's credibility—and credibility, especially with patients and prospective patients, is, after all, what the struggle to maintain confidentiality is all about.

*The Federal confidentiality regulations promulgated in July, 1975, clearly recognized the need for adequate legal representation: "... [E]xperience has demonstrated that independent counsel may be of crucial importance. The leading case construing 21 U.S.C. 1175, *People v. Newman*, ... would never have been presented to the courts but for the fact that legal counsel for Dr. Newman was furnished on a *pro bono publico* basis by a private law firm. In an entirely different case, a United States District Court appears to have issued a wholly inappropriate order under 21 U.S.C. 1175 in a case in which the treatment program was operated by an agency of the United States Government, and either was unrepresented, or was represented by the same attorney who represented the agency seeking the order" (83). Because of this recognition, the new regulations specifically state: "Any application [for a court order to secure confidential information] ... shall be denied unless the court makes an explicit finding to the effect that the program has been afforded the opportunity to be represented by counsel independent of counsel for the applicant, and in the case of any program operated by any department or agency of Federal, State, or local Government, is in fact so represented" (84).

7

Confidentiality: Development of Program Policies and Procedures

INTRODUCTION

The orientation of the NYC MMTP regarding confidentiality of patient records was initially expressed as a broad, and in retrospect meaningless, generalization: "The Program will maintain confidentiality of patient records." This policy was considered so self-evident and unambiguous that explicit guidelines and procedures relating to confidentiality were not included in the first Policy and Procedures Manual prepared by the Program in July, 1971.

As the NYC MMTP patient population grew, the frequency of demands for access to patient information grew proportionately; by 1973, when 10,000 patients were enrolled, it was not at all unusual for several subpoenas to be pending at once. In addition to having records subpoenaed, less official demands were received from an almost endless variety of sources, including the District Attorneys and the Police Department, the City Fire Marshall, the State professional licensing authority, the Federal Bureau of Investigation, the Immigration and Naturalization Service, the State Drug Abuse Control Commission, narcotics enforcement agencies at all levels of government, parole and probation officers, the Bureau of Child Welfare, Family Court, relatives and acquaintances of patients, and individuals engaged in every imaginable type of research. The one characteristic common to virtually all of the inquiries was the acknowledgement that while confidentiality, in general, was essential, in the particular case in question an exception should be made. The rationale in each instance was felt to be so compelling that the usual arguments for maintaining patient privacy did not apply: "But we're trying to capture an arsonist." "This case involves a kidnapping." "We believe this patient is smuggling illegal immigrants into the country."

"I'm writing a Ph.D. thesis and I need a quick look at a sampling of patient records."

The intense interest which has been focused on the records of Program patients is not surprising. By definition, every applicant for treatment identifies himself (herself) as a criminal who has not only been engaged in the illegal act of possession of narcotics and the paraphernalia associated with its use, but who has also generally supported the high price of a physical dependence on heroin through criminal activities. In addition, there is the extraordinary prejudice which society at large, and law enforcement agencies in particular,* harbor against patients and former patients; the adage "once an addict, always an addict" persists, and little distinction is made between the heroin user on the street and the patient receiving medical and ancillary care in a clinical setting. Finally, unlike the elusive street addict, applicants and patients by the tens of thousands are known to be conveniently listed in the files maintained by large treatment programs such as the NYC MMTP. Addiction treatment program records are consequently a logical pond in which to fish for suspects.

THE PROBLEMS OF INCONSISTENCY

In establishing and implementing a policy of absolute confidentiality, the NYC MMTP was hampered by the practices of other methadone programs. The 1972 Procedure Manual of the Santa Clara County Methadone Program, one of the most prestigious and widely known programs in the country, stated that, "The names and addresses of patients entering the program are forwarded to all law enforcement agencies. . . . Requests for information about patients by law enforcement officials should be answered in a very circumspect manner. It is reasonable to confirm that a particular patient is or is not currently on the program, but any additional information must be regarded as part of the confidential medical records of the clinic. . . . When a patient is discharged, however, this fact is reported to all the agencies to whom the original report of his entry onto the program was made. The same policy is followed if a patient is absent for a period of two weeks" (87).† A

*A survey of attitudes of police chiefs in 27 major cities of the United States concluded: "The prevailing tone [with respect to addiction treatment] in the interviews was one of skepticism. Treatment hadn't worked" (85). Methadone treatment, in particular, was ". . . controversial in police circles, and among the chiefs interviewed the predominant attitude was not favorable" (86).

†The experience of the NYC MMTP is that the enquirer's primary interest almost invariably is limited to determining whether an individual is enrolled in the Program, and what his (her) address is. An additional and somewhat related question, asked especially by parole and probation officers, is whether the individual has been discharged from treatment.

similar orientation was expressed by a methadone program in New Orleans, which also routinely provided names and addresses of clients to the police (88). Undoubtedly a great many other addiction treatment agencies in New York City and elsewhere did likewise.

An additional problem in implementing the internal policies of the NYC MMTP was created by the abuses of secondary sources to whom the Program must report. It has not been unusual for an individual to state: "We were already told by the Department of Social Services that Mr. Z. is a patient in one of your clinics; all we want to know is which clinic he attends".*

Consistency within the Program itself is of primary importance in maintaining credibility. While occasional deviations from established policies and procedures are inevitable in a large program such as the NYC MMTP,† these instances can be minimized by the clear definition of terms:

In the light of Program experience, the definition of "patient" was expanded to include applicants for treatment and former patients, as well as those individuals who are currently enrolled.

"Patient information" was not defined explicitly until a District Attorney attempted to persuade a court that photographs were not part of the "medical record" and thus not covered by the usual rules which apply to confidentiality of treatment information. It would obviously vitiate the intent of the laws, regulations and policies governing confidentiality if patient identity were excluded from the protection given other patient information. The current definition of patient information is intended to be all-inclusive: ". . . all reports, records, photographs, or data maintained in connection with the operation of the Program. It includes the fact that a person is currently in the Program, was in the Program, or has ever applied to the Program, as well as any information which may be communicated orally regarding a patient" (89).

The term "Program" has, from the outset, included the NYC MMTP Central Office as well as each of the component treatment units, and access to patient records is not limited to the staff in the clinics.

*For several years, addicts were required by the New York City Department of Social Services (D.S.S.) to prove that they were enrolled in addiction treatment programs to be eligible for welfare assistance. When confirmation was provided by the Program, pursuant to written authorization of the patient, it became part of the client record maintained by D.S.S., which refused to apply any special confidentiality provisions to such data.

†For example, a woman whose pocketbook was stolen took it for granted that the thief was a patient in one of the Program's clinics which happened to be in the neighborhood; the Unit Supervisor, in flagrant violation of Program policies, permitted her to review the photographs of all enrolled patients. Ironically, this incident took place in the midst of the court battle stemming from my refusal to divulge photographs subpoenaed by a Grand Jury in connection with a homicide case (see Chapter 6).

Since almost all of the clinics comprising the NYC MMTP are administered under contract by hospitals, it was necessary to make explicit reference to "hospital records" which identify patients as participants in the Program. Although such reference is incorporated in the confidentiality section of the Policy and Procedures Manual and is contractually binding on the hospitals, no satisfactory safeguard has been developed to ensure that institutional records are, in fact, afforded the same stringent protection which applies to all other Program records.

THE RATIONALE FOR MAINTAINING CONFIDENTIALITY

When demands for information are refused, the Program is frequently accused of being indifferent, or overtly hostile, to the needs and the concerns of society. Ironically, the protection of the community is one of the primary objectives in maintaining confidentiality, without which addicts would not be attracted into treatment. The underlying premise which guides the Program's policies is that addicts, if denied meaningful and acceptable treatment, will exact a tremendous toll on the general population because of the antisocial life style which is associated with illicit drug use.

An area of particular concern is the crime attributed to narcotic addicts. Although controversy exists regarding both the dollar cost of addiction to society and the causal relationship between drug use and crime, society clearly benefits when large numbers of addicts enter treatment (this is especially true of methadone maintenance, with its demonstrated ability to retain patients and assist them in assuming productive lives).

Consequently, policies which are intended to facilitate the apprehension and prosecution of an individual criminal, but simultaneously discourage thousands from seeking treatment, will prove counterproductive. It was this conclusion which prompted Congress to endorse the confidentiality provisions of the 1972 Drug Abuse Office and Treatment Act: ". . . the strictest adherence to the provisions of this section [on confidentiality] is absolutely essential to the success of all drug abuse prevention programs. Every patient and former patient must be assured that his right to privacy will be protected" (90).*

*The same rationale was restated by the Special Action Office for Drug Abuse Prevention in introducing the specific confidentiality regulations authorized by the 1972 Act: "If society is to make significant progress in the struggle against drug abuse, it is imperative that all unnecessary impediments to voluntary treatment be removed. . . . The only effect of [the addict's] enrollment is to diminish the likelihood of his continued criminal conduct, and if the price of this is to isolate the records generated by the enrollment itself, this is a small price indeed in light of the social benefits" (91).

Another area which has received considerable publicity is the apparent association between drug addiction and child abuse and neglect (92). By providing medical care and appropriate ancillary services to large numbers of former heroin addicts, the Program obviously helps their children as well. Regrettably, the potential impact of this assistance is frequently overlooked by child welfare agencies, which demand complete access to patient records in the course of investigating individual cases. In refusing such access, the Program has attempted to explain that if it were no longer in a position to assure patients and prospective patients of confidentiality, many thousands of children would suffer as a result.

The justification for strict confidentiality of patient information is not to protect criminals, child abusers, or any other antisocial individuals who might be patients in the NYC MMTP. Rather, it is to protect *society*, which in countless ways bears the enormous burden associated with drug addiction.

EXCEPTIONS TO THE RULE

Disclosure with Patient Consent

An unyielding policy of absolute confidentiality will inevitably conflict in certain instances with the patients' interests. It would be ridiculous to refuse to inform a medical facility of a patient's status in an emergency situation, when such information is recognized as vital to the individual's survival. Similarly, there are many occasions when the patient, in his (her) own interest, wishes to have certain information released to employers, probation or parole officials, insurance companies, and perhaps even to friends or relatives. Such consensual release of information is expressly permitted by the confidentiality regulations of the Federal government, and by the policies and procedures of the NYC MMTP.* Certain conditions, however, must be met:

Disclosure requires the written consent of the patient

The consent must specify precisely what information is to be released, to whom, and for what purpose

*It is of interest to note that in the case of venereal disease records maintained by the Department of Health, the New York City Health Code precludes the release of information even with patient consent (93). This absolute prohibition against disclosure under any circumstances also applies to information contained in the New York City Narcotics Register. The rationale is persuasive: if individuals are empowered to authorize disclosure of sensitive information, they may readily be coerced by others to do so even when it is not in their own best interests.

The NYC MMTP insists that a consent for the release of patient information be contemporaneous

The last condition is extremely important although, regrettably, it is not a prerequisite of consensual disclosure in the Federal regulations. An informed, voluntary consent requires that the patient know the precise nature of the information to be released; this condition can hardly be met when disclosure is authorized for the future release of urinalysis results, counseling notes, etc. Further, the relative advantages and disadvantages of permitting the release of information are determined by current circumstances, which will generally change over time. Authorization for disclosure which is signed long before the fact would legally justify release of information even if the patient subsequently decides that such release is contrary to his (her) interests.* For these reasons, the policy of the NYC MMTP has been to refuse to honor consent for the release of information which is not contemporaneous. The Policy and Procedures Manual specifies: "No patient shall be permitted to sign a release form which is blank, which has not been completely filled out prior to signing, or which provides for the release of information at a future date" (95).

A frequent argument raised by those who demand patient information without contemporaneous consent is that they are seeking disclosure only to "help the patient." Probation Department personnel, for example, often state that they will return a client to custody if assurance is not given that the individual is doing well in treatment. The NYC MMTP, however, has consistently maintained that agencies must prevail upon their clients to authorize release of the required information. If an agency has lost contact with a client, the Program generally offers to take the name of the individual in question and relay a message, if indeed he (she) is a patient, but the delivery of such a message is neither confirmed nor denied, since that would reveal the person's status in the Program.

Disclosure without Patient Consent

There are four situations in which disclosure of confidential information is made by the NYC MMTP without the authorization of the patient:

In the case of a medical emergency

To prevent multiple simultaneous enrollment in more than one methadone program

*This issue has particular relevance in the case of addicts who are released from custody by the criminal justice system on condition that they enroll in a treatment program. With respect to such patients, the Federal confidentiality regulations not only permit, but expressly mandate, that the initial open-ended consent to disclosure be irrevocable (94).

For purposes of audit, evaluation, and research
With the authorization of an appropriate court order, in cases where crimes are committed by patients in Program facilities

Medical Emergencies

In medical emergencies, three conditions must be met before disclosure by the NYC MMTP is made without patient consent:

There must be reasonable grounds for believing that a *bona fide* medical emergency exists, which threatens the life or health of the patient
There must be an indication that release of information from the patient's NYC MMTP record is essential for effective treatment
There must be assurance that the patient is medically unable to sign a release form permitting the disclosure to be made, or reason to believe that delay in obtaining written consent would jeopardize the patient's treatment

Preventing Multiple Simultaneous Enrollment in More than One Methadone Program

From its inception, the NYC MMTP has participated in the Methadone Information Center operated by The Rockefeller University, a computerized registry established by the State to prevent multiple simultaneous enrollment; identifying information on every person enrolled in a methadone maintenance program in the metropolitan New York area is contained in the registry. Although the NYC MMTP has found that the "problem" of multiple enrollment is minimal,* City (97) and State (98) regulations continue to mandate participation in the system, and these requirements have not been challenged by the Program [a similar requirement by the Federal Food and Drug Administration was dropped in 1974 (99).]

Audits, Evaluation, and Research

All methadone programs are obliged to permit the various Federal and State regulating agencies to spot check records for compliance with existing laws and regulations governing methadone treatment. Although there has never been any evidence that the agencies involved have abused this authority, the potential exists for using an audit as a subterfuge for gaining access to confidential information. The following incident heightened the Program's apprehension concerning audits: In September, 1974, the Deputy Director of the NYC MMTP received a call from a Group Supervisor of the Drug

*The experience of the NYC MMTP agrees with that of methadone programs in Washington, D.C., where only 20 alleged cases of attempted multiple enrollment were uncovered by a centralized "footprint registry" in the course of processing some 5000 admissions (96).

Enforcement Agency (D.E.A.), asking for information about an individual who was under investigation and believed to be a patient. The request was denied, whereupon the agent candidly stated that he could obtain the information surreptitiously in the course of a routine inspection of clinic records. Protesting this conversation with the D.E.A. District Director, we elicited a formal response which acknowledged that gathering confidential information in the course of an audit, to aid in a criminal investigation of a patient, was both inappropriate and illegal (100). Despite the assurance in that particular case, there is no way to eliminate the ever-present threat to patients' privacy which is inherent in any disclosure to agencies permitted to review clinical records.

Since the NYC MMTP is supported entirely through public funds, outside evaluation, requiring virtually unlimited access to patient files, has always been accepted as a necessary complement to the internal analyses of Program performance. Independent evaluation has been carried out by the Methadone Evaluation Committee, chaired by Dr. Frances R. Gearing of the Columbia University School of Public Health. Relying on verbal assurances, more implicit than explicit, the Program has never insisted upon formal guarantees for the protection of confidential information released to the Evaluation Committee. In retrospect, though there has been no evidence that patients' privacy has been compromised, the lack of a written agreement setting forth the conditions under which the data would be maintained was irresponsible.

In few areas has the demand for confidential information been as insistent, and refusal met with as much indignation, as in the case of research. Due to the extraordinary size of the NYC MMTP and the comprehensiveness of its data, innumerable requests have been received from researchers seeking access to Program records. Cooperation with these projects, however, has been on a highly selective basis, and any study which entails providing names or other identifying information to third parties has been routinely turned down.*

Two specific research projects to which the NYC MMTP has consistently supplied confidential patient information on all admissions, without patient consent, are the New York City Narcotics Register and the State Office of Drug Abuse Services (O.D.A.S., previously known as the Drug Abuse Con-

*For instance, several follow-up studies which have been implemented in New York involve determining the current status of former patients with the help of the Police Department, parole and probation agencies, Department of Social Services, the Social Security Administration and other agencies. The Program has refused to permit names of patients or former patients to be submitted by researchers to *any* outside agency. Disclosure by researchers to third parties was eventually prohibited in revised Federal confidentiality regulations which went into effect in August, 1975 (101).

trol Commission). In the case of the Narcotics Register, the New York City Health Code mandates that reports of known or suspected drug addicts be submitted by any person who "... has knowledge of or gives care to a narcotics addict or drug abuser" (102), but the Health Code also includes an absolute prohibition against the release of any information which identifies individuals for any reason whatever (103). The legal protection afforded the files of the Register has never been challenged in the ten years of its existence.

The contractual obligation to report names and other sociodemographic information to the O.D.A.S. on all patients (at the time of admission and at termination) has created considerable concern. The O.D.A.S. serves not only as a funding and regulating agency, but also as a provider of treatment services to involuntary clients who are certified and committed by the courts. For all practical purposes, the distinction between the O.D.A.S. and a law enforcement agency is merely semantic: The O.D.A.S. defines clients who leave its facilities as "absconders" and "escapees"; its officers issue warrants and return recalcitrant clients to institutions. In light of the Office's legislated responsibilities as a custodial agency for certified addicts, there is inevitably a strong temptation to utilize the information from voluntary programs as a means of locating thousands of clients for whom warrants are outstanding. This temptation must be especially difficult to resist since the O.D.A.S. Data Center routinely produces special listings, by reporting program, of patients who previously absconded from its facilities.

Despite the fact that there exists no concrete evidence implicating the O.D.A.S. in any abuse of the information it receives, the dual mandate of the Office as an enforcement agency and an addiction treatment and research organization led to an increasing sense of concern. In December, 1974, the NYC MMTP notified the O.D.A.S. that patient admission and termination information henceforth would be identified by a unique number, but would not include name, address, or other identifying data. In response, the Office insisted on the immediate resumption of reporting of all information, including names, and stated that financial support would be discontinued if the Program failed to comply (104). The timing of this confrontation unfortunately coincided with the emergence of New York City's severe fiscal crisis. With the specter of a loss to the City of almost $4 million in State aid, and in the absence of Federal support for the Program's position, the City soon backed down. Reporting was reinstituted, with the hope that new Federal regulations, due to be promulgated during the first half of 1975, would protect programs against such a reporting requirement.

The revised regulations, published in proposed form in May, 1975, did, in fact, prohibit Federal and State agencies from maintaining any form of "directory" or "listing" of patients in addiction treatment programs in connection with audit or regulatory functions (105). Paradoxically, however, they left State agencies with the authority to *mandate* disclosure of any and all patient information "... for the purpose of conducting scientific research or long-term evaluation studies" (106). The self-proclaimed research functions presented by the State as the rationale for submission of identifying data on all patients cannot be challenged; programs which are dependent upon the State for funding, accreditation or licensure have no recourse but to comply with any demand which is made.† Despite strenuous protests by the NYC MMTP, these new regulations went into effect on August 1, 1975.

Disclosure Pursuant to Court Orders

According to Federal regulations, addiction treatment program records may be disclosed pursuant to a court order which is issued on the basis of a finding of "good cause"; in assessing good cause, "... the court shall weigh the public interest and the need for disclosure against the injury to the patient, to the physician–patient relationship, and to the treatment services" (109).

Through the end of 1974, the NYC MMTP had never been compelled to make disclosure based on court orders initiated by an outside source. However, there have been instances where the Program itself sought a court order permitting it to disclose information without patient consent. These cases involved criminal activities perpetrated by patients on the Program premises.

The first such instance which arose is illustrative. A patient who was quite distinctive in appearance because of his size and hair color entered one of the Program clinics in April, 1974, wearing a stocking mask. The patient's identity was so unmistakable that when he approached the nursing station one nurse immediately commented to a fellow staff member: "Why do you suppose G——— is wearing that stocking over his face?" The patient proceeded to draw a gun and seize a considerable amount of methadone. Although this crime took place late on a Friday afternoon, I was able to obtain a court order

*This blanket authority of State agencies to demand unlimited access to patient information for alleged research purposes is in direct conflict with the stated intent of the regulations, "... to leave [the decision to make disclosure for research purposes] for interpretation on a case-by-case basis by those who must apply it in practice: the researchers who seek the information, and the programs which supply it" (107). Also, the Federal regulations state: "Patient identifying information may not be disclosed to a funding source, as such, whether with or without patient consent. ... [I]t is clear that Congress did not intend funding sources, as such, to have access to patient identifying information" (108). Nevertheless, it is solely through the threat of withholding funds that the New York Office of Drug Abuse Services has been able to compel programs to submit "research" data.

in less than 3 hours authorizing release of the patient's name, address, and photograph to the local police precinct.*

In another case, a patient assaulted a Unit Supervisor, hitting him over the head with a telephone and causing a concussion. A counselor immediately called the police and revealed the patient's name and address; since this was in direct violation of Federal regulations, the City's Corporation Counsel subsequently refused to seek a court order permitting the release of additional identifying information, including the patient's photograph. The patient was never apprehended, and the case served to emphasize to the staff the necessity of adhering to the procedures which apply in such instances.

*The epilogue to this case is that the police, armed with the identifying information, failed to apprehend the thief; several months later he was shot and killed following an attempted robbery of another methadone program in New York City.

8

Methadone Dosage and Duration Of Treatment

INTRODUCTION

This chapter discusses the NYC MMTP procedures with respect to:

- Informing patients of their dosage
- The use of solid versus dissolved medication
- Methadone dosage manipulation and the prescribing of nonopiate, mood-altering drugs
- Services for patients following voluntary detoxification

INFORMING PATIENTS OF THEIR DOSAGE

The NYC MMTP initially attempted to keep dosages secret from patients, assuming that this policy would allay patient concern regarding the amount of methadone prescribed, that there would be less manipulation of the staff, and that a better staff–patient relationship would be established. Many patients, however, viewed the policy as paternalistic, and staff members soon began to question the premise underlying the "blind" dosage approach. It was apparent that patients did not stop thinking and worrying about the dosage level, and there was an almost universal expression of concern that the dose being administered was inappropriate.* Six months after the Pro-

*The program in Palo Alto, California, while maintaining a double-blind dosage protocol, found that ". . . a majority of patients in all [dosage] groups regard their dose as too low" (110). The experience of the NYC MMTP, and others, was that patients were concerned about being given too much as well as too little medication: "Patients are not supposed to know their dosage

gram began, an unexpected opportunity arose which permitted a comparison of the existing procedures with a clinical situation in which all patients were informed of their dosage.

In June, 1971, several thousand methadone patients were left without care when a private program in New York City was abruptly closed by Federal authorities. In order to provide continuity of treatment for these individuals, emergency referrals were arranged to other private and public programs, and approximately 400 were sent to the NYC MMTP. To accommodate these transfers, the Program converted a decommissioned Staten Island ferry boat into a clinic facility. Since medication was initially administered and dispensed by Public Health nurses with no prior experience in addiction treatment, and without the availability of pharmacist support, the Program was obliged to use "Diskets"* which the nurses could dissolve on the spot for consumption in the clinic; take-home doses were dispensed undissolved.

Obviously, patients receiving a given number of 40-mg Diskets immediately knew their precise dosage. To the surprise of many staff members, arguments over methadone dosages very rarely occurred, even though dosage levels varied widely, and patients could quite easily determine by observation the amount of medication being administered to others. In view of this experience, the procedures of the NYC MMTP were changed in the fall of 1971, and all patients were subsequently told the exact amount of medication ordered for them. The feeling of both the staff and the patients has continued to be overwhelmingly in favor of this open policy.†

SOLID VERSUS DISSOLVED MEDICATION

As noted above, the NYC MMTP initially dissolved all medication in order to keep patients from knowing their dosages. Once the need for secrecy was no longer a factor, the many advantages of dispensing medication for take-

*"Disket" is the trade name of an Eli Lilly methadone preparation, a scored 40-mg tablet which can readily be broken by hand into four 10-mg quarters.

†The same experience was reported by the Palo Alto program: in the course of a research project, patients were not only advised of the precise amount of methadone being prescribed, but permitted (within limits) to make adjustments at will. With the uncertainty removed, very few patients availed themselves of the opportunity to change the dose, despite their previous conviction that the dosage was inadequate (112).

---

of methadone, and they resent this. One girl [sic!], for example, complained that she was feeling high and suspected that the nurse had increased her dose. She felt that her dosage was her business and that at the very least she would be informed so as to know what to expect. . . . [P]atients continued to negotiate for more or less methadone on the basis of perceived side effects"(111).

home in solid form became apparent.* From the patient's perspective, it was far easier to carry one small bottle with several days' tablets than a separate bottle for each day's medication. (This was especially relevant for those patients who visited the clinic on the way to work.) The need for "locked boxes," previously employed by the Program to lessen the likelihood of accidental ingestion by children in the patients' homes, became obsolete, to the relief of many patients who claimed the conspicuous boxes made them targets for thieves. The inconvenience of having to refrigerate medication dissolved in Tang or Kool-Aid was also eliminated.

The economic and logistical advantages for the Program of solid medication were numerous. The required number of "child-proof" bottles was drastically reduced, as was the need for medication labels; several days' medication could be dispensed in one bottle for take-home consumption, with instructions regarding the number of tablets to take each day. Depending on the quality of the bottles and caps purchased, they could generally be used on more than one occasion. It was also considerably easier for the nursing staff to place a specified number of tablets in a bottle than to have to dissolve each day's supply separately.

In March, 1972, an official of the Food and Drug Administration told a meeting of all metropolitan-area methadone program directors in New York that the F.D.A. had decided to prohibit the dispensing of liquid methadone. In explaining the rationale for this decision, it was argued that dissolved medication lent itself to "skimming" on a large scale at the pharmacy and clinic level. Most programs that dispensed liquid methadone used stock solutions prepared ahead of time from powdered methadone which, if diverted for illicit use, could be readily dissolved and injected. In a relatively large facility diversion of as little as 5% of the medication could represent a large quantity, and yet even if the discrepancy were detected, it would probably be attributed to an acceptable degree of pharmacist error.† Subsequently, however, the F.D.A. did an about-face and within a year had mandated that all programs dispense dissolved medication only (113).

Ironically, the F.D.A.'s rationale for insisting upon dissolved methadone was identical to its earlier endorsement of solid medication: there would be

*The NYC MMTP has always administered medication in solution for consumption in the clinics. In addition to ensuring that patients actually drink the methadone given to them, the Disket used by the Program was known to cause gastric irritation if taken without prior dissolving.

†Just prior to the conversion to Diskets, the NYC MMTP arranged for samples of medication prepared by pharmacists in the various contract hospitals to be quantitatively analyzed; discrepancies were found to be the rule rather than the exception, and in some cases amounted to as much as 30%. This generated considerable concern not only with respect to possible diversion of the drug, but on grounds of clinical safety and efficacy; these findings added to the urgency with which the NYC MMTP changed to tablet methadone.

less likelihood of illicit diversion. Street addicts, if given a choice, were known to prefer purchasing tablets since the dose could be determined with certainty, while dissolved methadone represented a danger either of being cheated or of unknowingly taking an overdose. Therefore, it was hypothesized that the demand for the drug on the illicit market would disappear if methadone were available in liquid form only. Predictably, black market methadone continued to be in demand, and the incidence of methadone overdose deaths among nonpatients in New York City increased sharply in the 6 months following implementation of the F.D.A. regulation in July, 1973: from 50 during the first half of the year to 131 in the last half (114).

After arguing in vain against this new ruling, the NYC MMTP had no choice but to comply. Nevertheless, the Program maintained its policy of advising patients of their dosage, and nurses have continued to prepare all medication by dissolving Diskets, rather than relying on stock solutions provided by hospital pharmacists.*

DISCOURAGING EXCESSIVE DOSAGE MANIPULATION AND PRESCRIBING OF NONOPIATE MOOD-ALTERING DRUGS

The futility of seeking to resolve all patient problems through the manipulation of methadone dosage and the use of other drugs has been recognized since the Program's inception. In this regard, the Program's Policy and Procedures Manual stresses the following precautions:

> The physician, the entire unit staff, and the patient must recognize that few individuals who have been receiving widely varying amounts of illicit narcotics will be able to change abruptly to regulated doses of methadone with absolutely no side effects. This is true regardless of the care which is exercised in determining appropriate medication schedules. Attempts to adjust dosages to the point where there are no complaints whatever are likely to produce constant frustration and cynicism among both staff and patients. . . . Patients should be encouraged to advise the staff of their response to medication. Physicians are urged to respond to patients' complaints firmly but not inflexibly; confidently, but not disinterestedly.
>
> Overemphasis on medication, especially methadone, sleeping pills and tranquilizers, will tend to reinforce an orientation which many addicts have prior to entering the Program that most, if not all, problems are solved by drugs. The Clinic staff must recognize that complaints related to sleep, sexual function and most other causes of anxiety (in the population at large no less than among our patients) usually are neither due to nor cured by medication (115).

*The Program's experience is that maximum control of methadone supplies can be assured only through the use of tablet-form medication, which permits an exact accounting of how many milligrams are received, administered and dispensed by the individual clinics.

The problem of overprescribing of psychotropic drugs is a problem which faces the medical profession at large; the fact that Valium is the most widely prescribed drug in America, and Librium the third most prevalent, is evidence of the extent of the problem (116). Although the NYC MMTP has been successful in keeping at a minimum the prescribing of mood-altering drugs by its own physicians, some patients continue to obtain such drugs from other sources.

SERVICES FOR PATIENTS FOLLOWING VOLUNTARY DETOXIFICATION

Recognizing that coercing patients to remain in treatment would be medically and morally unconscionable, and diametrically opposed to the principle that all patients must be voluntary, the Program has a firm commitment to provide every assistance to patients who opt for detoxification. Accordingly, overt or subtle pressure to dissuade patients wishing to withdraw from methadone has been avoided, and former patients are assured top priority should they seek readmission following voluntary termination; in such cases there is no minimum interval between discharge and readmission, and relapse to narcotic use is not a prerequisite.

Some staff members, however, felt that detoxified individuals should not be discharged at all. The argument was advanced that in order to avoid applying pressure on patients to continue taking methadone, the provision of medical, vocational, legal, and all other ancillary services should not be made contingent upon the administration of medication; in other words, it was suggested that patients should be offered the option of remaining indefinitely "active" even after detoxification.

This argument was initially rejected due to the extraordinary demand by many thousands of addicts who were forced to wait months for admission because of limited capacity. Every patient who remained on the active census following detoxification would, in fact, deny admission to a heroin addict who desperately wanted methadone treatment. If the Program had viewed its therapeutic regimen as a continuum leading to a state of total abstinence (as is true of almost all programs today), then it clearly would have been paradoxical to discontinue services when a patient achieved the final "phase" of treatment. This, however, was not the objective of the Program. Rather, the NYC MMTP was designed to provide methadone maintenance; supportive services were viewed as an essential adjunct to treatment with methadone. The clinic staffing was barely adequate to provide ancillary services to the caseload of patients receiving methadone; obviously, it could not provide such services to nonmethadone clients as well.

Nevertheless, the policy that all patients be promptly discharged following detoxification generated increasing concern among clinic staff, and in the middle of 1973 a compromise was reached between the opposing viewpoints. Voluntarily detoxified patients were thereafter permitted to remain in active status, and have continued access to all the services of the Program, for a period not to exceed 3 months following the last dose of methadone.* Subsequent experience with the 3-month "grace period" revealed that only a very small proportion of patients returned to the clinics following detoxification unless they had decided to request resumption of methadone treatment.†

*To ensure that analysis of patient retention in the Program would be meaningful, the NYC MMTP continued to define the "official termination date" as the date of last medication.

†This experience has been reported by other methadone maintenance programs as well, and is reflected in the difficulty of obtaining follow-up information on patients after detoxification (117–119).

9

The Role of Social and Psychiatric Services

INTRODUCTION

Much of the controversy surrounding methadone maintenance treatment reflects the philosophical differences which pervade almost every aspect of addiction treatment. That there are divergent viewpoints is not surprising, since with few exceptions this is true of all areas of medicine. Nor is the lack of consensus undesirable; it would be as inappropriate to apply a "standard regimen" for the management of addiction as it would be to insist that all cases of cancer be treated exclusively by surgery or exclusively by radiation.

Some critics of methadone maintenance treatment, however, have avoided the substantive issues and dealt solely with straw men which they themselves have created. The primary example of this tendency to focus on nonissues is the insistence that ancillary services must be made available to patients along with the medication itself. Contrary to the implication of this frequently repeated assertion, no responsible proponent of methadone treatment has ever seriously suggested that programs limit their efforts solely to the administration and dispensing of medication.

The very first paper published by Dole and Nyswander expressed their conviction that ancillary services were an essential component of the treatment regimen: "In our opinion, both the medication and the supporting program are essential. . . . We believe that methadone has contributed in an essential way to the favorable results, although it is quite clear that giving of medicine has been only part of the program" (120).* The admonition that

*This view has been consistently expressed by Dole and Nyswander in subsequent papers: "In the treatment of addiction and other chronic diseases, medicines should be prescribed only as part of a larger program of rehabilitation" (121). "The medical procedure—stopping heroin

ancillary services are indispensable to a successful methadone maintenance program is accepted by all programs; no one has advocated the provision of methadone in a vacuum.* The kinds of services which are needed, however, and the special role, if any, of psychiatric and psychological counseling, are still open to debate.

PSYCHOTHERAPY AS AN ANCILLARY SERVICE

Prior to the introduction of methadone maintenance, the underlying premise upon which almost all addiction treatment rested was that addicts, by definition, were emotionally disturbed individuals whose condition required psychotherapy in one form or another. The rejection of this assumption, one of the most revolutionary aspects of the therapeutic regimen proposed by Dole and Nyswander, was based on empirical evidence rather than on theory: "It must be emphasized that the absence of routine psychiatric treatment did not stem from indifference or lack of clinical resources; all patients [were] seen by qualified psychiatrists on admission and, informally, at frequent intervals thereafter. . . . The lack of formal psychotherapy in the treatment program reflected the experience of the professional staff that routine psychotherapy was not needed for rehabilitation of the patients that we had stabilized on methadone" (127).

In retrospect, the observations of Dole and Nyswander are not surprising. Since addicts represent an extremely heterogeneous population with respect to age, sex, ethnicity, national origin, educational and social levels, economic status, etc., it would be extraordinary if psychiatric illness were a common bond. It is especially unlikely that there could be a universal *causal* relation-

*Reflecting the popular consensus among those involved in methadone treatment, regulations of the Federal Food and Drug Administration since 1972 have explicitly required that ancillary medical and social services be part of the treatment regimen (125). Nevertheless, methadone maintenance continues to be criticized as a ". . . new conceptualization of what addiction is and how it is best treated, i.e., with medication rather than rehabilitative therapy" (126).

---

addiction with methadone—is simple, but the social problems of the street addict will continue to disable him unless effective social helps are also given" (122). "In the complex task of rehabilitating an addict, methadone (or any other medication) is only an adjunct. . . . The main services needed by a methadone program . . . are helps in housing, school placement, job training, and employment. Without such help the patient is likely to be trapped in his past, even if he stops using heroin" (123). ". . . [O]ur programs are usually called 'methadone maintenance programs.' This popular label puts the emphasis on what is merely the medicinal aspect of the treatment. More importantly, the clinics should be rehabilitation programs, not merely dispensaries. . . . Specifically, the program must help open the way to better jobs and housing for patients, provide opportunities for education, defend the patients against injustices" (124).

ship between two such vague and ill-defined concepts as "addiction" and "mental illness."*

Just as in the general population, there will inevitably be some methadone patients who might benefit from psychotherapy. The policy of the NYC MMTP with respect to psychiatric and psychological services is precisely the same as that which applies to all other ancillary services: in those cases where they are believed to be indicated, they should be made available.

SUPPORTIVE SOCIAL SERVICES

In addressing the practical problems of employment, education and training, housing and the resolution of outstanding legal cases, most methadone programs have focused primarily not on alleged shortcomings of the patients themselves but rather on external, societal barriers to rehabilitation. The major impediment in overcoming these obstacles is the almost universal discrimination faced by methadone patients. Decades of ineffective efforts to "cure" addiction have lead to frustration, and a consequent reluctance by the general public to accept the concept of "ex-addict" as other than a euphemism for "junkie." Opinions expressed by public officials and the people who staff treatment programs have reinforced this cynicism:

The Federal Food and Drug Administration has decreed that no methadone patient can be routinely trusted with more than a 3-day supply of medication, and to merit even this degree of confidence requires at least 2 years of continuous treatment (130).

The New York State Legislature has legally defined methadone maintenance patients as "addicts" for purposes of criminal certification to the Drug Abuse Control Commission (131). The practical implication of this statute is that the courts, in ordering involuntary commitment, may not distinguish between patients enrolled in methadone maintenance programs and heroin addicts who maintain an illicit, debilitating, antisocial narcotic dependence.†

The United States Post Office, in 1972, acknowledged: "We presently make no distinction between heroin and methadone users for purposes of employment" (132).‡

*Thomas Szasz, a psychiatrist, has cogently argued that both "drug abuse" and "mental illness" do not even exist except as functions of popular morality (128, 129).

†Prior to the Legislature's action, the Mental Hygiene Act employed a definition of "addict" which excluded individuals who were physically dependent upon narcotics ". . . taken under the supervision of a physician in the course of accepted medical practice." The exclusion no longer applies to those whose medical treatment is related to previous drug abuse.

‡Almost three years later, the Postal Service was ordered by a Federal Court to lift its ban on employing methadone patients (133).

The Mount Vernon Housing Authority in Westchester County, New York, justified the exclusion of methadone patients from its facilities by quoting the former Governor of New York, who had concluded: "We have achieved very little permanent rehabilitation [of addicts], and have found no cure" (134). The Appellate Court agreed with the Housing Authority's premise that, since any distinction between methadone patients and heroin addicts is at best temporary, the same discriminatory policy should be applied to both (135).

A physician who directed a methadone maintenance clinic in Washington, D.C., scoffed at the reliability of urine specimens which were collected under the direct observation of "... so-called ex-addict counselors, some of whom were receiving methadone maintenance treatment themselves" (136). (When a program director expresses his conviction that methadone patients, employed as counselors, cannot even be trusted to observe patients urinating, it is not surprising that the public at large refuses to trust them with more essential functions.)

An evaluation of a methadone maintenance program in Philadelphia referred to four counselors as follows: "All four, despite their treatment and 14 months of employment as counselors, were still being maintained with daily doses of methadone. Hence, all four were, in fact, still addicts" (137).*

"Rehabilitation" is generally used to describe the ultimate goal of patients to be reintegrated into the general community. The indispensable prerequisite, however, is not merely the patient's own readiness, willingness and capability to return to a productive role in society, but society's acceptance of the patient. The experience of the NYC MMTP has consistently been that the latter is by far the greater stumbling block, and the supportive services provided by the Program have been developed accordingly. Despite

*The assertion that methadone patients are "still addicts" is a widely heard criticism, and the rationale for much of the persistent discrimination. Even in a strictly technical sense, "... the term *addiction* has been used in so many ways that it can no longer be employed without further qualification or elaboration" (138). As commonly employed, however, the implication of the rubric "addict" goes far beyond physiological phenomena of tolerance and dependence: "Addiction and addict have been used so often that the words have developed a cultural rather than a scientific meaning, connoting disapproval and deprecation" (139). This connotation is in accord with the popular definition of addiction as "The compulsive and uncontrolled use of habit-forming drugs, beyond the period of medical need, or under conditions harmful to society" (140). It also agrees with the criteria of "drug addiction" proposed by the World Health Organization: "(i) an overpowering desire or need (compulsion) to continue taking the drug and to obtain it by any means; (ii) a tendency to increase the dose; (iii) a psychic and generally a physical dependence on the effects of the drug; and (iv) detrimental effects on the individual and on society" (141). Most other definitions are similar, and stress the harm to the individual and society associated with "addict" drug use (142, 143). Clearly, none of these definitions apply to the methadone maintenance patient.

the Program's efforts, however, it is usually the patient's ability to conceal his or her status as a methadone patient which is the decisive factor in determining whether reintegration will be possible.

Employment, one of the most important factors in ultimate treatment outcome, is a case in point. Together with patient referrals to educational and training programs, major emphasis has been placed on job development, and in this respect there have been few successes in opening up job opportunities with major employers.* Some have refused even to discuss modifying policies which preclude the hiring of methadone patients, while others set certain "conditions" which are impossible for the Program to accept. Thus, some employers demand a firm "guarantee," or "certification," that a patient referred to them for work will not return to drug use,† and the Program is asked to "report" any patient who terminates treatment (or has a positive urinalysis or other clinical evidence of difficulty) after being hired. The imposition of such conditions would not only conflict with the Program's policies regarding confidentiality of patient records, but would also be contrary to the ". . . strong conviction that job performance should be the sole criterion for continued employment. To allow the employer to become involved in the treatment aspects of rehabilitation leads to paternalism. And paternalism is just another form of discrimination" (148).

The development of meaningful and effective supportive social services has been the most difficult challenge faced by methadone maintenance programs. Experience has confirmed and strengthened the premise which has been the keystone of methadone maintenance treatment since its introduction ten years ago: programs must work with their patients in seeking to overcome the many barriers to successful rehabilitation.

*One notable exception was the Program's role in persuading the New York City Department of Personnel to adopt the following policy: "No ex-addict, methadone-maintained or drug-free, will be refused employment solely on the basis of his previous addiction . . . except where current medical requirements bar such employment" (144). The qualification refers primarily to the uniformed services (fire, police, and sanitation), but even these agencies have recently begun hiring ex-addicts to fill nonuniformed positions (145). Other programs in the State have not been so fortunate in eliminating conflicting policies of local governmental agencies. The experience of a county-funded methadone maintenance program in Syracuse, New York, is not atypical: ". . . a county department fired an employee when it learned that she was on methadone, apparently without realizing the irony involved in one county agency undermining the efforts of another and, by so doing, forcing a person onto county-funded work relief" (146).

†With respect to certification, the New York City Commission on Human Rights, following extensive hearings on the question of job discrimination against rehabilitated addicts, noted: ". . . [T]here is something fundamentally repugnant about certifying an individual as an 'ex-addict.' Most of the drug treatment experts who testified at the hearings were reluctant to endorse a certification process, no matter how constructed. Certification runs not only the risk of stigmatization but also places too much dependence on the judgement of a single individual who may or may not be objective, fair or qualified to make a valid assessment of job readiness (147)."

10

The Irrelevance of Success

INTRODUCTION

There are almost as many distinctive addiction treatment approaches as there are individual programs; even where the administration of methadone forms a common bond among different programs, the philosophies, policies, and procedures are widely divergent. *The unique feature which characterizes the original "methadone maintenance" approach introduced ten years ago is the acceptance of methadone as a medication, devoid of any inherent negative value: the drug is used in order to achieve a desired clinical result; effectiveness is measured solely by improvement in the patient's status; the dosage of the drug is not a criterion of treatment outcome; and the treatment regimen is continued until it no longer elicits the desired response, or until the underlying condition is resolved.*

In all these respects, the management of narcotic dependence proposed by Dole and Nyswander parallels the medical treatment of other illnesses. In most clinical situations, the amount of medication prescribed is recommended on the basis of experience, and in the absence of serious side effects attendant to the use of a drug, the "conservative" approach is generally to give more rather than less, in order to provide a margin of safety. Even where the drug employed is an addictive, abusable substance such as a barbiturate, the same orientation applies; in the management of epilepsy with phenobarbital, the primary focus is on controlling the disease, and moral qualms regarding the prescribed dosage or duration of medication do not justify subjecting patients to the risk of persistent seizures. Moral qualms, however, have pervaded the field of methadone maintenance treatment since its inception, and consequently the regimen introduced a decade ago has been drastically altered.

METHADONE MAINTENANCE: THE BASIS FOR DISSONANCE

In introducing methadone maintenance as a new therapeutic approach to drug addiction, Dole and Nyswander recognized that the anticipated opposition would be based on moral rather than medical grounds. There was a deep-rooted belief that "... prescription of medication would do no more than gratify a bad habit, and therefore that it could not possibly contribute to rehabilitation" (149). The American Medical Association, as early as 1921, had urged "... an end to all manner of so-called ambulatory [i.e., maintenance] treatment of narcotic addicts" (150). In a joint statement with the National Research Council in 1963, only weeks before Dole and Nyswander initiated clinical studies with methadone, the Association reaffirmed its position: "Continued administration of drugs for maintenance of addiction is not a bona fide attempt at cure, nor is it ethical treatment [of addiction]. . . ."* An equally unambiguous condemnation of maintenance treatment had been voiced earlier by the Judiciary Committee of the United States Senate: "We believe the thought of permanently maintaining drug addiction with 'sustaining' doses of narcotic drugs to be utterly repugnant to the moral principles inherent in our laws and the character of our people" (153). The unprecedented results of the Dole–Nyswander treatment did not change the prevailing attitudes, and as late as 1970 the American Medical Association continued to question the propriety of substituting methadone for heroin and "... maintain[ing] such dependence for an indefinite period, perhaps for life" (154).

The fact that nonnarcotic drugs used in the management of substance abuse are generally free of controversy indicates that the rejection of methadone maintenance treatment is based on the moral, and irrational, premise that methadone "substitutes vodka for gin." The dosage of Antabuse employed in alcoholism is rarely the subject of discussion, let alone debate, and "weaning" the former alcoholic from Antabuse is a goal which is viewed with almost total indifference by the clinician, the patient and the general public. These issues are similarly inconsequential with respect to narcotic antagonists: few workers in the field know or care what the "usual" or "best" dose of cyclazocine or naltrexone is; little attention has been focused on the optimal means of discontinuing the administration of these drugs; and no attempt has been made by regulatory agencies to limit the number of months that they may be prescribed. The critical difference between these drugs and methadone is that the latter is pharmacologically classified as a narcotic. The

*This position was warmly endorsed by the Bureau of Narcotics in a "Concurring Statement": "The Bureau is pleased to note that the American Medical Association has reaffirmed its position opposing the establishment of community ambulatory clinics for ... the continuing maintenance of addicts on narcotics" (152).

conclusion is inescapable: methadone remains identified as a euphorigenic drug which exerts its influence by keeping patients "doped up," all the facts to the contrary notwithstanding.

The assumption that the administration of any narcotic, under any circumstances, will produce euphoria is simply inaccurate. The initial, carefully controlled studies by Dole and Nyswander demonstrating that patients maintained on constant doses of methadone experience no mood-altering effect from the drug have been confirmed by other, independent investigators; they have been considered beyond dispute by knowledgeable clinicians and pharmacologists for many years. Nevertheless, the medical community's bias against maintenance treatment with narcotics has remained largely impervious to the facts:

In one of the earliest articles denouncing methadone maintenance treatment, published in the *Journal of the American Medical Association* as a "Critical Commentary," the author concluded: "'Stabilization,' in other words, is just a euphemistic term to indicate that when heroin addicts receive a sufficiently high euphorogenous dose of methadone, they no longer have any craving for the euphorogenous effects of heroin" (155).*

A medical journal article asserted that methadone maintenance patients were reduced to "narcotized zombies" (158).

Some clinicians, having experienced the frustrating failure of other forms of addiction treatment, viewed the success of methadone maintenance as proof that the medication must produce "psychic gratification" (159), and reasoned that persons on methadone are ". . . satiated to the effects of opiates and, therefore, demonstrate reduced illicit heroin self-administration" (160).

DOSAGE AND DURATION OF TREATMENT: CHANGING ATTITUDES

In introducing methadone maintenance treatment, Dole and Nyswander defined the pharmacological objectives as: "(1) the relief of narcotic hunger, and (2) induction of sufficient tolerance to block the euphoric effects of an average illegal dose of diacetymorphine [i.e., heroin]" (161). The importance

*An article by the same author, in which he states that methadone maintenance involves ". . . simply substituting the euphoric action of methadone for the euphoric action of heroin by administering massive doses of the former," (156) was reprinted in 1968 by the New York State Narcotic Addiction Control Commission as an "especially noteworthy article on narcotic addiction" which deserved a wider audience (157).

of the latter effect was underscored in 1966, when the Committee on Problems of Drug Dependence of the National Research Council defined the Dole–Nyswander research with methadone as a "... project serving to test the hypothesis that... the administration of methadone *in amounts sufficient to produce a high level of tolerance* will result in the narcotic dependent person losing his inclination toward continued abuse of illicit narcotics" (162, emphasis added). Four years later, in 1970, the World Health Organization Expert Committee on Drug Dependence still described methadone maintenance as "... the continuing daily oral administration of methadone under adequate medical supervision, the dose being adjusted (a) to prevent the occurrence of abstinence phenomena, (b) to suppress partially or completely any continuous preoccupation with taking of drugs of the morphine type [i.e., to suppress "drug hunger"], and (c) *to establish a sufficient degree of tolerance and cross-tolerance to blunt or suppress the acute effects of such agents*" (163, emphasis added). One of the hallmarks of the original methadone maintenance concept, therefore, was the use of medication to establish a high degree of tolerance to narcotics. Although the early programs frequently relied on dosages in the range of 80–120 mg of methadone to achieve this effect, the specific dosage used for an individual patient was generally viewed with disinterest. The focus was on the patient, and the patient's response to treatment.

The dramatic increase in the late 1960's and early 1970's in the number of addiction treatment programs throughout the country utilizing methadone, however, was accompanied by a growing preoccupation with lowering the maintenance dosage. Decreasing the amount of medication prescribed became an end in itself, for which the rationale was considered so self-evident that it required no elaboration. Those program directors who did seek to explain their departure from the original, highly successful protocol pointed to experimental studies which alleged that treatment outcome is not appreciably affected by dosages used. In this connection the most widely publicized findings have been those of Goldstein and his co-workers (164–167). The double-blind research design employed in these studies, however, which prevented both the patients and the staff from knowing the dosages prescribed, created an artificial setting wholly different from that of programs which adjust dosages on the basis of individual patient assessment, and make no secret of the amount prescribed.* Consequently, the experimental conclusions have little relevance to the clinical management of patients. This

*In the early months of operation, the NYC MMTP attempted to keep patients from knowing their dosages, and noted an almost universal preoccupation with dosage levels; virtually all patients believed the amount prescribed was either too high or too low. The adverse effect of this anxiety, which has also been reported by other programs (168, 169), may overshadow differences in treatment outcome associated with various dosage levels.

was evident in subsequent studies by Goldstein, in which patients were not only advised of the dose of methadone ordered, but allowed (within limits) to make adjustments themselves; under these circumstances, a reduction in heroin use was associated with dosage increases in some cases (170). Whether these findings are the result of psychological or pharmacological factors, or both, there are indeed patients who do better, objectively and subjectively, when maintained at dosages of approximately 100 mg than at lower levels.

Nevertheless, increasing numbers of clinicians have lowered the amount of methadone which they are willing to prescribe, and established inflexible upper limits of 60 mg, or less. The debate between low-dose advocates and those who continue to prescribe higher doses has received considerable attention, and unfortunately has obscured the more fundamental issue: assuming the results of treatment are satisfactory, why should it matter whether they are achieved with 50 or 150 mg of methadone? Rigid policies of uniform adherence to *any* dosage conflict with the axiom that medical treatment should be based on the clinical course of the individual patient. The concern of program staff with dosages rather than patients, however, is the rule rather than the exception.*

Preoccupation with lowering the maintenance dosage of methadone has been exceeded only by the emphasis which total detoxification has received. In a step which is without precedent in the practice of medicine, a limit has been imposed on the duration of methadone maintenance treatment; the Food and Drug Administration now demands that a physician provide written justification for extending the administration of methadone beyond the arbitrary time frame which is permitted.† The F.D.A. explicitly acknowledged the political pressure which motivated its decision: "The Honorable Paul G. Rogers, Member of Congress from Florida, Chairman of the Subcommittee on Public Health and Environment of the Committee on Interstate and Foreign Commerce, U.S. House of Representatives, has written the Commissioner of Food and Drugs to request revision of the regulations governing methadone . . . to include a requirement for discontinuance of methadone after 2 years of treatment unless, based on clinical judgement, the patient's status indicated that treatment with methadone should be con-

*This orientation is shared by the Federal Food and Drug Administration, which has decreed that when more than 100 mg are prescribed by the physician, daily clinic attendance is mandatory; the degree of social rehabilitation demonstrated by the patient is totally inconsequential (171).

†The orientation which this regulation reflects has been espoused by the former Director of the National Institute of Mental Health, Division of Narcotic Addiction and Drug Abuse (the forerunner of the National Institute on Drug Abuse): "It is most important to recognize methadone maintenance for the crutch that it is, a *temporary* support which is to be discarded as soon as the client has changed his sick attitudes, values and rationalizations" (172).

tinued for a longer period of time" (173). According to the perverted logic underlying this ruling, the fact that a patient is doing well is presumptive evidence that treatment should be terminated, and only in those cases where therapy has been relatively *unsuccessful* can its continuation be condoned.

Departing from its usual practice of soliciting public comment prior to promulgating new regulations (174), the F.D.A. explained that the imposition of a time limit with respect to methadone treatment was immediately necessary in order to "... protect the health and safety of patients treated with methadone" (175). Although this claim was totally unsupported by the extensive data regarding the effects of long-term methadone administration, the message conveyed to patients as well as staff was that methadone treatment is a dangerous and undesirable modality which can only be tolerated as a temporary expedient.

CONCLUSION

In retrospect, the most destructive impact on methadone maintenance treatment has come from the seemingly more moderate critics who tolerated the use of methadone, but with certain qualifications, especially with respect to dosage and duration of treatment. The "endorsement by the Federal Government of the methadone maintenance treatment modality," (176) and its "strong commitment to the ... massive expansion of methadone maintenance programs throughout the country," (177) has amounted to no more than the grudging approval to utilize methadone, but only within a therapeutic framework diametrically opposed to that which formed its original foundation. Today, the utilization of methadone represents only a modification of the drug-free approach, and a total repudiation of methadone maintenance treatment as employed so successfully by Dole and Nyswander and the few early programs that sought to emulate their experience. Despite the fact that administration of methadone for more than 21 days continues to be labeled "methadone maintenance," this form of treatment no longer exists.

11

The Rationale for Ambulatory Detoxification Treatment

INTRODUCTION

The inability of short-term detoxification to achieve permanent abstinence is well established. At the same time, however, most workers in the field of addiction also believe that any treatment modality which does not aim for total "cure" is irrevelant to the management of addicts. Accordingly, virtually all reports in the literature evaluate detoxification services by the same criteria which are applied to long-term chemotherapeutic and drug-free approaches*; the conclusions based on the degree to which abstinence and behavioral change are maintained after withdrawal are, inevitably, quite dismal. In published studies it is rare for even 10% of patients beginning withdrawal to remain free of drug usage following discharge, regardless of the setting in which treatment is provided or the duration of time over which detoxification is carried out (179–187).

With the focus of evaluation on long-term "success," most reports have dismissed detoxification as a futile effort: "Results of detoxification have been uniformly disappointing across the country. . . . Most addicts return to narcotic abuse very soon after treatment" (188). "Review of the empirical data presently available fails to demonstrate that detoxification, per se, regardless

*One exception is found in the assessment of treatment modalities included in the Drug Abuse Council's Report to the Ford Foundation: "The most straightforward way to help a heroin addict is to detoxify him . . . Detoxification has several clear benefits for both the addict and society. Even if the addict does not intend to stay off drugs, it reduces his habit and decreases its cost. This spares him the hassle and society the crime costs of his addiction for some period, even if only a few days, after the process is complete. For some addicts, it is also a step toward rehabilitation. After repeated failures to remain detoxified, they become ready for other modalities. It is valuable, especially for anyone who believes that addicts should be treated more humanely than they are at the present time and that bandaids can be valuable things" (178).

of technique, is in any way substantially related to achievable social, psychological or vocational goals, or to sustained abstinence" (189). "Methadone withdrawal by itself can not be considered definitive treatment, because experience has shown that most addicts require a great deal of social and psychological support to remain drug-free after detoxification" (190).

Although ambulatory detoxification is rarely accepted as a meaningful treatment in its own right, it is frequently afforded a role as a preliminary component of long-term treatment modalities, to eliminate a prospective client's physical dependence on narcotics prior to admission. The assumption that ". . . withdrawal is only the first and the least important step in the treatment of narcotic addiction" (191) would be true if one takes the narrow view that "success" can only be defined as lasting abstinence. Such a premise, however, ignores the frustrating reality that, to date, the problem of drug addiction has proven notoriously resistant to the myriad therapeutic approaches which have been applied.

THE PERSPECTIVE OF THE NEW YORK CITY AMBULATORY DETOXIFICATION PROGRAM

In February, 1971, the Health Services Administrator sent to the Mayor's Narcotic Control Council a draft proposal for a multifaceted detoxification program, to include both in-patient and out-patient withdrawal services, and a "crisis intervention" component which would provide medication on a one-time basis to alleviate acute symptoms of narcotic abstinence. At that time the New York City Methadone Maintenance Treatment Program was just getting under way, and the City Administration planned to increase the capacity of both methadone and drug-free programs by more than 400%, to a total of 50,000 patients.* With an estimated 150,000 addicts in New York City, it was readily apparent that even this extraordinary expansion would still leave the majority of heroin-dependent individuals with no care whatever; these comprised the target population for the detoxification program which was contemplated.

From the outset, the major emphasis in the H.S.A. proposal was on ambulatory detoxification, which had a cost–benefit ratio considerably greater than that of either of the other two components.† Basing its analysis

*This ambitious goal was achieved within 2 years, during which the census of patients being treated in addiction programs in New York City increased from slightly more than 12,000 to almost 53,000 (192).

†In-patient detoxification and crisis intervention were almost immediately deleted from the H.S.A. proposal since it was not clear that there would be a significant demand for these services once a network of out-patient clinics had been established.

on the conservative assumption that less than 1% of patients would remain drug-free for an extended period of time after withdrawal, and that for the remainder recidivism would occur within 2 weeks, the H.S.A. nevertheless concluded that the extremely large number of addicts who would want detoxification, and who could be accommodated at relatively low cost in outpatient clinics, justified implementation of a City-operated program (193).

The objectives of detoxification were initially summarized as follows: "Relief of addict suffering and reduction of the danger of overdosing, reduction of addict-caused crime in New York City, and provision of referral services to other treatment programs" (194). It was postulated that a safe, legal alternative to even one day's self-administration of street heroin, if provided to tens of thousands of addicts yearly, would inevitably benefit the general community as well as the patients themselves; that a positive treatment experience in a short-term detoxification program would influence at least some patients to seek long-term care; and that the anticipated demand for detoxification would confirm that addicts themselves perceived the program as beneficial.*

The aims of the New York City Ambulatory Detoxification Program were stated consistently in many contexts subsequently. In a proposal to the Office of Economic Opportunity submitted in May, 1971, the need for ambulatory detoxification was explained as follows: "The existence of a large number of heroin addicts in New York City, most of whom do not voluntarily seek long-term treatment, suggests the value of a service which would allow an addict, even temporarily, to reduce his habit" (196). In the City's "Comprehensive Plan for the Control of Drug Abuse," released in November, 1971, the new Program was described as an effort to "... intervene in the lives of previously unreached addicts" (197). The clinical goals enumerated in the NYC ADP Policy and Procedures Manual (198) were:

> To provide during each day of treatment a safe, legal and effective alternative to the physical need to self-administer illicit naroctics.
>
> To eliminate the patient's present physical dependence on narcotics through the administration of decreasing doses of methadone until, after about seven days, a drug-free state is achieved.
>
> To motivate patients to seek long-term treatment for their narotic addiction.
>
> To provide referral services to appropriate long-term treatment programs.
>
> To provide screening and follow-up as indicated for acute and chronic medical conditions, whether related to addiction or not.

Notable by its consistent omission from all references to Program objectives was the achievement of permanent abstinence. To prevent frustration

*It was known that in-patient detoxification at the Morris J. Bernstein Institute of Beth Israel Medical Center was in considerable demand: there were reported to be between 800 and 1200 addicts awaiting admission for narcotic withdrawal in late 1970 (195).

among Program staff and disenchantment of funding sources and the general public, it was essential to distinguish between realistic and unrealistic goals. With respect to funding sources, however, the Program's candor also produced disappointment. Skepticism regarding program objectives which failed to include permanent abstinence was the prevailing attitude of the National Institute of Mental Health when the NYC ADP sought support in the summer of 1971. Expressing concern that "serial detoxification of the same patient without intensive followup [would become] a substitute for treatment" (199), N.I.M.H. requested several revisions of the Program protocol with progressively greater emphasis on the mechanisms for patient referral to and from long-term treatment facilities. Although these changes were implemented in the initial clinics of the NYC ADP, the fundamental doubts of N.I.M.H. regarding the utility of out-patient narcotic withdrawal as a distinct treatment entity could not be overcome, and after more than a year of fruitless negotiation the City gave up the attempt.

The unwillingness of N.I.M.H. to support a program which, from its inception, attracted unprecedented numbers of addicts,* was especially frustrating given the existing situation in New York City in 1971–1972. Even the most ambitious plans to expand chemotherapeutic and drug-free programs would leave about 100,000 heroin addicts with no alternative to continued, daily, illicit drug use. The plight was most obvious in the case of more than 10,000 applicants for methadone maintenance who were on "waiting lists," and for whom no temporary relief from the physical dependence on narcotics was readily available.

Fortunately, other funding sources were available to the NYC ADP. The Program's primary objectives remained essentially unchanged, and it continued to operate as an independent entity rather than as a subsidiary unit of a comprehensive treatment agency. Eligibility for admission has never been made contingent upon a commitment by the applicant to pursue a goal of total rehabilitation†; while orientation and referral of interested patients to long-term programs has consistently been a secondary therapeutic goal, it has never been permitted to take precedence over the narrower aim of detoxification per se.

*In the first 12 months of operation, beginning in July, 1971, over 10,000 individuals were admitted to the NYC ADP.

†By contrast, another, independently operated detoxification program in New York demands that applicants first attend at least four consecutive sessions at a neighboring drug-free Community Service Center as a prerequisite to enrollment (200).

12

Organization of the Program

The question of which City agency would operate the new detoxification program was the focus of considerable debate. The Addiction Services Agency, responsible for funding and monitoring most drug-free programs in the City, sought control by arguing that since the NYC ADP would involve referrals to and from long-term programs, optimal coordination could be achieved by unifying the administrative authority.

Health Services Administrator Gordon Chase, on the other hand, felt that the Program would be implemented most rapidly under the direction of the H.S.A., and pointed to the experience of the New York City Methadone Maintenance Treatment Program (NYC MMTP), which had opened fourteen facilities in four months. Furthermore, it was argued that since detoxification is primarily a medical procedure, the Program should be organizationally located in the Department of Health, an agency of the Health Services Administration. In the end, it was decided to follow the same course which had been chosen for the City's Methadone Maintenance Treatment Program. The A.S.A. would provide the funds, and the H.S.A. would be responsible for the operation of the Program.

Fearing considerable pressure to combine organizationally the NYC ADP and the NYC MMTP, I was one of the few H.S.A. officials who did not share Chase's enthusiasm for the new Program. Although funding would be provided for hiring NYC ADP Central Office staff, I was apprehensive that extensive demands upon the limited Methadone Maintenance Program personnel would nevertheless be made. Of greater importance, I was concerned that if the administration of the two programs were combined, the objectives of each might be compromised. Clinically, the NYC MMTP had already experienced tension among patients as well as staff members when the two modalities were juxtaposed geographically (a NYC MMTP clinic had been established in Delafield Hospital, and shared cramped basement quarters with an independent ambulatory detoxification program); the potential clearly existed for similar friction at the central level. I also felt that to be optimally effective, both the maintenance and detoxification programs should remain distinct entities, a difficult task if both were operated under the aegis of the same office.

Nevertheless, Chase was anxious to unify the administration of the two programs, and within several months I was persuaded to accept the added responsibility for directing the operation of the New York City Ambulatory Detoxification Program. Fortunately, the negative consequences which I had feared did not materialize. Within the Central Office, a clear delineation of functions was maintained between the two staffs, and only the Deputy Director and I had responsibilities covering both programs. Clinically, there was virtually no contact between the staffs except at occasional joint training sessions.

In retrospect, the major shortcoming of the organizational unification was that the more visible Maintenance Program overshadowed the NYC ADP for the next several years. The attention of the public, as well as of professionals in the field of addiction, centered on the NYC MMTP, while the New York City Ambulatory Detoxification Program, one of the most ambitious and successful drug treatment programs in the country, was generally overlooked.

13

Selected Policy Issues

INTRODUCTION

The character of an out-patient detoxification program is determined primarily by its admission criteria and procedures, and by the medical guidelines which govern treatment, especially dosage limitations and the duration of the detoxification regimen. The orientation of the New York City Ambulatory Detoxification Program (NYC ADP) with respect to these issues is discussed in this chapter.

ADMISSION CRITERIA

The criteria for admission to the NYC ADP are the following.

1. *Only voluntary applicants are eligible for admission.* As in the case of the NYC MMTP, "voluntary treatment" is defined pragmatically as a therapeutic relationship in which the program is under no implicit or explicit obligation to report to any outside individual or agency regarding the patient's admission, progress in treatment, or termination.

2. *The applicant must have a primary physical dependence on narcotics.* In applying this criterion, major reliance is placed on the history of drug usage given by the applicant. If there is an obvious inconsistency in the history (e.g., if a daily heroin consumption of only one or two "bags" is reported by someone allegedly addicted for a considerable period of time), or if suspicion is aroused during the medical examination (e.g., by the absence of "track marks" in an individual claiming many years of intravenous heroin use), the applicant is generally referred to an in-patient facility,

where it is possible to provide continuous observation before and after the administration of medication.*

The weight given self-reported drug history reflects the assumption that there is very little incentive for nonaddicts to seek admission: the relatively low dosage of methadone initially prescribed is rapidly reduced, and discontinued altogether within one or two weeks; diversion of prescribed methadone is impossible since all medication is administered and consumed in the clinic under the direct observation of the nursing staff; nonaddicted "experimenters" are unlikely to be tempted by the small amount of methadone provided by the Program, since a preliminary intake interview, complete physical examination, and extensive laboratory tests always precede the administration of medication. Despite the safeguards inherent in the protocol, however, the possibility that a nonaddict might apply to the NYC ADP obviously can not be ruled out entirely.

Rather than employ sophisticated, time-consuming, and expensive techniques in an effort to identify the occasional applicant who should be excluded, the NYC ADP has focused its energies and resources on implementing admission procedures which will permit prompt treatment of those who want and need care. A major factor in determining this policy has been the realization that, to date, no screening methods exist which are both reliable and consistent with Program goals:

Insisting upon *routine preadmission urinalysis* results which are positive for opiates entails a delay of at least one or two days, and involves considerable expense. Furthermore, urine testing only suggests that a drug has recently been taken; it sheds no light on the frequency or duration of use, or the extent to which dependence and tolerance have developed. The nonaddict who is determined to be admitted would simply be encouraged to use heroin once or twice in order to "pass" the urine screening test.

Requiring *confirmation of prior addiction treatment* would conflict with the stated aim of the NYC ADP to attract the previously "unreachable" addict; it would also compromise confidentiality, and necessitate delays in the admission process.

Withholding treatment until *physical signs of the abstinence syndrome* appear† would be paradoxical for a program whose aim is to prevent the discomfort associated with withdrawal.

*Referral for in-patient treatment is also made when applicants indicate a concurrent history of heavy barbiturate or alcohol use, in view of the reported hazards associated with the detoxification of the poly-drug addict. Approximately 5% of applicants have been referred for these reasons.

†Such a procedure is suggested by the Food and Drug Administration (201).

At best, an elaborate screening process might serve to protect the Program from adverse criticism, but it would do so at the expense of those the Program is intended to serve. In this regard, there has been a constant fear that a news reporter would make a spurious application to the NYC ADP in order to document the "laxity" of the admission procedure. This actually occurred on one occasion, and in that instance the reporter gave up the attempt before the preadmission physical examination had been carried out.

3. *The applicant may not be simultaneously enrolled in any other clinic which administers methadone or any other narcotic or narcotic antagonist.* Prior to admission, the NYC ADP routinely checks against its own patient listing to ensure that the applicant is not currently enrolled.* The instances of attempted multiple enrollment in more than one Program clinic have been exceedingly rare. This is to be expected in view of the low dosages of methadone used in withdrawal treatment, the short duration of detoxification, and the nature of the admission procedures of the NYC ADP. It is also clear that the only completely reliable means of thwarting an applicant who is determined to receive medication in two facilities simultaneously is through the use of a fingerprint (or footprint) registry in which all chemotherapeutic programs in the metropolitan area would participate; even if legally and technically feasible, there would be an almost universal refusal of programs to be included in such a system.

4. *If an applicant has previously been treated at any detoxification clinic, admission is not permitted within 28 days of last medication.* This requirement is enforced only with respect to the component clinics of the NYC ADP, since no mechanism is available to identify individuals who may have been detoxified recently in other programs.

The initial rationale for insisting on a 28-day interval between admissions was based on the limited intake capacity of each clinic (100 new patients weekly), and the Program's objective of providing detoxification to as many addicts as possible. It was not the intent of the NYC ADP to supplement the capacity of long-term treatment programs, but rather to provide a different, more limited service to addicts who did not seek long-term care. Accordingly, it was necessary to limit the duration of the detoxification regimen, and at the same time prevent the spurious "termination" and "readmission" of patients from one day to the next. Otherwise, the NYC ADP could have become, *de facto*, a low-dose methadone maintenance program.

The length of the "waiting period" between admissions was the subject of considerable debate, with many staff members favoring a reduction to three

*Detoxification programs in New York City do not participate in the "Methadone Information System" operated by The Rockefeller University, which includes patients in maintenance programs only (see page 53).

or even two weeks. An analysis of Program readmissions, however, found that fewer than 10% of former patients who reapplied did so during the first four weeks following the 28-day interval; it was therefore concluded that there was little need to reduce further the minimum time period between treatment episodes.

5. *Applicants under 18 years of age must have written consent of a parent or guardian, except in the case of "emancipated minors."* This requirement has been retained primarily on the advice of the Department of Health General Counsel's office.

PROCEDURES RELATED TO APPLICATION AND ADMISSION

Application and admission procedures have remained essentially unchanged since the NYC ADP began:

Every potential applicant to one of the Program's clinics is interviewed by a counselor, who explains the objectives and operation of the Program. An Application Form is completed which contains identifying information, sociodemographic history, and the pattern of drug use. Two items substantiating identification are required.

The applicant must sign a copy of the General Information and Program Rules, and the Program's Consent to Treatment Form.

If the applicant is under 18 and does not meet the definition of "emancipated minor," a Parental Consent Form must be signed by a parent or guardian.

A medical history is obtained by a physician or nurse, and a general physical examination is performed. No applicant may receive medication without a complete physical examination being recorded in his (her) chart.

The following medical screening tests are ordered routinely at the time of admission: chest x-ray and/or skin test for tuberculosis; hemoglobin or hematocrit; serology; sickle cell test for all black and Hispanic applicants; and a Pap smear, gonnorhea smear, and pregnancy test for all women. Additional diagnostic tests are ordered at the physician's discretion.

Prior to completing the admission process and administering the first dose of medication, the clinic contacts Central Office to ascertain whether the applicant is, or has been within 28 days, a patient in the Program. (The result of this telephone check is given immediately to the clinic staff.)

Initially, the detoxification "cycle" began (i.e., medication was initiated) only one day each week. This policy was based on the assumption that if treatment commenced for all patients on the same day, screening, dispensing of medication, record keeping, and other administrative procedures would be facilitated. In April, 1972, however, in order to reduce the waiting period between application and admission (which could be as long as 6 days), a decision was made to admit patients twice a week. The result was dramatic: in the first 3 months following the change, the number of applications increased from an average of 53 per clinic per week to 72. Furthermore, the loss of applicants failing to return as scheduled to begin treatment decreased from 18% to 8%. Although other factors unrelated to Program policies may have been associated with this improvement, the NYC ADP began in early 1973 to provide same-day admission for all eligible applicants from Monday through Friday. Contrary to expectations, these changes did not appreciably compound the clerical or dispensing tasks of the clinic personnel.

DOSAGES

At the outset the Program strongly recommended, but did not mandate, that the initial methadone dosage not exceed 40 mg and that for the first 2 or 3 days the dosage be split, with half administered in the morning and half in the afternoon. The latter recommendation was ignored by most clinics when it became apparent that patients did equally well with a single daily dose and were generally reluctant to make two trips each day to the facility. In the light of this experience, Program guidelines were subsequently modified, and by 1973 a single daily methadone dose was routine in all Program clinics.

The policy regarding the amount of initial medication, however, created far more difficulty. Several clinic physicians, emphatically supported by the counseling staff,* insisted that it was possible to gauge an applicant's "habit size" with a reasonable degree of accuracy, and that dosage flexibility was essential to permit appropriate, individualized treatment. Reluctant to mandate inflexible dosage limits, I permitted the administration of dosages considerably higher than the suggested maximum of 40 mg, although with growing concern.

The implementation of a rigid policy regarding dosage limitations followed an incident in January, 1972, when an 18-year-old patient was admitted to one of the Program's clinics and given a starting dose of 60 mg. Six hours later the patient was dead, and the clinical history and toxicological findings at autopsy strongly suggested that the cause of death was acute methadone

*In the NYC ADP approximately one-third of the counselors are ex-addicts.

intoxication. I immediately sent a directive to all clinics prohibiting the administration of more than 30 mg of methadone in a single dose; no exceptions to these limits were permitted under any circumstances. In the following three years, in which there were almost 50,000 admissions to the Program, no other fatalities attributed to administered methadone occurred. Clinics have rarely resorted to the option of referring patients with particularly high dependence to in-patient facilities, and the dropout rate prior to completion of detoxification has not been affected by this change in dosage policy.

DURATION OF TREATMENT

When the Program began, a limit to the duration of detoxification treatment seemed indicated both to accommodate the anticipated demand and to distinguish the treatment regimen from low-dose maintenance. If the NYC ADP were to achieve its stated objective of making ambulatory detoxification available promptly to all eligible addicts who sought this service, it was clear that patients seeking long-term care would have to be referred to other sources which existed in the community.

The original limit of 7 days was based on reports from other programs that this time period was generally sufficient to withdraw most addicts from their heroin dependence with minimal discomfort; it was also based on the expectation that clinic capacity would be inadequate to accommodate all the applicants. Although there were over 12,000 admissions to the NYC ADP during the first 12 months of operation, however, the daily patient load rarely exceeded 50 patients per clinic. Consequently, it was decided to permit clinics to "hold over" patients for an additional week (i.e., the maximum duration of treatment permitted was 2 weeks). Despite this added flexibility, the prescribed course of detoxification has remained 7 days for the great majority of admissions, and there has been very little pressure from either the clinic staff or patients to extend further the duration of treatment.

Part II

ANALYSIS OF PROGRAM EXPERIENCE, 1970–1974

Summary of Findings
Chapters 14–21

Summary of Findings

Chapters 14–21

Applicants to the Maintenance and Detoxification Programs

There were over 58,000 applications for admission to the New York City Methadone Maintenance Treatment Program (NYC MMTP) from its inception in November, 1970, through the end of 1974. In the 3.5 years after the New York City Ambulatory Detoxification Program (NYC ADP) began in July, 1971, almost 70,000 applications were received. These figures take on added significance since these programs represent less than half the methadone treatment capacity in the City.

The major findings regarding applications to the two programs include:

The number of applications to both programs reached a peak in the third quarter of 1972, when almost 5500 individuals applied to the Methadone Maintenance Program, and applicants to the Detoxification Program reached 7000.

Following a sharp drop in the fourth quarter of 1972, the demand for treatment in the Ambulatory Detoxification Program again increased markedly in 1973 and 1974, while the number of applicants to the Methadone Maintenance Program leveled off at approximately 2000 in each 3-month period.

A striking increase in applications to the New York City Methadone Maintenance Treatment Program from residents in the immediate vicinity of new clinics was found when the Program expanded into previously unserved areas.

Over half of all applicants to the Methadone Maintenance Program from 1971 through 1974 did not enter treatment. The major causes of attrition were the inability to locate applicants at the address given and the failure of applicants to respond when notified to report for admission screening. The attrition rate was generally similar for subgroups of applicants as defined by year of application, and by selected demographic, social and drug-use characteristics.

Descriptive Analysis of Patients Admitted to the Maintenance and Detoxification Programs

The demographic, social, and drug-use characteristics of patients, as reported at admission screening, were analyzed for over 20,000 admissions to the New York City Methadone Maintenance Treatment Program, and for approximately 65,000 admissions to the New York City Ambulatory Detoxification Program.

Among the major findings are the following:

The admissions to the two programs were almost identical with respect to their distributions by age and sex. Less than 50% of the patients were over 25 years of age at the time of admission, and 75% were men.

Approximately 50% of those admitted to the NYC MMTP were black, with the remainder fairly evenly divided between whites and Hispanics. Almost 65% of the Detoxification Program admissions were black, and less than 10% were white.

The duration of addiction was similar for admission cohorts of both programs, with the peak years of onset of heroin use 1967, 1968 and 1969. Differences in the duration of addiction were associated with the age of patients at the time of admission.

Patients entering the NYC MMTP and the NYC ADP differed with respect to prior addiction treatment history. About 75% of the Detoxification Program admissions had no prior long-term treatment, compared to 50% of the Maintenance Program admissions. Among NYC MMTP admissions, only 20% had been treated previously in abstinence programs.

Over two-thirds of the patients entering the NYC MMTP had not completed high school, and an equal proportion were neither employed nor receiving job training or schooling at the time of enrollment.

Of the Maintenance Program admissions, almost 60%, by self-report, had previously used barbiturates, and 10% reported excessive alcohol consumption at the time of entering treatment. Three-quarters of the patients had been arrested at least once, and half had one or more prior convictions.

Methadone Dosage Levels of Patients in the Maintenance Program

Beginning in 1972, the frequency distributions of methadone dosages prescribed for all patients in the NYC MMTP have been determined monthly, based on computerized medication records. Analysis of the dosage patterns revealed the following:

Between June, 1972 and December, 1974, there was a marked decrease in the proportion of patients maintained at 100 mg of methadone, or more, per day: from 69% to 16%; during the same time period, the proportion of patients receiving 50 mg or less increased from 3% to 30%.

Among NYC MMTP patients in treatment at the end of 1974, those who were older, had been in the Program longer, and who were white were more likely to be receiving higher dosages of methadone.

Assessing Progress in Patients Enrolled in the Maintenance Program

Four parameters of progress toward rehabilitation were analyzed for 11,157 patients in treatment in the NYC MMTP at the end of December, 1974: drug abuse (including excessive consumption of alcohol); gainful occupation (employment, schooling and, homemaker activities); welfare status; and arrests.

The major findings include:

Approximately 20% of all patients were reportedly abusing one or more drugs during the last two months of 1974. Overall, 5% were abusing heroin, and the proportion decreased among cohorts with progressively longer treatment exposure.

In the case of heroin, cocaine, and alcohol abuse, a higher prevalence was noted among blacks and among patients who were older; barbiturate and amphetamine abuse was more prevalent among whites and among women.

The proportion of patients gainfully occupied was markedly higher among patients in treatment 1–12 months than was reported at the time of admission to the NYC MMTP (51% and 31%, respectively); there was no appreciable further increase, however, among patients with 13–24 months or 25–36 months of treatment exposure.

Work stability, as measured by length of time in the same job, was strongly associated with increasing time in treatment; 61% of working patients enrolled in the NYC MMTP for over 3 years were employed continuously for more than 12 months.

Employment and welfare status varied among the demographic subgroups, and the differences were consistent with those in the general community: women, black and Hispanic patients, and patients over 40 years of age were far less likely to be gainfully occupied, and more likely to be receiving public assistance.

Less than 3% of the patient population was arrested during the 2-month period of observation. Increasing time in treatment, employment, and lack of evidence of drug or alcohol abuse were associated with a decreased likelihood of arrest.

Retention and Termination of Patients in the Maintenance Program

There were 20,653 individuals admitted to the NYC MMTP from its inception in November, 1970, through December, 1974. The retention and termination experience was determined for all patients, and for subgroups defined by demographic, social, and drug-use characteristics. Strictly administered criteria of admission and termination, and an effective control system operated by the Program's Central Office, ensured that every individual who had received even one dose of methadone was included as an admission, and that patients were terminated when methadone treatment was discontinued.

The key findings include:

Overall, 65% of the patients were retained in continuous, active treatment for 1 year; 47% remained for 2 years, and 35% for 3 years following admission.

There was a remarkable similarity in the retention and termination experience of all of the diverse subgroups of patients studied.

Retention was not found to vary with clinic size; the experience of patients admitted to NYC MMTP units with an average census of 250 or less, 251–400, and more than 400 was almost identical.

There was a considerable decline in retention rates for cohorts admitted in successive years from 1971 through 1973. The decline was found to reflect primarily an increase in terminations initiated by the patients themselves.

A sharp peak in the rate of voluntary withdrawal for all patients, regardless of length of time in treatment, was associated with the promulgation by Federal and State agencies in 1973 of restrictive regulations governing methadone treatment.

Irrespective of length of time in treatment, an increased likelihood of termination was found to be associated with lack of gainful occupation, and with reported use of illicit drugs or excessive alcohol consumption.

Readmission of Patients following Termination from the Maintenance Program

Through the end of 1974, 10,401 patients were terminated for causes other than death, following their first admission to the New York City Methadone Maintenance Treatment Program. The readmission experience of these individuals, through June, 1975 was analyzed.

The major findings include:

The cumulative rate of readmission to the NYC MMTP for all patients was 13.9% by the end of 1 year following termination, and 20.1% by the end of 2 years.

The highest readmission rates were observed for patients terminated because of incarceration, and for those voluntarily withdrawing from treatment (27.3% and 20.1%, respectively, within 2 years after discharge).

Among patients voluntarily terminated, as well as those discharged for all other reasons, the readmission rates did not vary with length of time in treatment prior to termination.

The readmission rate of patients voluntarily leaving the Program more than doubled for cohorts terminated in successive years from 1972 to 1974, while the rates remained constant for patients discharged for all other reasons.

Retention rates of patients following readmission to the NYC MMTP were considerably lower than those of patients admitted to the Program for the first time; one year after enrollment, the rates were 50% and 65%, respectively.

Patients who voluntarily withdrew from treatment following first admission had the highest retention upon readmission; higher retention rates during the second treatment episode were also associated with longer duration in treatment following first admission.

Reports to the New York City Narcotics Register before and after Admission to the Maintenance Program

The reporting history to the New York City Narcotics Register, from all agencies and from criminal justice system sources in particular, was analyzed for all patients, and for subgroups defined by retention in the NYC MMTP and by reason for termination.

The following are the major findings:

The proportion of patients reported to the Narcotics Register each 6-month period steadily increased during the 3 years prior to enrollment; following admission, there was a sharp decline in the reporting rate from all sources, and from criminal justice system agencies in particular.

There was a strong correlation between the decline in postadmission reporting to the Register, and retention in the NYC MMTP; for those patients who remained in continuous treatment for at least 2 years, the likelihood of one or more reports from any agency, and from criminal justice system agencies specifically, declined by about 40% in the 24 months after enrollment, compared to the same time period prior to admission.

Four out of five patients remaining in the Program for 2 years were not reported from a criminal justice system source while in treatment.

Patients who were terminated from the NYC MMTP had a considerably greater likelihood of being reported to the Register while still in treatment than did those who continued in the Program, and the disparity was observed long before termination occurred.

Following termination, almost half of the former patients were reported to the Narcotics Register within 6 months, and by 36 months after discharge, the proportion exceeded 70%.

Overall, the likelihood of being reported to the Register during the year preceding admission and in the first 12 months after termination was very similar. For those patients who remained in treatment for at least 1 year, however, the posttreatment reporting, from all agencies and from criminal justice system agencies in particular, was considerably reduced.

Patients voluntarily withdrawing from treatment had a markedly lower reporting rate after termination than did patients who were discharged from the NYC MMTP for all other reasons; this was especially true with respect to reports from criminal justice system agencies.

The Ambulatory Detoxification Program: Duration of Treatment and Referral to Long-Term Treatment Programs

The experience of the NYC ADP was analyzed with respect to the Program's primary objectives: to eliminate physical dependence on narcotics; to provide a safe, legal alternative to the physical need to self-administer illicit narcotics; and to motivate patients to seek long-term treatment and facilitate appropriate referral.

The major findings include:

From July, 1971 through the end of 1974, there were 63,500 admissions to the NYC ADP, and 375,000 patient-days of treatment were provided.

Providing patients and staff the option of extending the period of detoxification from 7 to 14 days was not associated with a significant change in average patient stay.

More than 9000 addicts, 15% of all admissions, entered long-term treatment programs as a result of referral by the NYC ADP staff.

The experience with respect to average patient stay and proportion of patients completing referral to long-term treatment programs was essentially the same for first admissions and for those who had previously been detoxified in the NYC ADP.

More than half of all completed referrals were to ambulatory drug-free programs. Although variations were noted in the proportion of patients in successive admission cohorts who entered different treatment modalities, an increase in completed referrals to one type of program was generally not associated with a decrease in the proportion entering others.

14

Applicants to the Maintenance and Detoxification Programs

INTRODUCTION

The New York City Methadone Maintenance Treatment Program (NYC MMTP), from its inception in November, 1970, through the end of 1974, received 58,388 applications for admission. The New York City Ambulatory Detoxification Program, which began accepting patients in July, 1971, received 68,925 applications by the end of 1974. These figures take on added significance when it is noted that the Methadone Maintenance Program is one of approximately 40 long-term methadone programs, and treats only one-third of all maintenance patients in the City; and the Ambulatory Detoxification Program provides less than half of the combined out-patient and in-patient detoxification capacity in New York City.

In this chapter, the following data are presented:

- The number of applicants to the two City-operated programs during each 3-month period from 1971 through 1974, by age, sex and ethnicity
- The disposition of applicants to the New York City Methadone Maintenance Treatment Program
- The relationship between the location of clinics and the area of residence of addicts applying for admission to the Methadone Maintenance Treatment Program

APPLICATION PROCEDURES AND SOURCES OF DATA

The New York City Methadone Maintenance Treatment Program

Applications for admission to the NYC MMTP are available in each of the Program clinics, as well as in 22 District Health Centers, in welfare centers, in the City prisons, and in most detoxification and addiction referral facilities which operate in New York City.* All applications are forwarded to the Program's Central Office, where they are checked for duplication and for the Program's admission criteria of age (18 years or older), duration of addiction (at least 2 years), and residence in New York City. Central Office then notifies the clinic nearest the applicant's home to schedule him (her) for admission screening; eligible applicants are scheduled in chronological order of application.

Every application is assigned one of the following "status" designations:

"Admitted"—applicants who have begun treatment in the NYC MMTP

"Scheduled for admission"—applicants who appear to meet the eligibility requirements of age, duration of addiction and residence, and who are awaiting admission screening by one of the Program clinics

"Ineligible - age"—applicants who are under 18 years of age

"Ineligible - duration of addiction"—applicants who have been addicted for less than 2 years

"Ineligible - residence"—applicants who do not reside in New York City

"Lost to followup"—applicants who can not be located at the address or phone number indicated on the Application Form, or who do not respond to at least three requests to report for admission screening

"Rejected - motivation"—applicants who, at the time of admission screening, indicate they do not want methadone maintenance treatment

"Rejected - other"—this designation is applied to applicants who are rejected by the clinic staff on the basis of serious multiple addiction, and for other, miscellaneous reasons

"Application withdrawn - in treatment elsewhere"—this status is assigned when applicants notify the Program that they have entered another addiction treatment facility and wish to cancel their application to the NYC MMTP

"Died"—determined by the NYC MMTP upon routine review of the death certificates of persons identified by the Chief Medical Examin-

*Over 90% of the applications received during the first 4 years of operation were filled out in the Program clinics.

er's Office as addicts; in addition, relatives and friends occasionally notify the Program of the death of an applicant

Implicit in these definitions is the fact that the status of applicants can change over time. Thus, when an individual who previously could not be located contacts the Program and provides a new address, he (she) is rescheduled for admission screening and the status is changed from "lost" to "scheduled for admission."

The information provided on each Application Form (Appendix III), as well as the status which is assigned, is key-punched and available for analysis. All data elements which comprise the applicant file can be corrected and updated.

Applications received from individuals who are already awaiting admission are designated "duplicates." Patients who have been terminated from the Program, however, must submit a new Application Form if they seek readmission.

The New York City Ambulatory Detoxification Program

Applicants for admission to the New York City Ambulatory Detoxification Program (NYC ADP) must apply in person at one of the Program's clinics. Admission criteria are current physical dependence on narcotics and residence in New York City. Since January, 1973, eligible applicants have been admitted on the same day they apply. Application Forms (Appendix VI) are forwarded by the clinics to Central Office at the end of every week.

Since treatment is initiated on the day of application, there is virtually no attrition of eligible applicants prior to admission. Former patients may be readmitted to the NYC ADP after an interval of four weeks following their last treatment in the Program; readmission requires completion of a new Application Form.

The NYC ADP data system is not computerized. Accordingly, all data must be tabulated by hand, thus limiting the analyses which are possible.

RESULTS

Applicants to the New York City Methadone Maintenance and Ambulatory Detoxification Programs (1971–1974)

The number of applicants to the NYC MMTP and the NYC ADP in each 3-month period from the inception of the programs through the end of 1974 is shown in Figure 14.1. The initial experience of the two programs was somewhat different. The number of applicants to the NYC ADP rose steadily

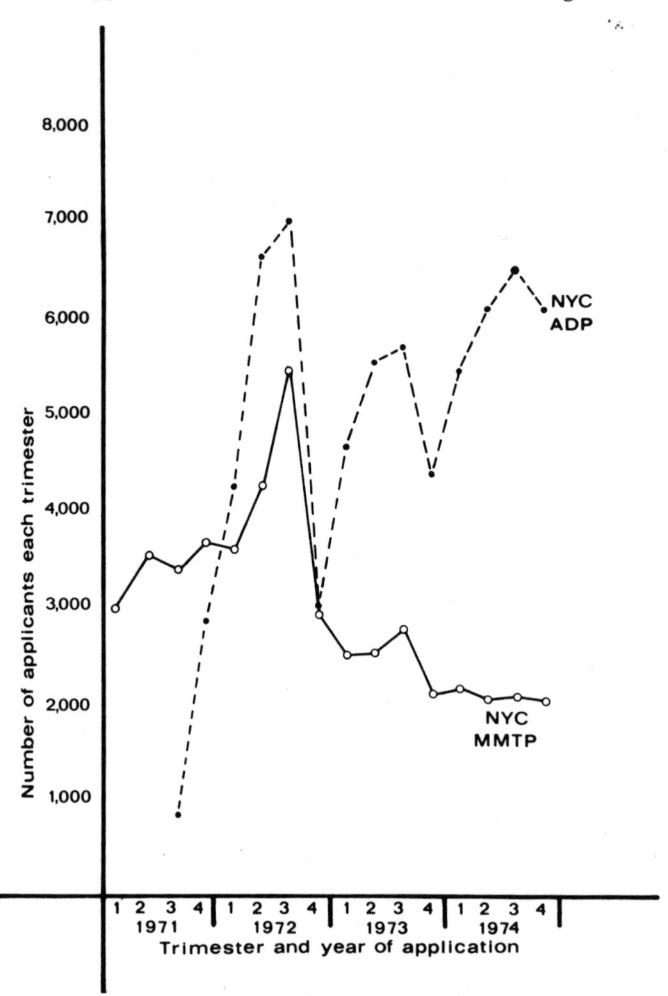

Figure. 14.1. Applicants to the NYC MMTP and NYC ADP, by trimester of application, 1971–1974. Excludes applications from individuals already awaiting admission. First quarter of 1971 includes applications to the NYC MMTP received in November and December, 1970.

from 859 during the first 3 months after the Program was begun in July, 1971, to 7004 during the corresponding 3 months of 1972. For the NYC MMTP, the number of applicants in each 3-month period from January, 1971 through March, 1972, was quite constant, ranging between 3000 and 3600.

The number of applicants to both programs peaked during the third quarter of 1972. Thereafter, applicants to the Methadone Maintenance Program dropped rapidly, leveling off at approximately 2000 per trimester from Oc-

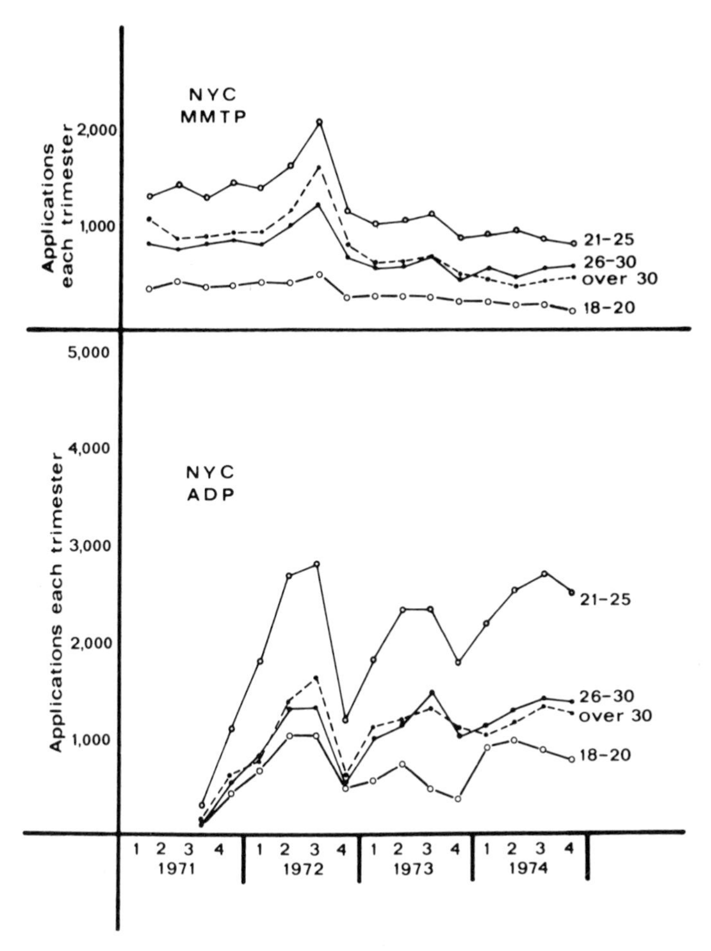

Figure 14.2. Applicants to the NYC MMTP and NYC ADP, by age group, by trimester of application, 1971–1974. Excludes applications from individuals already awaiting admission. First quarter of 1971 includes applications to the NYC MMTP received in November and December, 1970.

tober, 1973 through the end of 1974. Applicants to the Detoxification Program, on the other hand, after dropping to less than 3000 in the last quarter of 1972, increased sharply in 1973 and again in 1974. Whereas the number of applicants to the NYC ADP was highest during the second and third trimesters of each of the 3 years of observation, there was no consistent seasonal variation in the case of applications received by the Maintenance Program.

The pattern of total applicants to the NYC MMTP and NYC ADP was similar for subgroups defined by age and sex (Figures 14.2 and 14.3, respectively). Figure 14.4, which shows the number of applicants to the programs

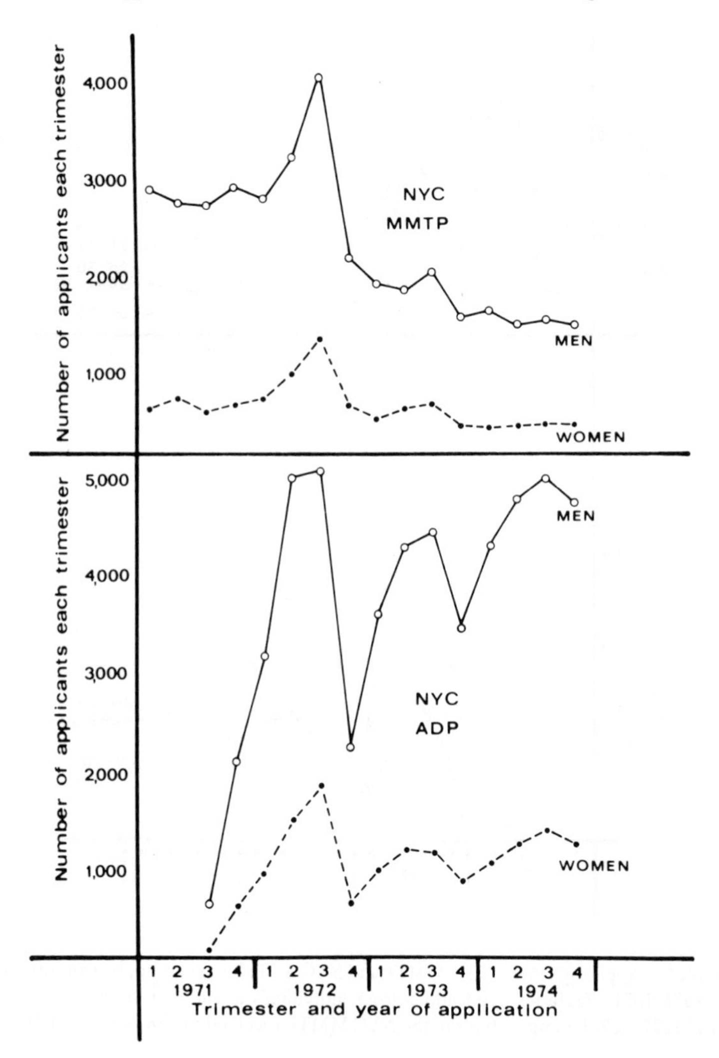

Figure 14.3. Applications to the NYC MMTP and NYC ADP, by sex, by trimester of application, 1971–1974. Excludes applications from individuals already awaiting admission. First quarter of 1971 includes applications to the NYC MMTP received in November and December, 1970.

by ethnicity, indicates that the peak experienced by both the NYC MMTP and the NYC ADP during the third quarter of 1972 comprised primarily black applicants. Except for that 3-month period, the patterns for whites, blacks, and Hispanics were similar.

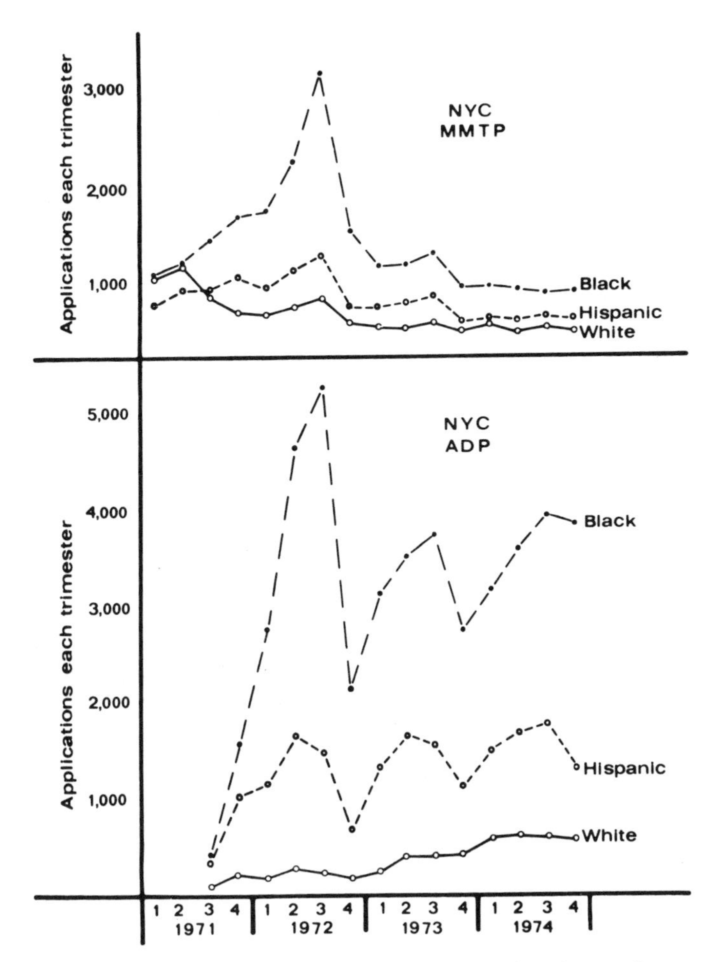

Figure 14.4. Applications to the NYC MMTP and NYC ADP, by ethnicity, by trimester of application, 1971–1974. Excludes applications from individuals already awaiting admission. First quarter of 1971 includes applications to the NYC MMTP received in November and December, 1970.

The Disposition of Applicants to the New York City Methadone Maintenance Treatment Program

Of the 58,388 applications for admission received by the NYC MMTP through December 31, 1974, 10,022 (17.2%) were duplicates, submitted by applicants already awaiting admission. The remaining 48,366 applications were analyzed according to their status as of March 31, 1975, providing for all subjects a minimum interval of three months following application.

All Applicants

Of all applicants, slightly less than half (46.6%) were admitted to the Program. Approximately 3% of the applicants were rejected for failure to meet the admission criteria of age, duration of addiction or residence in New York City, and an additional 3% were rejected at the time of screening for lack of motivation or for other reasons. Over 2000 applicants (4.2% of the total) notified the NYC MMTP that they had entered other treatment programs.

It is known that 426 applicants died before they could be admitted to the Program. At the end of March, 1975, only 174 individuals who applied on or before December 31, 1974 were scheduled for admission; the remaining 41.3%, almost 20,000 applicants, were "lost to follow-up."

Disposition by Year of Application

Table 14.1 shows the disposition of individuals who applied for admission to the NYC MMTP each year, from 1971 through 1974. The lowest proportion of admissions and, correspondingly, the highest "lost to follow-up" rate was noted for the 1972 applicants.

Disposition of Applicant Subgroups Defined by Demographic and Social Characteristics, and by Self-Reported Drug Abuse History

The status of the 18,083 unduplicated applications for admission to the NYC MMTP, submitted during 1973 and 1974,* was determined for applicant subgroups defined by selected characteristics.

The disposition for specific sex, ethnic, and age groups is shown in Table 14.2. There were essentially no differences between men and women. With respect to ethnicity, somewhat fewer blacks started treatment; whites were more likely to have been rejected for failure to meet Program criteria (age, duration of addiction, or residence), and less likely to be "lost to follow-up," than black and Hispanic applicants.

Applicant groups defined by age at the time of application showed only minor differences in the likelihood of starting treatment. The youngest group, under 21 years old, was considerably more likely to be rejected because of Program criteria. Those over 40 years of age at the time they applied for treatment had a greater likelihood of dying before admission, and were more likely to be rejected by the clinics on the basis of the screening interview. The older the applicant, the greater the likelihood of being "lost to follow-up."

*At the end of 1972, the Application Form was modified; comparable data are not available for earlier applicants.

TABLE 14.1

Disposition of Applicants to the NYC MMTP, 1971 through 1974, by Year of Application

		Status of Applicants (Percent) as of March 31, 1975						
Year Applied	Number of Applicants	Started Treatment	Sched. for Admission	Rejected for Age, Duration or Resid.	Lost to Follow-up	Rejected by Clinic	Entered Other Program	Died
Total	48,366 (100%)	46.6	0.4	3.4	41.3	3.2	4.2	0.9
1971[a]	14,114 (100%)	49.7	0.0	2.9	41.2	1.5	3.6	1.1
1972	16,169 (100%)	38.9	0.0	3.7	48.4	2.2	5.7	1.1
1973	9,858 (100%)	48.2	0.6	3.9	36.3	4.9	5.4	0.7
1974	8,225 (100%)	54.6	1.2	3.0	33.9	5.9	1.0	0.3

[a] Includes 604 applicants in 1970.

TABLE 14.2

Disposition of Applicants to the NYC MMTP, 1973 and 1974, by Sex, Ethnicity, and Age at Time of Application

Group	Number of Applicants	Status of Applicants (Percent) as of March 31, 1975						
		Started Treatment	Sched. for Admission	Rejected for Age, Duration or Resid.	Lost to Follow-up	Rejected by Clinic	Entered Other Program	Died
Total	18,083 (100%)	51.1	0.9	3.5	35.2	5.4	3.4	0.5
Men	13,769 (100%)	50.9	0.9	3.4	36.0	5.2	3.2	0.5
Women	4,314 (100%)	51.8	0.9	3.9	32.7	6.0	4.1	0.6
White	4,067 (100%)	53.3	0.9	5.5	27.6	7.6	4.6	0.5
Black	8,309 (100%)	49.1	0.8	2.9	39.1	4.6	2.9	0.6
Hisp.	5,374 (100%)	54.2	1.0	2.8	34.3	4.4	3.1	0.4
Under 21 years	1,775 (100%)	49.1	0.8	10.2	30.7	5.9	3.0	0.3
21–25 years	7,704 (100%)	52.5	0.8	3.3	34.7	5.2	3.2	0.3
26–30 years	4,509 (100%)	52.2	1.1	2.7	35.3	5.1	3.3	0.4
31–40 years	3,126 (100%)	48.4	0.8	2.0	38.8	5.1	4.0	0.9
Over 40 years	969 (100%)	43.8	1.1	1.9	39.6	7.9	4.1	1.5

Table 14.3 shows the disposition of applicants according to employment and welfare status, prior arrest history, and source of referral. Employed applicants were more likely than unemployed to enter treatment. Applicants receiving public assistance at the time of application were more frequently rejected by the clinics; they were also more likely to enter another addiction treatment program.

Applicants with one or more self-reported arrests were less frequently rejected for failing to meet the Program criteria of age, duration of addiction or residence, than those with no prior arrest history.

The greatest differences are those associated with the source of referral. Of the 2271 applicants referred by detoxification programs, only 34% were admitted, while 61% of referrals from long-term addiction treatment programs began treatment in the NYC MMTP (the latter category includes transfers from other methadone programs). The experience of the two largest applicant groups, however, self-referrals and those referred by family or friends, was almost identical.

The disposition of applicants by age of first heroin use and previous methadone maintenance or drug-free treatment history is shown in Table 14.4. Only minor differences are noted among these subgroups.

The Relationship between Clinic Location and Residence of Applicants to the New York City Methadone Maintenance Treatment Program

In order to investigate the relationship between the establishment of NYC MMTP clinics and the number of applications from the surrounding areas, the United States Postal Service ZIP codes of residence of applicants were analyzed with respect to the location and opening dates of Program facilities (there are 100 ZIP code areas in New York City). The first four clinics, which opened in November, 1970, were excluded from the study since applications were not accepted prior to their opening.

A total of 40 NYC MMTP clinics were established between January, 1971 and October, 1973. Facilities were located in each of the five boroughs, with the number of Program clinics ranging from one in Staten Island to fifteen in Manhattan. The number of applications received from the ZIP code area in which each of these facilities was located was determined for the 2 months preceding the opening, the month in which the clinic began admitting patients, and for the following 2 months. The data were analyzed separately for the 16 Program clinics which were established in ZIP codes in which methadone maintenance facilities already existed (whether operated by the NYC MMTP or under other auspices), and for the 24 clinics which, at the time they began admitting patients, represented the only source of

TABLE 14.3

Disposition of Applicants to the NYC MMTP, 1973 and 1974, by Employment and Welfare Status at Time of Application, Prior Arrest History, and Source of Referral

Status at Time of Application	Number of Applicants	Status of Applicants (Percent) as of March 31, 1975						
		Started Treatment	Sched. for Admission	Rejected for Age, Duration or Resid.	Lost to Follow-up	Rejected by Clinic	Entered Other Program	Died
Total	18,083	51.1	0.9	3.5	35.2	5.4	3.4	0.5
Employed	3,922 (100%)	57.5	0.8	4.2	29.1	4.9	3.2	0.3
Unemployed[a]	14,161 (100%)	49.4	0.9	3.3	36.8	5.5	3.4	0.6
On welfare	4,528 (100%)	48.9	0.9	2.6	32.7	7.7	6.3	0.9
Not on welf.[a]	13,555 (100%)	51.9	0.9	3.8	36.0	4.6	2.4	0.4

Prior arrest	13,339 (100%)	50.4	0.9	2.9	35.9	5.7	3.5	0.6
No arrests[a]	4,744 (100%)	53.1	0.8	5.2	33.1	4.3	3.2	0.3
Referred by								
Family or friends	7,726 (100%)	54.0	1.0	3.3	32.8	5.3	3.1	0.6
Self	4,652 (100%)	55.1	1.0	3.3	30.9	6.3	3.0	0.4
Detox program	2,271 (100%)	34.4	0.3	3.6	55.5	2.9	2.6	0.6
Long-term treat. prog.	846 (100%)	60.5	1.1	3.1	19.0	7.7	8.4	0.2
Drug referral program	429 (100%)	56.6	0.5	3.0	30.3	4.4	4.7	0.5
Hospital	388 (100%)	49.0	1.5	3.4	34.5	6.2	4.4	1.0
Welfare department	229 (100%)	44.5	0.4	5.2	34.9	8.3	5.7	0.9
Other and no answer	1,542 (100%)	42.0	1.2	5.1	42.6	4.8	3.7	0.6

[a] Includes applicants who failed to respond to this item.

TABLE 14.4

Disposition of Applicants to the NYC MMTP, 1973 and 1974, by Age of First Heroin Use and Prior Addiction Treatment History

Addiction History	Number of Applicants	Status of Applicants (Percent) as of March 31, 1975						
		Started Treatment	Sched. for Admission	Rejected for Age, Duration or Resid.	Lost to Follow-up	Rejected by Clinic	Entered Other Program	Died
Total	18,083 (100%)	51.1	0.9	3.5	35.2	5.4	3.4	0.5
Age first used heroin (years)								
Under 16	5,155 (100%)	50.9	0.9	3.6	35.1	5.9	3.1	0.6
16–17	5,246 (100%)	52.1	1.1	3.2	34.3	5.4	3.4	0.5

18–20	4,351 (100%)	50.8	0.8	3.3	35.9	5.3	3.4	0.5
21–25	2,298 (100%)	50.2	1.0	3.0	36.7	4.8	3.9	0.5
26–30	677 (100%)	49.8	0.4	5.0	35.6	3.4	4.3	1.5
Over 30	283 (100%)	54.1	0.0	3.9	32.9	6.0	2.8	0.4
Prior addiction treatment[a]								
None/no ans.	4,788 (100%)	48.9	0.9	5.6	38.6	4.0	1.8	0.3
Prev. meth. maintenance	7,044 (100%)	54.8	1.0	2.4	28.3	8.0	5.0	0.6
Prev. drug-free	3,388 (100%)	52.2	0.8	2.7	34.4	5.9	3.3	0.7
Prev. detox-ification	10,784 (100%)	51.7	0.9	2.6	35.0	5.6	3.6	0.6

[a] Treatment categories are not mutually exclusive.

TABLE 14.5

Applications to the NYC MMTP from ZIP Code Area in Which Program Facilities Are Located, from Two Months before to Two Months after Clinic Opening

Preexisting Clinic(s) in Same ZIP Code Area	Number of NYC MMTP Clinics[a]	Number of Applications from ZIP Code Area in Which Clinic Is Located, during Specified Time Period				
		Second Month preceding Opening	First Month preceding Opening	Month Clinic Opened	First Month after Opening	Second Month after Opening
Yes	16	274	235	251	284	231
No	24	279	349	706	752	864

[a] Clinics opened January, 1971 through October, 1973.

methadone maintenance treatment in the area. The results are shown in Table 14.5.

In the case of clinics which were established in ZIP code areas where methadone treatment facilities already existed, there was essentially no change in the number of applications received from local residents before, during and after the clinic openings. The situation was markedly different with respect to Program clinics which opened in areas where no other methadone treatment sources were available. In the month of opening, and in the subsequent 2 months, applications more than doubled compared to the 2 months preceding the opening.

DISCUSSION

The large numbers of applicants seeking admission to the New York City Methadone Maintenance and Ambulatory Detoxification Programs demonstrate the attractiveness of these programs to the target population. The figures take on added significance in view of the many other sources of addiction treatment, and of chemotherapy in particular, which are available in New York City.

The steady increase in applications received by the Ambulatory Detoxification Program in the 15 months following its inception was not observed in the case of the Methadone Maintenance Treatment Program. Within two months after the first NYC MMTP clinics opened, addicts were applying at a fairly constant rate of about 3000 to 3500 per 3-month period. This plateau, which persisted for 15 months, appears to reflect the large gap which existed between demand for methadone maintenance and treatment capacity when the NYC MMTP began.

The approximately 2000 applications received by the Maintenance Program in each quarter of 1974 represented a marked decline from the peak level of almost 5500 applicants in the third quarter of 1972. Viewed in isolation, this might suggest that there had been a corresponding decline in the prevalence of heroin addiction in New York City. The persistent increase in demand for ambulatory detoxification during the same period of time, however, does not support such a conclusion.

The sharp drop in applicants seeking admission to the NYC MMTP is probably in part a consequence of increasingly restrictive regulations imposed on maintenance programs by Federal and State authorities since the end of 1972, as well as of the growing disenchantment with methadone maintenance treatment in the general community (see Chapter 10). Another possible factor, which has received little attention in the professional literature to date, is the proximity of the treatment facilities to the target population. City-wide, there has been a small, but consistent excess capacity among all methadone maintenance programs since early 1973, and this has been the rationale for halting further expansion. The experience of the NYC MMTP, however, suggests that a large potential demand exists in currently unserved neighborhoods, which would surface if additional clinics could be opened.

The high proportion of applicants to the NYC MMTP who are not subsequently admitted suggests that, for many addicts, the decision to seek treatment is tenuous. Overall, half of the applicants to the NYC MMTP did not follow through and begin treatment, and the experience was similar for subgroups defined by age, sex, ethnicity, and social and drug abuse history. The length of the interval between application and admission appears to be an important factor; thus, from 1972 to 1973, when the waiting period was reduced from many months to a few weeks, there was an associated decline in the proportion of applicants lost to follow-up. Nevertheless, even in 1974, when most applicants could be admitted in a matter of days, only 55% began treatment, and one-third were "lost."

Since the NYC MMTP consistently maintained a census very close to capacity, the attrition of applicants created little concern at either the clinic or the Central Office level. In retrospect, however, it is clear that "success" ought not to be measured solely in terms of outcome as observed in those applicants who are admitted. The fact that 20,000 addicts who initiated contact with the NYC MMTP were "lost," without treatment having been provided, must be considered in evaluating the Program's impact on those who want and need services, and on the general community.

15

Descriptive Analysis of Patients Admitted to the Maintenance and Detoxification Programs

INTRODUCTION

A description of the demographic, social, and drug use characteristics of patients entering addiction treatment programs is important for several reasons. It permits a more meaningful evaluation of program effectiveness, since outcome measures are a function both of the therapeutic regimen provided and of the population being served. Insight is also obtained with respect to the applicability and acceptability of the treatment services to the target population. In the case of programs which are as large as those discussed here, the data are useful on a broader scale as well; although the subjects in the study are self-selected and limited by established program admission criteria, analysis of the data on tens of thousands of patients can help further the understanding of the natural history of addiction.

SOURCES OF DATA

The New York City Methadone Maintenance Treatment Program

For every patient entering the New York City Methadone Maintenance Treatment Program (NYC MMTP), an "Admission Screening Form" (Appendix IV) is completed by the clinic counseling staff and submitted to the Program's Central Office. Responses are provided by the patients, and no attempt is made to verify the information with outside sources.

Administrative procedures of the Program provide for monitoring by Central Office to ensure that all Admission Screening Forms are submitted by the clinics. Since the information collected at the time of admission was substantially modified in content and format during the latter half of 1972, consistent data are not available for patients entering the NYC MMTP prior to 1973. Consequently, except for age, sex and ethnic distributions, the descriptive information presented is limited to individuals admitted in 1973 and 1974. Only the data obtained at the time of the first Program admission are included.

Additional data were obtained from a cooperative study carried out by the NYC MMTP and the New York City Narcotics Register, analyzing the preadmission reporting history to the Register for all Methadone Maintenance Program patients.*

The New York City Ambulatory Detoxification Program

A combined application and admission form (Appendix VI) is completed at the time of application to the New York City Ambulatory Detoxification Program (NYC ADP). Responses are obtained from the applicants and entered by the clinic staff; as in the case of the NYC MMTP, no attempt is made to substantiate the information provided.

Since the Ambulatory Detoxification Program data system is not computerized, it has not been feasible to analyze the data as comprehensively as in the case of the Maintenance Program. In particular, it should be noted that the data are not based on first Program admissions only, and thus do not represent unduplicated individuals.

RESULTS

The findings presented below are grouped into three major sections: admissions to the New York City Methadone Maintenance Treatment Program; admissions to the New York City Ambulatory Detoxification Program; and a comparison of patients admitted to the respective programs during 1973 and 1974.

*The New York City Narcotics Register is prohibited by law from disclosing any information with respect to individuals who have been reported (202). Consequently, all findings related to Narcotics Register reporting history presented here and in subsequent chapters are based on aggregate data which describe the experience of predefined cohorts. The operation of the Register is described in more detail elsewhere (203–205).

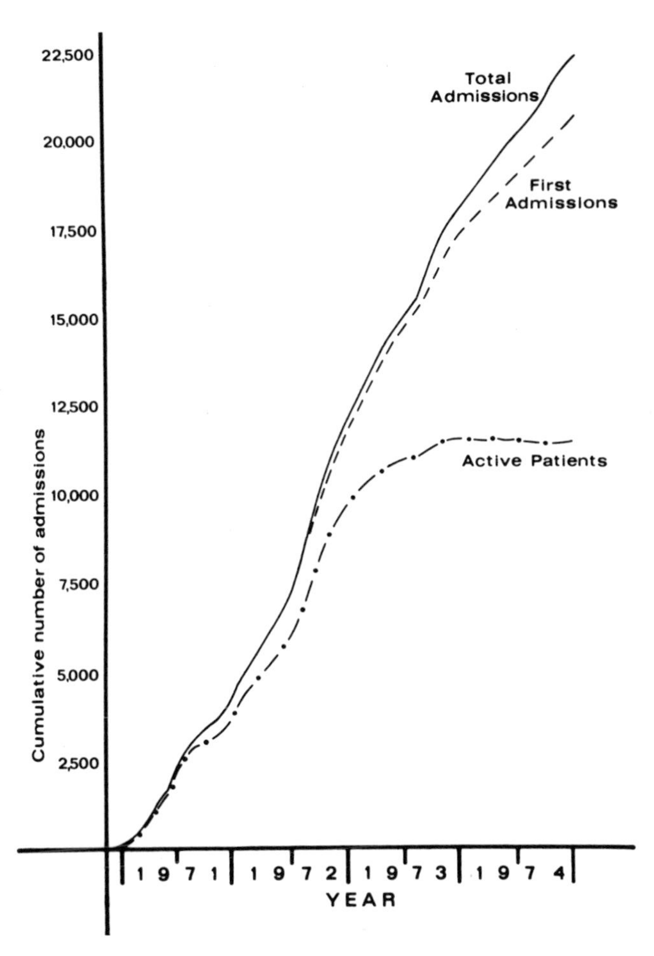

Figure 15.1. Cumulative total admissions, first admissions, and active patient census, NYC MMTP, 1970–1974. The NYC MMTP began admitting patients in November, 1970.

I. Admissions to the New York City Methadone Maintenance Treatment Program

Admissions to the NYC MMTP from 1970 through 1974

The cumulative number of admissions and readmissions to the NYC MMTP rose steadily following the inception of the Program in November, 1970, and by the end of 1974 had reached 22,292 (Figure 15.1). Since there were 1639 (7.4%) readmissions, the total number of individuals entering the NYC MMTP during this period was 20,653. During 1974, the last year studied, the number of terminations approximated that of admissions, and the Program census remained stable at about 11,400.

Table 15.1 shows the total number of admissions, subdivided into first admissions and readmissions, during each 6-month period. Although the percent of readmissions steadily increased, over 75% of the 2237 admissions in the last half of 1974 were never previously enrolled in the Program.

*Age, Sex, and Ethnic Distributions of Admissions Each Year (1971–1974)**

Age. The age distribution of first admissions to the NYC MMTP changed only slightly over the course of the first 4 years of the Program's operation (Table 15.2). Specifically, there was a gradual increase in patients 21–25 years of age, and a corresponding decline in the proportion over 30. Approximately one out of every six admissions was less than 21 years old.

Sex. Three-fourths of all first admissions to the NYC MMTP were men. As shown in Table 15.3, the proportion of women was somewhat lower in 1971 than in the subsequent 3 years.

Ethnicity. Of the 20,653 individuals admitted to the NYC MMTP through the end of 1974, approximately half were black, while the remainder were almost evenly divided between white and Hispanic (Table 15.4). During the first year of the Program's operation, 1971, slightly fewer blacks than whites were admitted; the number of black patients admitted during the following 2 years, however, was well over twice that of whites. By 1974 the disparity diminished somewhat.

Selected Social Characteristics of Patients Admitted in 1973 and 1974

Tables 15.5–15.12 show selected social characteristics of patients who entered the NYC MMTP for the first time during 1973 and 1974.

Drug Abuse Patterns of Patients Admitted in 1973 and 1974

Age Started Daily Heroin Use. The age distribution of first daily heroin use is shown in Table 15.13. The modal age is 16 years, and the median is 16.8.

Calendar Year of First Heroin Use. As shown in Table 15.14, 1968 was the peak year of onset of heroin use among patients first admitted to the NYC MMTP in 1973 and 1974. Of the 8706 patients responding, 43% indicated onset in the 3-year period from 1967 to 1969. One out of every six patients reported onset in 1960 or earlier.

It was found that while 1968 was the modal year of onset for both men and women admitted in 1973 and 1974, the proportion of women in each of the more recent years of onset, 1968 through 1972, was considerably greater

*A more detailed breakdown of age within sex within ethnic group by year of admission is shown in Appendix IX.

than that of men (Table 15.15). The year of first heroin use varied to an even greater extent with the age of patients at admission. Specifically, for the youngest patients, age 18–20 at the time of admission, the peak year was 1969; for patients 21–30 years of age the peak year was 1968; and for patients 31–40 years old when they entered the NYC MMTP, the mode was within the five year period 1956–1960. In the oldest age group, those over 40, more than 60% reported onset of heroin use prior to 1951.

Patients were grouped with respect to calendar year of first heroin use, and distributed according to their 6-month period of admission in 1973–1974. The results are shown in Table 15.16. With the exception of patients who started using heroin in 1970, the largest proportion of each group entered the Program during the first half of 1973, the number declining in each of the three subsequent 6-month periods. The greatest decline was for those patients with the earlier years of onset of heroin use. For patients who began using heroin in 1970, the proportion admitted during each half-year remained essentially unchanged.

Average Cost per Day of Heroin Habit. The average cost per day of heroin, as self-reported by patients first admitted to the NYC MMTP in 1973 and 1974, is shown in Table 15.17.

Preadmission Use of Nonopiates and Excessive Alcohol. Table 15.18 shows self-reported use of nonopiate drugs and excessive alcohol consumption prior to admission to the NYC MMTP in 1973 and 1974. The categories are not mutually exclusive.

Longest Period of Voluntary Abstinence from Narcotics. Over 60% of the patients entering the NYC MMTP in 1973 and 1974 reported voluntary (i.e., noninstitutional) abstinence from narcotics for a period of at least one month since the onset of addiction. One out of eight patients indicated they had been abstinent for over a year since becoming addicted (Table 15.19).

Previous Methadone Maintenance and Drug-free Treatment. Almost 50% of the patients admitted to the NYC MMTP for the first time in 1973 and 1974 indicated previous addiction treatment in a methadone maintenance or drug-free program (Table 15.20). One-third of the patients had been in methadone maintenance treatment (since the cohort is limited to first NYC MMTP admissions, the prior source of treatment in all cases was an unaffiliated program). One out of five patients had been enrolled in a drug-free program.

Self-Reported Arrest and Conviction History of Patients Admitted in 1973 and 1974

One or more preadmission arrests were reported by 75% of the patients first admitted to the NYC MMTP in 1973 and 1974 (Table 15.21). The charges and disposition of the cases were not obtained.

The number of preadmission convictions was also asked of all new patients; the results are shown in Table 15.22.

Reporting History to the New York City Narcotics Register prior to Admission

Preadmission Reports to the Narcotics Register from Any Agency. Of the 20,653 individuals admitted to the NYC MMTP through the end of 1974, 17,292 (83.7%) had previously been reported to the New York City Narcotics Register. While the proportion previously reported varied somewhat among the cohorts entering treatment in successive years from 1971 to 1974, it never fell below 80% (Table 15.23).

*Preadmission Reporting History to the Narcotics Register from Criminal Justice System Agencies.** Table 15.24 shows, for each admission cohort, the preadmission reporting history to the Narcotics Register from criminal justice system (CJS) agencies.

The percentage of patients with CJS reports prior to admission gradually decreased from 60% of those admitted in 1971 and 1972, to 50% of those entering in 1974. More striking, however, is the variation in the proportion of patients with a CJS agency report during the 6-month period immediately preceding admission: from 11.3% in 1971 to 19.0% in 1972, followed by a sharp decline to less than 10% for 1973 and 1974 admissions.

Preadmission Reports to the Narcotics Register from Other Methadone Maintenance and Drug-free Addiction Treatment Programs: Comparison with Responses of Patients. Although about 20% of patients entering the NYC MMTP in 1973 and 1974 indicated prior treatment in drug-free addiction programs, only 7% were reported from such agencies to the Narcotics Register. With respect to methadone maintenance treatment, the correlation between patient self-reporting and Register data is far closer: 33% of the 1973–1974 admissions stated they had received methadone maintenance treatment in the past, and 27% had been reported to the Register by maintenance programs prior to enrollment in the NYC MMTP. In both cases, it is possible that part of the discrepancy is due to treatment obtained outside of New York City.

Preadmission Reports to the Narcotics Register from In-patient and Out-patient Detoxification Programs. The in-patient detoxification unit of the Morris J. Bernstein Institute (MJBI), and the out-patient clinics of the New York City Ambulatory Detoxification Program, are the two largest detoxification resources in the City. Both programs have consistently submitted reports to the Narcotics Register on all admissions, and almost half the NYC

*Criminal justice system agencies are defined as the police, corrections, parole, and probation departments.

MMTP patients had been admitted previously to one or both of these detoxification facilities.

Table 15.25 shows the reporting history to the Register from MJBI and the NYC ADP, of patients entering the Methadone Maintenance Treatment Program in successive years from 1971 to 1974. Subsequent to the start of the NYC ADP in the latter half of 1971, the proportion of patients with previous reports from MJBI decreased steadily, from 32% in 1971 to 18% in 1974. On the other hand, the proportion of patients with previous reports from the Ambulatory Detoxification Program increased rapidly, from 2% of 1971 NYC MMTP admissions to 28% of the 1972 admission cohort, rising further to 36% in 1973, and 38% in 1974.

Since 1972, more than two-thirds of the NYC MMTP patients previously reported to the Narcotics Register from the NYC ADP had been reported within the 6 months preceding admission; in 1973 and 1974, these recently detoxified patients totalled fully 25% of all admissions to the NYC MMTP. By contrast, the majority of the most recent reports from MJBI preceded admission by more than 12 months; less than 5% of all admissions to the Maintenance Program had received in-patient detoxification, as reported from MJBI, within 6 months prior to admission.

It was found that 7939 patients entering the NYC MMTP from 1972, the first full year of operation of the Ambulatory Detoxification Program, through 1974, had preadmission reports to the Narcotics Register from MJBI and/or the NYC ADP. Of these patients, less than 17% had been reported from *both* programs, and the proportion was remarkably constant in each of the 3 years, ranging from 17.5% in 1972 to 14.7% in 1974.

Relationship of Age of First Daily Heroin Use to Age of First Arrest

The self-reported age of first daily heroin use and the age of first arrest (if any) were analyzed for patients admitted to the NYC MMTP during 1973 and 1974.

The overall likelihood of any preadmission arrest decreased slightly with increased age of onset of daily heroin use (Table 15.26). There was also found to be a decreased likelihood of having a first arrest *after* onset of addiction, among those patients becoming addicted at later ages, as shown in Table 15.27. Of those patients with daily heroin use beginning at age 14–17, who had not been arrested previously, almost two-thirds were arrested after addiction began; among patients without an arrest prior to becoming addicted at age 26–30, only 41% were subsequently arrested. However, since exposure to arrest following onset of heroin use may have been longer for those with onset at age 14–17, as compared to those with onset at age 26–30, this observation may simply be an artifact.

The data were further analyzed to determine the temporal relationship between age of first arrest and the age at which daily heroin use began. It was found that the peak age of onset of addiction consistently coincided with or preceded the age of first arrest (Table 15.28). It was also noted that the interval between the two events increased with increasing age of first arrest; that is, the greater the age when first arrested, the longer the average arrest-free period following onset of daily heroin use.

II. The New York City Ambulatory Detoxification Program

Admissions to the NYC ADP from 1971 through 1974

The first NYC ADP clinic began accepting patients in July, 1971. By the end of 1974, there had been almost 64,000 admissions, and over 38,000 individuals had been treated one or more times (Figure 15.2).

As shown in Table 15.29, there was an increasing proportion of readmissions in each successive 6-month period; even during 1974, however, the last year included in this analysis, over 10,000 addicts were admitted to the NYC ADP for the first time.

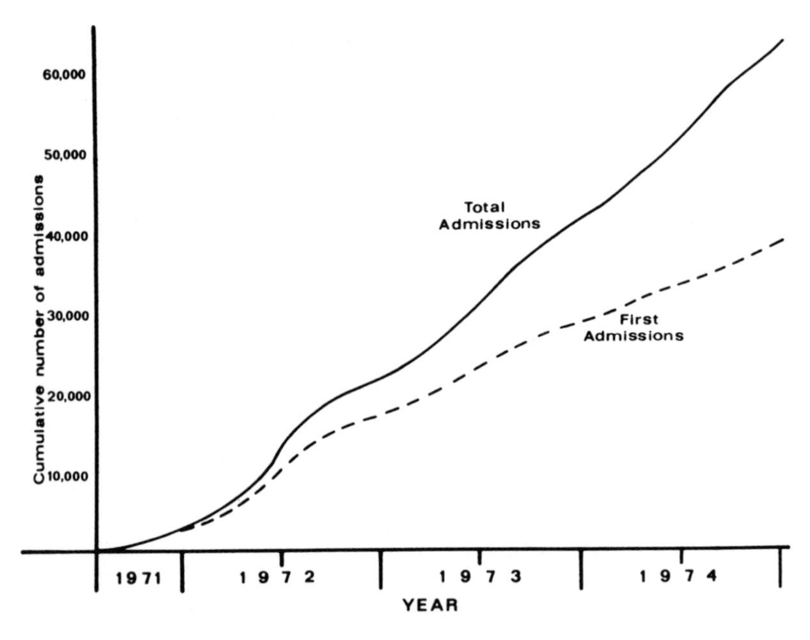

Figure 15.2. Cumulative total admissions and first admissions, NYC ADP, 1971–1974. The NYC ADP began admitting patients in July, 1971.

Age, Sex, and Ethnic Distributions of Admissions to the NYC ADP (1971–1974)

The age, sex, and ethnic characteristics of all admissions to the NYC ADP during each year, from 1971 through 1974, are shown in Table 15.30. There have been only slight changes with respect to age and sex distributions in successive years, but the ethnic pattern has changed considerably. While blacks comprised 53% of all admissions in 1971, they increased to 71% in 1972, and subsequently declined to 65% and 60% in 1973 and 1974, respectively. The percentage of Hispanic patients declined during these 3.5 years, and whites consistently represented less than 10% of the total.

Prior Addiction Treatment History and Duration of Addiction of Admissions to the NYC ADP in 1974

Data obtained at the time of enrollment were analyzed with respect to prior addiction treatment and duration of addiction for a systematic sample of admissions to the NYC ADP in 1974. Specifically, every patient was included who entered the Program during the following 12 weeks: weeks 11–13, 24–26, 37–39, and 50–52. The sample comprised 5387 admissions, 23.5% of the 1974 total.

Overall, slightly more than 11% reported prior methadone maintenance treatment only, and an equal proportion drug-free treatment only; less than 5% of the total had prior experience in both types of programs. Almost three-quarters of all admissions had never had any form of long-term treatment for addiction.*

The frequency with which prior long-term treatment was reported varied with duration of addiction, as shown in Table 15.31. Patients with more than 20 years of addiction had the most frequently reported history of previous treatment, but even among this group, three out of five said they had never been enrolled in either a methadone maintenance or a drug-free program.

Of the patients with neither prior methadone maintenance nor drug-free treatment, two-thirds reported previous detoxification, and this proportion approached 80% for those patients addicted for more than 15 years (Table 15.32). Nevertheless, of the entire sample of 5387 admissions, 1322 (25%) reported never having had any previous addiction treatment at all, neither long term nor detoxification.

The median years of addiction were calculated separately for patients categorized according to their prior treatment experience. As shown in Table 15.33, the medians for the different subgroups ranged from 4.6 to 7.1 years.

*In order to obtain some indication of the validity of responses with respect to prior treatment, patients reporting no previous methadone maintenance were checked against the records of admissions to the NYC MMTP; less than 1% had been enrolled.

III. Comparison of 1973–1974 Admissions to the NYC MMTP and NYC ADP

Demographic Characteristics

The demographic characteristics of patients first admitted to the NYC MMTP in 1973 and 1974, and of all admissions to the NYC ADP during these two years, are shown in Table 15.34. There are essentially no differences between the programs in the age and sex distributions. With respect to ethnicity, there are proportionately fewer whites, and more blacks, among the admissions to the NYC ADP.

Employment and Welfare Status

During 1973 and 1974, there was little difference in employment and public assistance status as reported by patients at the time of admission to the New York City Methadone Maintenance and Ambulatory Detoxification Programs. The percentage of admissions who were employed was 23.4% for the NYC MMTP, and 19.4% for the NYC ADP. Of the patients admitted to the Maintenance Program, 27.2% were receiving public assistance, compared to 23.0% of admissions to the Detoxification Program.

Previous Addiction Treatment History

The treatment experience prior to enrollment in the NYC ADP was analyzed for a sample of 1974 admissions only; therefore, the comparison between the two programs was limited to 1974 data.

As shown in Table 15.35, the previous treatment histories of the patients admitted to the two programs are markedly different. Admissions to the Ambulatory Detoxification Program were much more likely to have had no prior long-term treatment; also, the proportion of patients with previous methadone maintenance treatment among NYC MMTP admissions was more than twice the corresponding proportion among NYC ADP admissions.

Years since Heroin Use Began and Duration of Addiction

Figure 15.3 shows the years since first heroin use (NYC MMTP) and the number of years since addiction began (NYC ADP), for patients admitted in 1974. Although the curves are quite similar, they represent responses to somewhat different questions: patients entering the Methadone Maintenance Program were asked the calendar year in which they first used heroin, while the Ambulatory Detoxification Program asked the number of years since onset of addiction. If the average interval between first heroin use and addiction were known, it would be possible to correct for this discrepancy. However, since this would involve shifting the NYC ADP curve to the right,

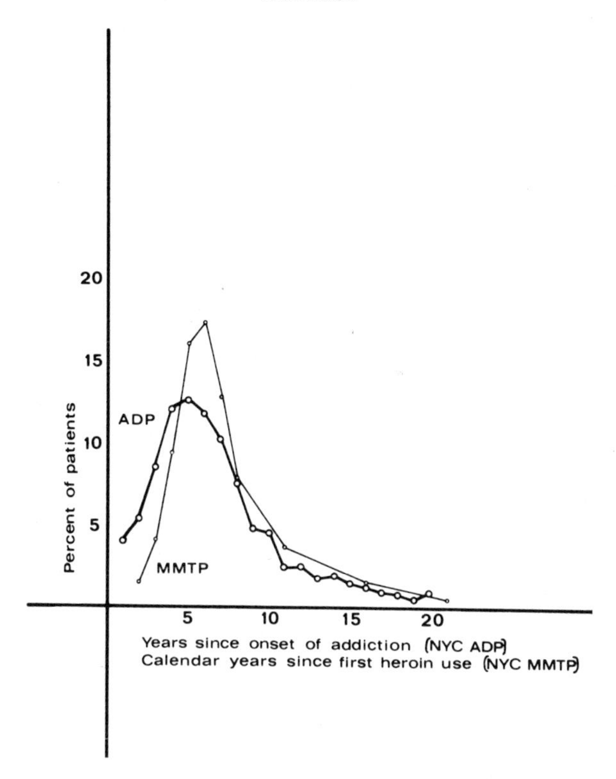

Figure 15.3. Years of heroin use by patients admitted during 1974 to the NYC MMTP [all first admissions to the NYC MMTP during 1974, excluding 41 patients (1.1%) for whom year of onset is not known; $N = 3549$] and NYC ADP (systematic sample of all NYC ADP admissions during 1974, comprising all admissions during weeks 11–13, 24–26, 37–39, and 50–52, excluding 14 patients for whom years since onset of addiction is not known; $N = 5373$).

it would appear that the results are in fact even closer than Figure 15.3 suggests.

DISCUSSION

The diversity of demographic and social characteristics of the patients entering the New York City Methadone Maintenance and Ambulatory Detoxification Programs supports the premise that there is no stereotype which can be applied to the narcotic addict. At the same time, it demonstrates that both maintenance and detoxification treatment are capable of attracting a very broad spectrum of the addict population. For instance, while methadone maintenance has frequently been viewed as a "treatment of last resort," acceptable mainly to the older addict with a history of repeated failure in other modalities, the data suggest otherwise; one of every six patients was under 21 years of age at the time of admission, and 80% had never had drug-free treatment.*

The duration of prior heroin use among admissions to the NYC MMTP and the NYC ADP is strikingly similar, as are the age and sex distributions. The difference noted with respect to ethnicity probably reflects the location of clinic facilities of the two programs. NYC ADP clinics, situated in predominantly black and Hispanic neighborhoods, attracted relatively few white patients; the NYC MMTP, on the other hand, with many more treatment units widely dispersed throughout the five boroughs, had an ethnic distribution which more closely paralleled the City-wide data of the New York City Narcotics Register (207).

There was a major disparity among the admissions to the two programs with respect to previous addiction treatment history. While almost half of the patients admitted to the Methadone Maintenance Program reported prior maintenance or drug-free treatment, this was true of only 28% of admissions to the Detoxification Program. It is especially significant that even among NYC ADP admissions with an addiction history of over 10 years, less than 40% reported any long-term treatment. Furthermore, among the large number of addicts entering the NYC ADP who had neither maintenance nor drug-free treatment in the past, two-thirds did have previous detoxification. These findings suggest that a sizable proportion of the addict population, while rejecting long-term treatment, is willing to accept the more limited services of a detoxification program. The corollary is also true: in the absence of detoxification facilities, there will be no therapeutic contact at all with a large segment of the addict community.

The difficulty of achieving social rehabilitation is underscored by the status of patients at the time of admission to the NYC MMTP: over two-thirds lacked a high school diploma, and an equal proportion were neither employed nor receiving job training or schooling; preadmission use of nonopiate drugs was the rule rather than the exception, with almost 60% of patients, by self-report, having used barbiturates, and 10% reporting excessive alcohol consumption; 75% had been arrested one or more times, and of these, one-third reported more than five arrests; while the specific charges and the disposition of the cases are not known, half of the patients had been convicted at least once.

*In a 1972 survey of 126 city and county drug abuse agencies, it was found that 101 (80%) required prior failure in an abstinence program as a condition of eligibility for methadone maintenance treatment (206). Had such an admission criterion been adopted by the NYC MMTP, four out of five patients would have been refused treatment.

Among first admissions to the NYC MMTP, the peak year of onset of heroin use was 1968. It was noted, however, that the year of onset varies considerably among different patient subgroups, especially as defined by age at time of admission. Attempts to extrapolate treatment program data to the general addict population in order to estimate incidence of addiction must take into account the characteristics of the patient cohort being studied, and the program eligibility criteria which may exclude certain age groups.

TABLE 15.1

Total Admissions, First Admissions, and Readmissions to the Maintenance Program Each Six-Month Period, 1971–1974

	Number of Admissions								
		1971		1972		1973		1974	
Type of Admission	Total 1971–1974	Jan–June	July–Dec	Jan–June	July–Dec	Jan–June	July–Dec	Jan–June	July–Dec
All	22,292 (100.0%)	2314[a] (100.0%)	2098 (100.0%)	2872 (100.0%)	4701 (100.0%)	2983 (100.0%)	2855 (100.0%)	2232 (100.0%)	2237 (100.0%)
First admissions	20,653 (92.6%)	2313 (100.0%)	2064 (98.4%)	2798 (97.4%)	4548 (96.7%)	2833 (95.0%)	2507 (87.8%)	1852 (83.0%)	1738 (77.7%)
Readmissions	1639 (7.4%)	1 (0.0%)	34 (1.6%)	74 (2.6%)	153 (3.3%)	150 (5.0%)	348 (12.2%)	380 (17.0%)	499 (22.3%)

[a] Includes 104 admissions in November and December, 1970.

TABLE 15.2

Age Distribution of Patients First Admitted to the NYC MMTP Each Year, 1971–1974

Age at Time of Admission (Years)	First Admissions (Percent)				
	Total 1971–1974	1971	1972	1973	1974
Number of Admissions	20,653	4377[a]	7346	5340	3590
Total	100.0	100.0	100.0	100.0	100.0
18–20	15.7	14.1	15.4	17.3	16.1
21–25	40.4	35.8	38.4	41.4	45.2
26–30	20.7	21.0	19.9	20.6	22.2
31–40	17.0	19.3	18.9	15.2	13.1
Over 40	6.1	6.8	7.4	5.4	3.4

[a] Includes 104 admissions in November and December, 1970.

TABLE 15.3

Sex Distribution of Patients First Admitted to the NYC MMTP Each Year, 1971–1974

Sex	First Admissions (Percent)				
	Total 1971–1974	1971	1972	1973	1974
Number of Admissions	20,653	4377[a]	7346	5340	3590
Total	100.0	100.0	100.0	100.0	100.0
Men	75.5	79.9	73.2	74.6	76.1
Women	24.5	20.1	26.8	25.4	23.9

[a] Includes 104 admissions in November and December, 1970.

TABLE 15.4

Ethnic Distribution of Patients First Admitted to the NYC MMTP Each Year, 1971–1974

	First Admissions (Percent)				
Ethnicity	Total	1971	1972	1973	1974
Number of Admissions	20,653	4377[a]	7346	5340	3590
Total	100.0	100.0	100.0	100.0	100.0
White	25.4	40.2	20.6	19.4	26.1
Black	45.8	35.3	52.1	47.1	44.0
Hispanic	28.1	23.5	27.0	32.7	29.4
Other/unknown	0.6	1.0	0.3	0.8	0.5

[a] Includes 104 admissions in November and December, 1970.

TABLE 15.5

Marital Status of Patients First Admitted to the NYC MMTP in 1973 and 1974

Marital Status at Time of Admission	First Admissions	
	Number	Percent
Total	8144[a]	100.0
Never married	4072	50.0
Married	1702	20.9
Widowed	98	1.2
Separated	1002	12.3
Divorced	301	3.7
Common-law	969	11.9

[a] Excludes 786 "no answer."

TABLE 15.6

Household Composition of Patients First Admitted to the NYC MMTP in 1973 and 1974

Household Composition at Time of Admission[a]	First Admissions	
	Number	Percent
Total	8778[b]	100.0
Lives alone	1501	17.1
With parents	2563	29.2
With spouse	2510	28.6
With children	1308	14.9
With other relatives	1009	11.5
With friends	1001	11.4
No stable arrangement	97	1.1

[a] Categories are not mutually exclusive.
[b] Excludes 152 "no answer."

TABLE 15.7

Religion of Patients First Admitted to the NYC MMTP in 1973 and 1974

Religion	First Admissions	
	Number	Percent
Total	8046[a]	100.0
Catholic	3773	46.9
Other Christian	2382	29.6
Jewish	161	2.0
Other non-Christian	177	2.2
None	1553	19.3

[a] Excludes 884 "no answer."

TABLE 15.8

Educational Level of Patients First Admitted to the NYC MMTP in 1973 and 1974

Educational Level at Time of Admission	First Admissions	
	Number	Percent
Total	8778[a]	100.0
Grade 9 or less	1773	20.2
Grade 10–12	4222	48.1
High School grad. or higher	2783	31.7

[a] Excludes 152 "no answer."

TABLE 15.9

Employment Status of Patients First Admitted to the NYC MMTP in 1973 and 1974

Employment Status at Time of Admission	First Admissions	
	Number	Percent
Total	8930	100.0
Employed	2090	23.4
Unemployed/no answer	6840	76.6

TABLE 15.10

Job Training or Schooling of Patients First Admitted to the NYC MMTP in 1973 and 1974

Receiving Job Training or in School at Time of Admission	First admissions	
	Number	Percent
Total	8930	100.0
Yes	491	5.5
No/no answer	8439	94.5

TABLE 15.11

Longest Period in One Job, Patients First Admitted to the NYC MMTP in 1973 and 1974

Longest Period in One Job	First Admissions	
	Number	Percent
Total	8930	100.0
Never worked/no answer	1545	17.3
1–6 months	1840	20.6
7–12 months	1759	19.7
13–24 months	1652	18.5
Over 24 months	2134	23.9

TABLE 15.12

Welfare Status of Patients First Admitted to the NYC MMTP in 1973 and 1974

Receiving Public Assistance	First Admissions	
	Number	Percent
Total	8930	100.0
Yes	2429	27.2
No/no answer	6501	72.8

TABLE 15.13

Age of First Daily Heroin Use of Patients First Admitted to the NYC MMTP in 1973 and 1974

Age Started Daily Heroin Use (Years)	First Admissions	
	Number	Percent
Total	8760[a]	100.0
Under 14	542	6.2
14	654	7.5
15	976	11.1
16	1318	15.0
17	1124	12.8
18	1029	11.7
19	668	7.6
20	573	6.5
21	401	4.6
22	296	3.4
23	211	2.4
24	181	2.1
25	180	2.1
26	111	1.3
27	99	1.1
28	80	0.9
29	45	0.5
30	44	0.5
Over 30	228	2.6

[a] Excludes 170 "no answers."

TABLE 15.14

Calendar Year of First Heroin Use of Patients First Admitted to the NYC MMTP in 1973 and 1974

Calendar Year of First Heroin Use	First Admissions	
	Number	Percent
Total	8742[a]	100.0
1972	63	0.7
1971	249	2.8
1970	673	7.7
1969	1245	14.2
1968	1420	16.2
1967	1128	12.9
1966	709	8.1
1961–1965	1769	20.2
1956–1960	775	8.9
1951–1955	329	3.8
1950 and earlier	382	4.4

[a] Excludes 188 "no answer."

TABLE 15.15

Calendar Year of First Heroin Use of Patients First Admitted to the NYC MMTP in 1973 and 1974, by Sex and Age at Time of Admission

	First Admissions (Percent)						
	Men	Women	18–20 Years	21–25 Years	26–30 Years	31–40 Years	Over 40 Years
Number of admissions	6716	2214	1502	3833	1899	1285	411
Total	100.0	100.0	100.0	100.0	100.0	100.0	100.0
Calendar Year of First Heroin Use							
1972	0.5	0.8	1.8	0.6	0.5	0.2	0
1971	2.1	5.2	4.6	2.9	2.3	1.6	0.2
1970	6.1	11.7	15.4	7.6	5.7	3.0	0.5
1969	12.4	18.2	27.3	15.4	9.3	4.0	1.5
1968	14.8	18.7	22.7	20.1	11.5	5.6	1.5
1967	12.8	12.1	13.2	17.4	10.0	4.5	2.7
1966	8.6	5.8	6.1	11.8	7.3	1.9	0.7
1961–1965	21.4	14.4	5.5	19.6	36.4	16.7	4.9
1956–1960	9.6	5.8	0.1	1.2	13.5	33.8	7.1
1951–1955	4.1	2.3	0.0	0.1	0.7	18.7	15.5
1950 and earlier	4.8	2.4	0.0	0.0	0.7	7.1	60.8
No answer	2.6	2.4	3.3	3.3	2.2	3.0	2.7

TABLE 15.16

Proportion of Patients First Admitted to the NYC MMTP Each Six-Month Period, 1973 and 1974, by Year of First Heroin Use

	Six-Month Period of Admission				
Calendar Year of First Heroin Use	Total 1973–1974	Jan–June 1973	Jul–Dec 1973	Jan–June 1974	Jul–Dec 1974
Total	8430[a] (100.0%)	2687 (31.9%)	2417 (28.7%)	1727 (20.5%)	1599 (19.0%)
1970	673 (100.0%)	171 (25.4%)	173 (25.7%)	165 (24.5%)	164 (24.4%)
1969	1245 (100.0%)	344 (27.6%)	338 (27.1%)	300 (24.1%)	263 (21.1%)
1968	1420 (100.0%)	426 (30.0%)	386 (27.2%)	307 (21.6%)	301 (21.2%)
1967	1128 (100.0%)	342 (30.3%)	342 (30.3%)	236 (20.9%)	208 (18.4%)
1966	709 (100.0%)	220 (31.0%)	215 (30.3%)	151 (21.3%)	123 (17.3%)
1961–1965	1769 (100.0%)	612 (34.6%)	521 (29.5%)	336 (19.0%)	300 (17.0%)
1956–1960	775 (100.0%)	281 (36.2%)	217 (28.0%)	134 (17.3%)	143 (18.5%)
1951–1955	329 (100.0%)	128 (38.9%)	107 (32.5%)	49 (14.9%)	45 (13.7%)
1950 and earlier	382 (100.0%)	163 (42.7%)	118 (30.9%)	49 (12.8%)	52 (13.6%)

[a] Excludes patients with year of onset later than 1970, who were not eligible for admission throughout the 2-year period, and "no answer."

TABLE 15.17

Average Cost Per Day of Heroin Habit of Patients First Admitted to the NYC MMTP in 1973 and 1974

	First Admissions	
Average Cost Per Day of Heroin Habit (Dollars)	Number	Percent
Total	6689[a]	100.0
1–25	1378	20.6
26–50	2749	41.1
51–100	2087	31.2
Over 100	475	7.1

[a] Excludes 2241 "no answer."

TABLE 15.18

Preadmission Use of Nonopiates and Excessive Alcohol by Patients First Admitted to the NYC MMTP in 1973 and 1974

Nonopiate Drug Use Prior to Admission[a]	First Admissions	
	Number	Percent
Total	8212[b]	100.0
Barbiturates	4738	57.7
Amphetamines	1519	18.5
Cocaine	2406	29.3
Excessive alcohol	797	9.7

[a] Categories are not mutually exclusive.
[b] Excludes 718 "no answer."

TABLE 15.19

Longest Period of Voluntary Abstinence from Narcotics following Onset of Addiction, Patients First Admitted to the NYC MMTP in 1973 and 1974

Longest Period of Voluntary Abstinence	First Admissions	
	Number	Percent
Total	8930	100.0
None/no answer	3469	38.8
1–3 months	2182	24.4
4–6 months	992	11.1
7–12 months	1134	12.7
Over 12 months	1153	12.9

TABLE 15.20

Previous Addiction Treatment History of Patients First Admitted to the NYC MMTP in 1973 and 1974

Previous Addiction Treatment History	First Admissions	
	Number	Percent
Total	8930	100.0
None/no answer	4839	54.2
Methadone maintenance only	2291	25.7
Drug-free only	1123	12.6
Methadone maintenance and drug-free	679	7.6

TABLE 15.21

Preadmission Arrests of Patients First Admitted to the NYC MMTP in 1973 and 1974

Number of Preadmission Arrests	First Admissions	
	Number	Percent
Total	8930	100.0
None/no answer	2261	25.3
1	1290	14.4
2	1097	12.3
3	880	9.9
4	609	6.8
5	515	5.8
6–10	1286	14.4
More than 10	992	11.1

TABLE 15.22

Preadmission Convictions of Patients First Admitted to the NYC MMTP in 1973 and 1974

Number of Preadmission Convictions	First Admissions	
	Number	Percent
Total	8930	100.0
None/no answer	4391	49.2
1	1591	17.8
2	839	9.4
3	629	7.0
4	325	3.6
5	241	2.7
6–10	563	6.3
More than 10	351	3.9

TABLE 15.23

Preadmission Reports to the Narcotics Register from any Agency, by Year of First Admission to the NYC MMTP, 1971–1974

Year	Number of First Admissions	Patients Previously Reported to the Narcotics Register	
		Number	Percent
Total	20,653	17,292	83.7
1971	4,377[a]	3,505	80.1
1972	7,346	6,381	86.9
1973	5,340	4,494	84.2
1974	3,590	2,912	81.1

[a] Includes 104 admissions to the NYC MMTP in November and December, 1970.

TABLE 15.24

Preadmission Reporting History to the Narcotics Register from Criminal Justice System Agencies, by Year of First Admission to the NYC MMTP, 1971–1974

		Percent of Patients with Most Recent Report to the Narcotics Register from a CJS Agency during Specified Preadmission Interval					
Year of Admission	Number of First Admissions	1–6 Months	7–12 Months	13–18 Months	19–24 Months	Over 24 Months	No Prior Report
Total	20,653	12.9	9.0	7.2	5.9	22.4	42.6
1971	4,377[a]	11.3	10.9	11.1	6.7	19.6	40.4
1972	7,346	19.0	9.5	5.3	6.4	21.5	38.3
1973	5,340	9.5	9.6	8.6	4.7	22.5	45.0
1974	3,590	7.5	4.7	4.3	5.8	27.1	50.7

[a] Includes 104 admissions to the NYC MMTP in November and December, 1970.

TABLE 15.25

Preadmission Reports to the Narcotics Register from the Bernstein Institute (In-patient Detoxification Service) and the NYC ADP, by Year of First Admission to the NYC MMTP, 1971–1974

		Percent of Patients Reported to the Narcotics Register from MJBI and from NYC ADP during Specified Preadmission Interval							
	Number of	1–6 Months		7–12 Months		Over 12 Months		No Previous Report	
Year of Admission	First Admissions	MJBI	NYC ADP	MJBI	NYC ADP	MJBI	NYC ADP	MJBI	NYC ADP
All	20,653	4.0	18.9	3.1	4.5	18.8	2.9	74.2	73.8
1971	4,377[b]	5.2	2.4	4.8	*a*	21.8	*a*	68.2	97.6
1972	7,346	5.0	21.3	3.7	5.8	20.3	0.5	71.0	72.4
1973	5,340	2.5	24.8	2.2	6.9	17.5	4.8	77.8	63.6
1974	3,590	2.5	25.8	1.1	3.6	14.0	8.3	82.4	62.3

[a] The NYC ADP began operation in July, 1971.

[b] Includes 104 admissions to the NYC MMTP in November and December, 1970.

TABLE 15.26

Likelihood of Arrest Prior to First Admission to the NYC MMTP in 1973 and 1974, by Age of First Daily Heroin Use

Arrest History Prior to Entering NYC MMTP	Age at Time of First Daily Heroin Use (Years)						
	All Patients	Under 14	14–17	18–20	21–25	25–30	Over 30
Total	8760[a] (100.0%)	542 (100.0%)	4072 (100.0%)	2270 (100.0%)	1269 (100.0%)	379 (100.0%)	228 (100.0%)
No arrest or no answer	2402 (27.4%)	125 (23.1%)	1030 (25.2%)	665 (29.2%)	388 (30.5%)	125 (32.9%)	69 (30.2%)
One or more arrests	6358 (72.5%)	417 (76.9%)	3042 (74.7%)	1605 (70.7%)	881 (69.4%)	254 (67.0%)	159 (69.7%)

[a] Excludes 170 "no answer" regarding age of first daily heroin use.

TABLE 15.27

Likelihood of First Arrest after Age of First Daily Heroin Use, by Age of First Daily Heroin Use; Patients First Admitted to NYC MMTP in 1973 and 1974

Arrest History prior to Entering NYC MMTP	Age at Time of First Daily Heroin Use (Years)[a]				
	Total (14–30)	14–17	18–20	21–25	26–30
Patients without arrest through the age of first daily heroin use	5318 (100.0%)	2947 (100.0%)	1394 (100.0%)	765 (100.0%)	212 (100.0%)
Patients first arrested following age of first daily heroin use	3120 (58.7%)	1924 (65.3%)	732 (52.5%)	377 (49.3%)	87 (41.0%)
Patients with no arrests following age of first daily heroin use	2198 (41.3%)	1023 (34.7%)	662 (47.4%)	388 (50.7%)	125 (58.9%)

[a] The age groups "less than 14" and "over 30" were not further broken down.

TABLE 15.28

Age of First Daily Heroin Use, by Age at Time of First Arrest; Patients First Admitted to the NYC MMTP in 1973 and 1974

Age at Time of First Arrest (Years)[a]	Number of Patients	Age of First Daily Heroin Use (Years)		Interval (Years) between Median Age of First Daily Heroin Use and Age of First Arrest[b]
		Mode	Median	
Total ages 14–30	5874	16	16.7	Not applicable
14	262	14	14.6	−0.1
15	414	15	15.1	+0.4
16	1187	16	15.5	+1.0
17	817	16	16.0	+1.5
18	818	17	16.9	+1.6
19	525	18	17.1	+2.4
20	414	18	17.3	+3.1
21	375	18	18.1	+3.4
22	232	18	18.6	+3.9
23	223	21	19.4	+4.1
24	148	22	20.5	+4.0
25	130	20	21.1	+4.4
26	96	25	23.0	+3.5
27	82	23	22.8	+4.7
28	61	28	24.8	+3.7
29	48	29	24.8	+4.7
30	42	27	25.0	+5.5

[a] The age groups "less than 14" and "over 30" were not further broken down.
[b] Calculated to the middle of the age-year of first arrest.

TABLE 15.29

Total Admissions, First Admissions, and Readmissions to the New York City Ambulatory Detoxification Program Each Six-Month Period July, 1971–December, 1974

	Admissions							
Type of Admission	Total July 1971–Dec 1974	1971 July–Dec	1972 Jan–June	1972 July–Dec	1973 Jan–June	1973 July–Dec	1974 Jan–June	1974 July–Dec
All admissions	63,559 (100.0%)	3,238 (100.0%)	9,488 (100.0%)	9,018 (100.0%)	9,463 (100.0%)	9,471 (100.0%)	10,879 (100.0%)	12,002 (100.0%)
First admissions	38,286 (60.2%)	2,979 (92.0%)	7,542 (79.5%)	6,413 (71.1%)	6,067 (64.1%)	5,237 (55.3%)	4,956 (45.6%)	5,092 (42.4%)
Readmissions	25,273 (39.8%)	259 (8.0%)	1,946 (20.5%)	2,605 (28.9%)	3,396 (35.9%)	4,234 (44.7%)	5,923 (54.4%)	6,910 (57.6%)

TABLE 15.30

Age, Sex, and Ethnic Distributions of All Admissions to the NYC ADP, 1971–1974

Demographic Characteristic	Total 1971–1974	Distribution during Specified Year of Admission			
		1971[a]	1972	1973	1974
All admissions	63,559 (100.0%)	3,238 (100.0%)	18,506 (100.0%)	18.934 (100.0%)	22,881 (100.0%)
Age (years)					
Under 18	572 (0.9½)	55 (1.7%)	225 (1.2%)	81 (0.4%)	211 (0.9%)
18–20	9,152 (14.4%)	554 (17.1%)	2,988 (16.1%)	2,146 (11.3%)	3,464 (15.1%)
21–25	26,187 (41.2%)	1,286 (39.7%)	7,587 (41.0%)	7,789 (41.1%)	9,525 (41.6%)
26–30	13,856 (21.8%)	638 (19.7%)	3,690 (20.0%)	4,459 (23.6%)	5,069 (22.2%)
31–40	10,487 (16.5%)	482 (14.9%)	3,035 (16.4%)	3,405 (18.0%)	3,565 (15.6%)
Over 40	3,305 (5.2%)	223 (6.9%)	981 (5.3%)	1,054 (5.6%)	1,047 (4.6%)
Sex					
Men	49,265 (77.5%)	2,424 (74.9%)	13,926 (75.3%)	14,873 (78.6%)	18,042 (78.9%)
Women	14,294 (22.5%)	814 (25.1%)	4,580 (24.7%)	4,061 (21.4%)	4,839 (21.1%)
Ethnicity					
White	4,352 (6.8%)	249 (7.7%)	703 (3.8%)	1,272 (6.7%)	2,128 (9.3%)
Black	40,902 (64.4%)	1,727 (53.3%)	13,176 (71.2%)	12,237 (64.6%)	13,762 (60.1%)
Hispanic	16,716 (26.3%)	1,162 (35.9%)	4,386 (23.7%)	5,179 (27.4%)	5,989 (26.2%)
Other/unknown	1,589 (2.5%)	100 (3.1%)	241 (1.3%)	246 (1.3%)	1,002 (4.4%)

[a] The NYC ADP began accepting patients in July, 1971.

TABLE 15.31

Prior Methadone Maintenance and Drug-Free Addiction Treatment Experience by Duration of Addiction for Sample[a] of Admissions to the NYC ADP in 1974

Prior Treatment History	Distribution (Percent) of Patients with Specified Duration of Addiction (Years)						
	Total	Less Than 2	2–5	6–10	11–15	16–20	Over 20
Number of admissions	5373[b]	213	2064	2068	543	251	234
Total	100.0	100.0	100.0	100.0	100.0	100.0	100.0
Methadone maint. only	11.4	4.2	9.3	11.7	14.7	17.5	20.5
Drug-free only	11.7	3.8	11.1	12.6	12.3	12.7	12.4
Both meth. maint. and drug-free	4.8	0.0	2.9	5.6	9.0	7.2	7.7
Neither methadone maint. nor drug-free	72.1	92.0	76.6	70.2	63.9	62.5	59.4

[a] Sample comprises all admissions during the following 12 weeks of 1974: weeks 11–13, 24–26, 37–39, and 50–52.

[b] Excludes 14 admissions for whom duration of addiction was not reported.

TABLE 15.32

Prior Detoxification Treatment of Patients Not Previously Enrolled in Long-Term Addiction Treatment Programs, by Duration of Addiction, for Sample[a] of Admissions to the NYC ADP in 1974

	Distribution (Percent) of Patients with Specified Duration of Addiction (Years)						
Prior Detoxification	Total	Less Than 2	2–5	6–10	11–15	16–20	Over 20
Number of patients with no previous long-term treatment	3,873[b]	196	1582	1452	347	157	139
Total	100.0	100.0	100.0	100.0	100.0	100.0	100.0
Previous detoxification	65.9	42.4	61.4	70.8	68.9	79.0	76.9
No previous detoxification	34.1	57.6	38.6	29.6	31.1	20.1	23.1

[a] Sample comprises all admissions to NYC ADP during the following 12 weeks of 1974: weeks 11–13, 24–26, 37–39, and 50–52.

[b] Excludes 14 patients for whom duration of addiction was not reported.

TABLE 15.33

Duration of Addiction Prior to Admission, by Prior Addiction Treatment Experience, for Sample[a] of Admissions to the NYC ADP in 1974

Prior Addiction Treatment Experience	Number of Patients	Median Years of Addiction
Total	5373[b]	5.7
No long-term or detoxification treatment	1322	4.6
No long-term treatment, but prior detoxification	2551	5.8
Drug-free only	626	5.8
Methadone maintenance only	614	6.6
Both drug-free and methadone maintenance	260	7.1

[a] Sample comprises all admissions to NYC ADP during the following 12 weeks of 1974: weeks 11–13, 24–26, 37–39, and 50–52.

[b] Excludes 14 admissions for whom duration of addiction was not reported.

TABLE 15.34

Age, Sex, and Ethnic Distributions of First Admissions to NYC MMTP, and All Admissions to NYC ADP, 1973–1974

Demographic Characteristic	Distribution (Percent)	
	NYC MMTP[a]	NYC ADP[b]
Number of admissions	8930	41,815
Total	100.0	100.0
Age (years)		
Under 18	Not applicable	0.7
18–20	16.8	13.4
21–25	42.9	41.4
26–30	21.3	22.8
31–40	14.4	16.6
Over 40	4.6	5.0
Sex		
Men	75.2	78.8
Women	24.8	21.2
Ethnicity		
White	22.1	8.2
Black	45.9	62.1
Hispanic	31.4	26.7
Other/unknown	0.7	3.0

[a] Unduplicated individuals.
[b] Includes readmissions.

TABLE 15.35

Preadmission Treatment History of Patients Entering the NYC MMTP and the NYC ADP in 1974

Previous Treatment History	Distribution (Percent)	
	NYC MMTP	NYC ADP
Number of admissions	3590[a]	5387[b]
Total	100.0	100.0
Methadone maintenance only	27.3	11.4
Drug-free only	12.4	11.7
Both methadone maintenance and drug-free	8.1	4.8
Neither methadone maintenance nor drug-free	52.1	72.1

[a] First admissions to the NYC MMTP in 1974.

[b] All admissions to the NYC ADP during the following twelve weeks of 1974: weeks 11–13, 24–26, 37–39, and 50–52.

16

Methadone Dosage Levels of Patients in the Maintenance Program

INTRODUCTION

The methadone dosages prescribed by the New York City Methadone Maintenance Treatment Program (NYC MMTP) are determined individually for each patient. The only limits imposed by the Program on its physicians are

- The initial dose of methadone may not exceed 40 mg
- No dosage increment or decrement may exceed 10 mg
- Dosages above 40 mg must be multiples of 10 mg; below 40 mg, multiples of 5 mg are permitted
- In compliance with Food and Drug Administration regulations (208), there is an upper limit of 120 mg per day (prior to promulgation of the Federal regulations in 1973, the Program's maximum dosage was 160 mg)

Although there has never been a limit with respect to *minimum* dosages, the initial orientation and in-service training of physicians and other professional and paraprofessional staff stresses the pharmacological rationale for maintenance dosages in the range of 80–100 mg (i.e., to achieve a high degree of cross-tolerance to all narcotics); conversely, it is emphasized that there is no justification for decreasing the dosage unless there is clinical indication to do so.

While the authority to order medication rests exclusively with the clinic physicians, other staff members are encouraged to participate in the evaluation of the patient's response to treatment and to recommend modification of the dosage level when this seems appropriate. Physicians are urged to consider the recommendations of the nonmedical staff, but without relinquishing the ultimate legal and professional responsibility which is their own.

Perhaps the most important determinant of the dosage level in the NYC MMTP is the individual patient's perception of his (her) own needs. Since 1971, each patient has known the precise amount of methadone prescribed. In the absence of evidence suggesting a continued illicit use of opiates, there is generally no basis for refusing a patient's request to lower the methadone dosage; within the limits established by Program policy and Federal regulations, there is also no rationale for maintenance at a dosage level lower than that requested by the patient.

Beginning in 1972, the frequency distributions of methadone dosages prescribed to all patients in the Program, as well as to those in each component clinic, have been determined monthly, based on the computerized medication records (see Chapter 3). In this chapter, the changing dosage patterns from 1972 through 1974 are described. Findings are also presented regarding the dosage levels prescribed for specified subgroups of patients defined by demographic characteristics and by length of time in treatment in the NYC MMTP.

FINDINGS

Distribution of Methadone Dosages (1972–1974)

At the end of June, 1972, when the analysis of methadone dosages in the NYC MMTP was first performed, the majority of patients (52%) were receiving 100 mg per day, and an additional 17% received more than 100 mg. As shown in Table 16.1, the pattern changed markedly during the following 2.5 years. By the end of 1974, the proportion of patients in the Program who were being maintained at 100 mg or more had declined from 69% to 16%, while at the other extreme, the proportion receiving 50 mg or less increased tenfold, from 3% to 30%.

Methadone Dosage and Length of Time in Treatment

Table 16.2 shows the dosage distributions, as of December, 1974, of patients grouped according to length of time in treatment in the NYC MMTP. There was found to be a direct association between the number of months since admission to the Program, and the proportion of patients maintained at methadone dosage levels of 100 mg or more.

TABLE 16.1

Distribution of Methadone Dosages of Patients in the NYC MMTP, 1972–1974

		Percent of Patients with Specified Dosage (mg)							
Date[a]	Number of Patients[b]	Total	Less than 40	40–50	60–70	80–90	100	110–120	More than 120
1972									
June	5,876	100.0	1.0	1.8	5.1	22.7	51.8	14.7	2.7
Dec.	9,329	100.0	1.7	3.5	6.4	29.6	45.6	11.7	1.6
1973									
June	10,128	100.0	4.1	6.9	11.4	34.9	41.5	1.3	0.1
Dec.	10,648	100.0	7.7	10.6	15.0	35.7	30.5	0.4	0.1
1974									
June	10,763	100.0	11.7	13.8	18.7	33.9	21.6	0.2	0.0
Dec.	10,487	100.0	13.3	17.0	21.3	32.0	16.3	0.1	0.0

[a] Data reflect the dosages prescribed for administration/dispensing during the last week of the month specified.

[b] Excludes patients temporarily receiving no methadone (e.g., due to incarceration or hospitalization), and those whose terminations were pending.

TABLE 16.2

Distribution of Methadone Dosages of Patients in the NYC MMTP as of December, 1974, by Length of Time in Treatment

		Percent of Patients with Specified Dosage (mg)						
Months in Treatment	Number of Patients[a]	Total	Less than 40	40–50	60–70	80–90	100	100–120
Total	10,487	100.0	13.3	17.0	21.3	32.0	16.3	0.1
1–6	1,799	100.0	7.8	19.2	31.4	34.7	6.9	0.1
7–12	1,447	100.0	10.2	17.9	26.8	37.2	7.9	0.0
13–18	1,424	100.0	12.3	19.2	23.4	35.1	9.9	0.1
19–24	1,303	100.0	13.7	17.9	18.8	35.8	13.6	0.2
25–30	1,974	100.0	12.8	17.2	16.2	33.9	19.9	0.1
31–36	1,052	100.0	14.0	15.8	14.3	26.2	29.8	0.0
37–42	684	100.0	14.5	14.9	15.1	25.9	29.7	0.0
43–48[b]	804	100.0	14.5	14.8	16.8	22.7	30.9	0.3

[a] Excludes patients temporarily receiving no methadone (e.g., due to incarceration or hospitalization), and those whose terminations were pending.

[b] Includes 41 patients in treatment more than 48 months.

TABLE 16.3

Distribution of Methadone Dosages of Patients in the NYC MMTP as of December, 1974 by Age and by Sex

Age (Years) and Sex	Number of Patients[a]	Percent of Patients with Specified Dosage (mg)						
		Total	Less than 40	40–50	60–70	80–90	100	110–120
Total	10,487	100.0	13.3	17.0	21.3	32.0	16.3	0.1
Age								
18–20	576	100.0	6.1	19.4	28.3	37.2	9.0	0.0
21–25	3,925	100.0	11.9	18.8	23.7	33.5	12.1	0.0
26–30	2,880	100.0	14.2	17.6	20.4	31.8	15.8	0.1
31–40	2,169	100.0	12.0	16.1	19.3	31.6	20.7	0.3
Over 40	937	100.0	9.6	14.3	14.7	31.5	29.6	0.3
Sex								
Men	7,785	100.0	11.5	16.8	21.1	33.2	17.4	0.1
Women	2,702	100.0	13.5	19.8	22.2	31.2	13.3	0.0

[a] Excludes patients temporarily receiving no methadone (e.g., due to incarceration or hospitalization), and those whose terminations were pending.

Methadone Dosage Levels and Demographic Characteristics of Patients

The distributions of dosages at the end of 1974 were determined for patient subgroups defined by age and sex (Table 16.3). Increasing age was found to be associated with higher dosage levels; patients over 40 were three times as likely to be maintained at 100 mg, or more, of methadone than those under 21. With respect to sex, no major differences were observed.

Table 16.4 shows the methadone dosage distributions for white, black, and Hispanic patients, according to length of time in treatment. For patients in treatment for more than 2 years, there was no consistent difference among the ethnic groups. Among more recently admitted patients, however, whites were about twice as likely to be maintained at the highest dosage levels (100 mg or more) as either blacks or Hispanics. The greatest disparity was noted in the case of patients who had entered the Program during the previous 6 months; of this cohort, 14% of white patients received 100 mg per day, compared to approximately 4% of black and Hispanic patients. The dosage distributions of black and Hispanic patients were generally similar, regardless of length of time in treatment.

TABLE 16.4

Distribution of Methadone Dosages of Patients in the NYC MMTP as of December, 1974 by Ethnicity and by Length of Time in Treatment

			Percent of Patients with Specified Dosage (mg)						
Months in Treatment	Ethnicity	Number of Patients[a]	Total	Less than 40	40–50	60–70	80–90	100	110–120
All	White	2636	100.0	12.1	16.7	19.0	29.9	22.0	0.4
	Black	4706	100.0	11.4	17.9	23.1	33.6	14.0	0.0
	Hispanic	3061	100.0	13.2	18.1	20.9	33.5	14.3	0.0
1–6	White	479	100.0	7.3	17.3	25.5	35.5	14.2	0.2
	Black	781	100.0	7.0	19.2	36.2	33.0	4.5	0.0
	Hispanic	532	100.0	9.6	20.9	29.7	35.9	3.9	0.0
7–12	White	401	100.0	11.0	16.5	24.4	36.7	11.5	0.0
	Black	601	100.0	8.8	18.5	32.4	34.9	5.3	0.0
	Hispanic	431	100.0	11.8	19.0	21.8	41.5	5.8	0.0
13–18	White	299	100.0	12.7	15.7	23.1	33.8	14.4	0.3
	Black	611	100.0	11.0	21.4	23.1	37.2	7.4	0.0
	Hispanic	497	100.0	14.1	18.9	24.3	33.6	9.1	0.0
19–24	White	271	100.0	12.2	12.9	15.9	32.8	25.1	1.1
	Black	599	100.0	12.9	19.5	17.7	39.1	10.9	0.0
	Hispanic	417	100.0	16.3	19.4	22.8	32.9	8.6	0.0
25–30	White	326	100.0	12.6	16.0	15.0	32.8	23.6	0.0
	Black	1110	100.0	12.9	16.9	17.6	34.5	18.1	0.0
	Hispanic	526	100.0	13.1	19.0	14.3	32.5	20.9	0.2
31–36	White	258	100.0	14.3	17.8	10.5	23.3	34.1	0.0
	Black	497	100.0	13.5	15.3	16.1	26.6	28.6	0.0
	Hispanic	295	100.0	14.6	14.9	14.2	28.1	28.1	0.0
Over 36	White	602	100.0	15.1	18.3	15.3	18.8	31.7	0.8
	Black	507	100.0	14.8	13.4	17.4	27.0	27.4	0.0
	Hispanic	363	100.0	14.0	11.3	15.4	26.4	32.8	0.0

[a] Excludes patients temporarily receiving no methadone (e.g., due to incarceration or hospitalization), and those whose terminations were pending.

DISCUSSION

Methadone dosages prescribed by physicians in the New York City Methadone Maintenance Treatment Program are a result of the interaction between patients and staff. Accordingly, the sharp drop in dosage levels observed between 1972 and 1974 reflects the attitudes of both, and is not a result of Program policy.

The findings confirm the experience of other programs in which patients are allowed considerable control over the dosages of methadone prescribed: very few opt for the maximum permissable levels (209, 210). This observation is in marked contrast to the behavior of addicts in experimental settings in which they are permitted to obtain morphine; under such circumstances, they typically demand all the morphine they can get (211, 212). This difference, of course, is not surprising: "The reason is, presumably, that the morphine addicts were free to use the opiate intravenously with the intent to get 'loaded' or 'high,' whereas this is neither intended nor possible with oral methadone . . . [since] the body simply adjusts its level of tolerance to whatever slow dosage changes are made. . ." (213).

On the other hand, while the lack of incentive to seek the highest possible methadone dosage is readily explainable, the motivation to reduce the maintenance levels, as observed in the NYC MMTP between 1972 and 1974, is not clear. The findings do indicate, however, that the dosage distributions, and the attitudes which they reflect, differ considerably among various subgroups of the patient population. Specifically, patients who are older, who have been in the Program for longer periods of time, and who are white are more likely to be receiving the higher dosages. These differences have no obvious explanation.

17

Assessing Progress of Patients Enrolled in the Maintenance Program

INTRODUCTION AND METHODOLOGY

A Patient Progress Report (Appendix V) is completed by clinic staff every other month for each patient enrolled in the New York City Methadone Maintenance Treatment Program. The data are analyzed centrally, and summary reports are prepared for each component treatment facility and for the total Program.

Four parameters of patient progress are analyzed in detail in this chapter:

- Drug abuse, including excessive consumption of alcohol
- Gainful occupation, including employment, schooling, and homemaker activities
- Status with respect to welfare (i.e., public assistance)
- Arrests

Abuse of drugs and alcohol is determined by counseling staff on the basis of direct patient evaluation as well as the results of urinalysis. Random testing of urines, usually weekly, is performed for morphine and quinine (as indicators of heroin abuse), barbiturates, amphetamines, and cocaine. The staff does not observe the collection of urine specimens.

Entries on the Patient Progress Reports regarding gainful occupation and welfare status are based primarily on self-reports of patients. With respect to arrests, the Program generally is contacted directly by the New York City Department of Corrections when a patient is incarcerated, in order to confirm the maintenance dose of methadone (detoxification is provided to narcotic-dependent individuals by the City's Prison Health Services); in addition, patients themselves notify Program staff of arrests in order to explain temporary absences from the clinic, and to seek referral for legal assistance.

The data presented here are based on the 11,157 patients enrolled in the NYC MMTP on December 31, 1974 and apply to the reporting period November–December, 1974. The demographic characteristics of these patients are shown in Table 17.1. In analyzing the results, comparisons are made between patient subgroups defined by length of time in treatment. Two major limitations must be kept in mind in interpreting the findings: by definition, patients grouped according to length of time in treatment represent different admission cohorts; secondly, the data reflect the experience only of those patients who "survived" (i.e., who were not terminated).

RESULTS

Drug and Alcohol Abuse

Abuse of One or More Drugs

One out of five patients enrolled in the NYC MMTP on December 31, 1974 was reportedly abusing drugs and/or alcohol during the preceding 2-month period (Table 17.2). There was little variation among patient subgroups defined by length of time in treatment, and by sex. Blacks, however, were more likely to be reported as abusing drugs or alcohol than either White or Hispanic patients, and the disparity was greater for patients in treatment longer periods of time. The greatest differences were associated with the age of patients at the time of the report, with older patients having a considerably higher likelihood of substance abuse regardless of length of time in treatment. For all age groups, however, increasing time in treatment was associated with a lower prevalence of drug abuse.

Heroin Use

Only 5% of all patients enrolled in the NYC MMTP at the end of December, 1974, had reportedly used heroin during the previous 2 months (Table 17.3). The proportion steadily decreased among patients with longer treatment experience, dropping from 7% among those enrolled for 12 months or less to 3% of those in the Program over 36 months.

There were only minor differences between men and women, but among the ethnic groups, blacks were more likely to be using heroin, regardless of length of time in treatment, than either white or Hispanic patients. For all ethnic groups, however, increasing time in treatment was associated with a lower proportion of heroin users.

Except for patients in treatment more than 3 years, the rate of heroin use showed a marked rise with increasing age. The disparity was greatest among patients enrolled for one year or less: only 4% of patients under 21 years of age were reportedly using heroin, compared to 13% of those over 40.

Barbiturate and Amphetamine Abuse

Approximately 4% of the patients reportedly abused barbiturates, and 2% abused amphetamines, during the last two months of 1974 (Tables 17.4 and 17.5, respectively). In the case of both drugs, abuse was more prevalent among women, and among whites. There were only minor differences among the age groups, and there was no consistent association between reported abuse of these drugs and length of time in treatment.

Cocaine Abuse

As shown in Table 17.6, slightly over 5% of all patients used cocaine during the 2-month reporting period. Prevalence was not related to length of time in treatment, and was only slightly greater in women than in men. Compared to black and Hispanic patients, whites were considerably less likely to be using cocaine. Regardless of duration of treatment in the Program, a far greater proportion of users was reported among the older age groups.

Excessive Alcohol Consumption

Only 4% of all patients were reportedly using excessive quantities of alcohol during November and December, 1974 (Table 17.7). For each cohort, the prevalence among blacks was more than twice that of whites, with Hispanic patients falling between these two extremes. There was a strong correlation between excessive alcohol consumption and increased age, but in only one subgroup was the proportion greater than 10% (patients over 40, in treatment for 25–36 months).

Concomitant Abuse of More Than One Drug

Table 17.8 shows a cross-tabulation of drugs of abuse during the last two months of 1974, for patients grouped according to length of time in treatment. It was found that the most common combined usage involved heroin and cocaine; although only 1% of the total population used both of these drugs, they represented 20% of all reported heroin users, as well as 20% of all cocaine users. Patients reportedly using excessive alcohol were the least likely to take other drugs concomitantly. Among patients using barbiturates, cocaine or excessive alcohol, the concomitant use of heroin declined with increasing time in treatment. This was not true, however, in the case of amphetamine users.

Gainfully Occupied Status

Patients Employed, in School or Homemakers

Of the patients in treatment in the NYC MMTP for 12 months or less, 52% were employed, in school or functioning as homemakers during the last 2 months of 1974. The corresponding proportion was 59% for patients in treatment 13–24 months, and 57% for those enrolled 25–36 months. The highest proportion of gainfully occupied patients, 65%, was reported for patients in treatment more than three years.*

Employment

The proportion of patients employed is shown in Table 17.9 for subgroups defined by demographic characteristics and by length of time in treatment. Overall, 41% of patients in treatment at the end of 1974 were working. The proportion of working patients varied little among those in treatment for up to 3 years (range, 39–42%), but increased among patients in treatment more than three years (of whom 50% were working).†

Considerable differences were noted among the various demographic subgroups. Men were almost three times as likely to be employed as women; whites had higher employment rates than either black or Hispanic patients; and patients at both age extremes (i.e., under 21 and over 40) were less likely to be working than those aged 21–40.

Employment stability, as measured by length of time in the current job, increased markedly with increased duration of treatment in the NYC MMTP (Table 17.10). Of working patients enrolled 6 months or less, 63% had obtained their job within the preceding 6-month period, while only 26% had been employed for more than one year. At the other extreme, among working patients in treatment more than three years, the distribution was reversed: 21% had been working at the same job for 6 months or less, and 61% had been with their current employer for over 12 months.

Welfare Status

At the end of December, 1974, 44% of the active patients in the NYC MMTP were receiving public assistance. The proportion increased from 32% of those enrolled for 12 months or less, to 45% and 56% of those in treatment for 13–24 months and 25–36 months, respectively; among patients in the Program more than three years, 45% were receiving welfare.

*By comparison, 31% of patients admitted to the NYC MMTP during 1973 and 1974 were gainfully occupied at the time they entered the Program (see Chapter 15).

†By comparison, 23% of patients admitted to the NYC MMTP during 1973 and 1974 were employed at the time they entered the Program (see Chapter 15).

Welfare status varied markedly with age, sex, and ethnic characteristics. There was a consistent association of increased likelihood of welfare support with increasing age. Women were twice as likely as men to be receiving public assistance. The proportion of black and Hispanic patients receiving welfare was almost double that of whites. The data are shown in Table 17.11.

Arrests

Of the 11,157 patients enrolled in the NYC MMTP on December 31, 1974, 299 (2.7%) were reportedly arrested during the preceding two months. The proportion decreased slightly with increasing time in the Program, from 3.7% of those enrolled one year or less to 1.8% of those in treatment for more than three years (Table 17.12). Men were more likely to be arrested than women; there was no consistent pattern with respect to age or ethnicity.

Table 17.13 shows the reported arrests during the last two months of 1974 for patients grouped according to drug abuse and employment status during this time period. Overall, reported drug users had a higher arrest rate than nondrug users. Among the former, those using heroin were most likely to have been arrested, and amphetamine and alcohol users the least likely; the differences, however, are small (range, 4.7%–3.0%). A considerable disparity was found for patients grouped by employment status. Overall, unemployed patients were more than twice as likely to have been arrested during November and December, 1974 than those who were working (3.6 and 1.4%, respectively). This relationship was observed regardless of the length of time in treatment.

DISCUSSION

Many factors limit the ability of addiction programs to evaluate the outcome of treatment. Ongoing follow-up of an admission cohort is precluded since patients constantly are being voluntarily and administratively terminated. Those who remain may differ markedly from those who leave, but these differences may be impossible to identify, let alone quantify. Even where there is a reasonable basis for concluding that patients (or specified subgroups of the patient population) do, in fact, show improvement with respect to various measures of "rehabilitation," a causal relationship between such improvement and the treatment services per se can rarely be established; personal as well as societal factors may be more important determinants of success or failure than the therapeutic regimen which is provided. The problem could be lessened if a random selection of applicants were to be denied treatment in order to serve as experimental "controls," but such a course would be ethically repugnant.

The data described here represent neither a prospective nor a retrospective analysis of patient progress following admission to treatment. Rather, they are *descriptive* of the experience of patients enrolled in the New York City Methadone Maintenance Treatment Program during the last 2 months of 1974.

Drug Abuse Patterns of Patients

Approximately 20% of all patients, regardless of length of time in treatment, were reportedly abusing one or more drugs during the 2-month period analyzed. Only 5%, however, were using heroin, the primary drug at the time of admission to the NYC MMTP. Furthermore, the prevalence of heroin use was lower for patients enrolled in the Program for progressively longer periods of time. A similar pattern was not found with respect to any of the other substances studied: barbiturates, amphetamines, cocaine, or alcohol.

Gainful Occupation

Even among patients enrolled in the NYC MMTP for more than three years, over one-third remained without gainful occupation. Although gainful occupation, and employment in particular, was markedly higher among patients in treatment for 1–12 months than was reported at the time of enrollment,* the proportion did not appreciably increase for those with 13–24 months or 25–36 months of treatment exposure. This suggests that while many patients quickly return to socially productive lifestyles, others remain unable to do so, despite the support which the Program attempts to provide. Such an hypothesis is supported by the findings with respect to job stability: among working patients, the proportion recently employed (three months or less) dropped from 40% of those enrolled for only 6 months to 11% of those in treatment more than 3 years. At the same time, the large percentage of employed patients who have been continuously employed in the same job for more than one year (48% of those in treatment for 25–36 months, and 61% of those in the Program for more than 3 years) indicates that job stability is very high among the patients of the NYC MMTP, once work is obtained.

The marked differences in employment associated with demographic subgroups are not unique to ex-addicts. Thus, women and minority groups were far less likely to be employed, as were those over 40 years of age. Until job

*Admission data based on patients entering the NYC MMTP in 1973 and 1974; see Chapter 15.

opportunities are expanded in the general community, addiction treatment programs will continue to have only limited success in assisting patients in these categories to gain employment.

Welfare Status

In general, the proportion of patients receiving public assistance was greater among cohorts in treatment for longer periods of time. This finding conflicts with data from previous years attributed to other methadone maintenance programs in New York City (214,215), in which welfare dependence was markedly reduced among patients with longer treatment exposure. The reason for this disparity is not clear.

As in the case of employment, welfare status varied considerably among the demographic subgroups, and the differences are consistent with those in the general community: a far greater proportion of women, black, and Hispanic patients, and patients over 40 years of age received public assistance.

Arrests

The proportion of patients arrested during the 2-month period of observation (2.7%) agrees with the postadmission reporting history from criminal justice system agencies to the New York City Narcotics Register (see Chapter 20). The data suggest that increasing time in treatment, employment, and lack of evidence of drug or alcohol abuse are all associated with a decreased likelihood of arrest.

TABLE 17.1

Demographic Characteristics of Patients Enrolled in the NYC MMTP on December 31, 1974 by Length of Time in Treatment

Group	Number and Percent of Patients in Treatment for Specified Period of Time (Months), as of December 31, 1974				
	Total	1–12	13–24	25–36	37–48[a]
All patients	11,157 (100.0%)	3,452 (100.0%)	2,888 (100.0%)	3,226 (100.0%)	1,591 (100.0%)
Sex					
Men	8,265 (74.1%)	2,594 (75.1%)	2,135 (73.9%)	2,294 (71.1%)	1,242 (78.1%)
Women	2,892 (25.9%)	858 (24.9%)	753 (26.1%)	932 (28.9%)	349 (21.9%)
Ethnic					
White	2,815 (25.2%)	938 (27.2%)	605 (20.9%)	629 (19.5%)	643 (40.4%)
Black	5,028 (45.1%)	1,481 (42.9%)	1,293 (44.8%)	1,705 (52.9%)	549 (34.5%)
Hispanic	3,235 (29.0%)	1,015 (29.4%)	959 (33.2%)	878 (27.2%)	383 (24.1%)
Other	79 (0.7%)	18 (0.5%)	31 (1.1%)	14 (0.4%)	16 (1.0%)
Age (years)					
Under 21	613 (5.5%)	371 (10.7%)	173 (6.0%)	69 (2.1%)	0 (0%)
21–25	4,193 (37.6%)	1,555 (45.0%)	1,152 (39.9%)	1,068 (33.1%)	418 (26.3%)
26–30	3,068 (27.5%)	854 (24.7%)	779 (27.0%)	902 (28.0%)	533 (33.5%)
31–40	2,302 (20.6%)	533 (15.4%)	545 (18.9%)	786 (24.4%)	438 (27.5%)
Over 40	981 (8.8%)	139 (4.0%)	239 (8.3½)	401 (12.4%)	202 (12.7%)

[a] Includes 42 patients in treatment more than 48 months.

TABLE 17.2

Reported Drug and/or Alcohol Abuse during November and December, 1974 by Length of Time in Treatment and by Demographic Characteristics of Patients Enrolled in the NYC MMTP on December 31, 1974

	Percent of Patients Reportedly Using One or More Drugs[a]				
		Months in Treatment as of December 31, 1974			
Group	Total	1–12	13–24	25–36	37–48
All patients	19.9	20.9	18.5	20.8	17.1
Sex					
Men	19.3	21.0	17.4	20.4	17.1
Women	21.4	20.6	21.6	21.8	22.1
Ethnic					
White	17.9	20.6	16.7	17.6	15.2
Black	22.5	21.8	21.7	23.3	23.8
Hispanic	17.2	19.2	15.0	18.0	15.4
Age (years)					
18–20	15.7	15.9	16.2	13.0	—
21–25	16.2	17.5	15.1	16.5	14.1
26–30	18.7	21.7	16.4	18.4	17.6
31–40	25.2	28.7	24.9	26.0	20.0
Over 40	29.4	37.4	29.3	29.2	24.1

[a] The number of patients in each group is shown in Table 17.1; percentages are based on those patients for whom the drug abuse item was completed on the Patient Progress Report for this time period (97% of all patients).

TABLE 17.3

Reported Heroin Abuse during November and December, 1974 by Length of Time in Treatment and by Demographic Characteristics of Patients Enrolled in the NYC MMTP on December 31, 1974

	Percent of Patients Reportedly Using Heroin[a]				
		Months in Treatment as of December 31, 1974			
Group	Total	1–12	13–24	25–36	37–48
All patients	5.3	7.1	5.4	4.1	3.4
Sex					
Men	5.4	7.0	5.7	4.4	3.6
Women	4.9	7.5	4.6	3.4	2.9
Ethnic					
White	4.4	7.0	3.6	2.2	3.6
Black	6.6	8.1	7.2	5.5	4.6
Hispanic	3.9	5.4	4.2	2.8	1.3
Age (years)					
18–20	3.8	3.8	4.0	2.9	—
21–25	4.3	5.8	4.4	2.6	3.2
26–30	5.3	7.7	4.9	4.2	3.7
31–40	6.7	10.9	7.7	5.2	3.1
Over 40	7.0	12.9	7.9	5.7	4.0

[a] The number of patients in each group is shown in Table 17.1; percentages are based on those patients for whom the drug abuse item was completed on the Patient Progress Report for this time period (97% of all patients).

TABLE 17.4

Reported Barbiturate Abuse during November and December, 1974 by Length of Time in Treatment and by Demographic Characteristics of Patients Enrolled in the NYC MMTP on December 31, 1974

	Percent of Patients Reportedly Using Barbiturates[a]				
		Months in Treatment as of December 31, 1974			
Group	Total	1–12	13–24	25–36	37–48
All patients	4.1	4.3	3.7	4.1	4.5
Sex					
Men	3.6	4.1	3.0	3.6	3.7
Women	5.5	4.9	5.7	5.4	7.1
Ethnic					
White	5.8	6.9	5.3	6.2	4.2
Black	3.6	3.3	3.6	3.5	5.4
Hispanic	3.3	3.3	2.7	3.6	3.7
Age (years)					
18–20	4.9	4.6	5.8	4.3	—
21–25	3.9	4.2	3.2	4.2	4.1
26–30	3.1	4.1	2.8	2.3	3.3
31–40	4.8	4.7	4.8	4.3	5.6
Over 40	5.9	4.3	4.6	7.2	5.6

[a] The number of patients in each group is shown in Table 17.1; percentages are based on those patients for whom the drug abuse item was completed on the Patient Progress Report for this time period (97% of all patients).

TABLE 17.5

Reported Amphetamine Abuse during November and December, 1974 by Length of Time in Treatment and by Demographic Characteristics of Patients Enrolled in the NYC MMTP on December 31, 1974

	Percent of Patients Reportedly Using Amphetamines[a]				
		Months in Treatment as of December 31, 1974			
Group	Total	1–12	13–24	25–36	37–48
All patients	1.8	1.7	1.9	1.9	1.7
Sex					
Men	1.6	1.7	1.4	1.7	1.7
Women	3.1	4.0	3.5	2.6	1.5
Ethnic					
White	3.0	2.8	3.6	3.5	2.4
Black	1.3	1.1	1.4	1.6	0.9
Hispanic	1.5	1.4	1.6	1.5	1.6
Age (years)					
18–20	1.6	1.9	1.2	1.4	—
21–25	1.8	1.5	2.2	1.8	2.2
26–30	1.6	1.3	1.8	1.8	1.7
31–40	2.2	2.4	2.0	2.5	1.4
Over 40	1.4	1.4	1.7	1.5	1.0

[a] The number of patients in each group is shown in Table 17.1; percentages are based on those patients for whom the drug abuse item was completed on the Patient Progress Report for this time period (97% of all patients).

TABLE 17.6

Reported Cocaine Abuse during November and December, 1974 by Length of Time in Treatment and by Demographic Characteristics of Patients Enrolled in the NYC MMTP on December 31, 1974

	Percent of Patients Reportedly Using Cocaine[a]				
		Months in Treatment as of December 31, 1974			
Group	Total	1–12	13–24	25–36	37–48
All patients	5.5	5.1	5.4	6.0	5.2
Sex					
Men	5.2	4.9	5.1	5.9	4.9
Women	6.1	5.8	6.2	6.3	6.2
Ethnic					
White	2.7	2.8	1.5	2.5	4.0
Black	6.8	5.7	7.7	7.0	7.1
Hispanic	5.7	6.2	4.8	6.6	4.5
Age (years)					
18–20	4.4	5.1	2.3	5.8	—
21–25	4.2	4.1	3.7	5.1	3.7
26–30	5.4	4.8	5.5	6.0	5.4
31–40	6.5	6.9	7.2	6.5	4.9
Over 40	9.1	10.8	10.9	8.0	8.2

[a] The number of patients in each group in shown in Table 17.1; percentages are based on those patients for whom the drug abuse item was completed on the Patient Progress Report for this time period (97% of all patients).

TABLE 17.7

Reported Excessive Alcohol Consumption during November and December, 1974, by Length of Time in Treatment and by Demographic Characteristics of Patients Enrolled in the NYC MMTP on December 31, 1974

	Percent of Patients with Reported Excessive Alcohol Consumption[a]				
		Months in Treatment as of December 31, 1974			
Group	Total	1–12	13–24	25–36	37–48
All patients	4.2	2.5	3.3	6.3	5.1
Sex					
Men	4.2	2.8	3.1	6.5	4.6
Women	4.2	1.7	3.9	5.6	7.1
Ethnic					
White	2.3	1.3	2.0	3.2	3.1
Black	5.9	3.9	4.6	7.7	8.4
Hispanic	3.2	1.7	2.4	5.6	4.0
Age (years)					
18–20	1.1	1.1	1.7	0	—
21–25	2.0	1.3	1.6	3.1	2.4
26–30	3.8	2.1	3.5	5.1	5.0
31–40	7.4	6.2	5.3	10.0	6.8
Over 40	9.0	8.6	7.1	11.0	7.2

[a] The number of patients in each group is shown in Table 17.1; percentages are based on those patients for whom the drug abuse item was completed on the Patient Progress Report for this time period (97% of all patients).

TABLE 17.8

Patterns of Reported Multiple Drug Usage during November and December, 1974, by Length of Time in Treatment of Patients Enrolled in the NYC MMTP on December 31, 1974

			Percent of Patients with Concomitant Use of Specified Drug[a]				
Reported Drug of Abuse	Months in Treatment	Number of Patients	Heroin	Barbs.	Amphet.	Cocaine	Excessive Alcohol
Heroin							
All patients		591	—	7.3	4.1	20.5	4.4
	1–12	246	—	7.7	1.6	16.3	4.1
	13–24	157	—	7.0	6.4	22.9	3.2
	Over 24	188	—	6.9	5.3	23.9	5.9
Barbiturates							
All patients		455	9.5	—	5.3	8.4	6.8
	1–12	148	12.8	—	3.4	6.8	7.4
	13–24	106	10.4	—	7.5	8.5	5.7
	Over 24	201	6.5	—	5.5	9.5	7.0
Amphetamines							
All patients		201	11.9	11.9	—	10.9	3.5
	1–12	57	7.0	8.8	—	7.0	1.8
	13–24	56	17.9	14.3	—	14.3	5.4
	Over 24	88	11.4	12.5	—	11.4	3.4
Cocaine							
All patients		608	19.9	6.3	3.6	—	3.1
	1–12	176	22.7	5.7	2.3	—	1.1
	13–24	155	23.2	5.8	5.2	—	2.6
	Over 24	277	16.2	6.9	3.6	—	4.7
Excessive alcohol							
All patients		467	5.6	6.6	1.5	4.1	—
	1–12	87	11.5	12.6	1.1	2.3	—
	13–24	95	5.3	6.3	3.2	4.2	—
	Over 24	285	3.9	4.9	1.1	4.6	—

[a] Percentages are based on those patients for whom the drug abuse item was completed on the Patient Progress Report for this time period (97% of all patients).

TABLE 17.9

Employment during November and December, 1974 by Length of Time in Treatment and by Demographic Characteristics of Patients Enrolled in the NYC MMTP on December 31, 1974

	Percent of Patients Reportedly Employed during Report Period[a]				
		Months in Treatment as of December 31, 1974			
Group	Total	1–12	13–24	25–36	37–48
All patients	41.4	38.5	42.3	39.6	49.9
Sex					
Men	49.7	44.8	51.1	49.8	57.2
Women	17.8	19.3	17.4	14.4	24.1
Ethnic					
White	56.2	53.2	56.0	55.6	61.3
Black	34.6	29.2	38.0	34.1	43.0
Hispanic	39.2	37.8	39.8	38.8	41.8
Age (years)					
18–20	34.9	33.4	36.4	39.1	—
21–25	43.0	40.7	43.8	41.3	53.8
26–30	43.8	37.9	45.8	42.4	52.5
31–40	40.2	39.0	39.6	37.2	47.9
Over 40	34.3	28.8	34.3	33.7	39.1

[a] Percentages are based on those patients for whom employment status was reported on the Patient Progress Report for this time period (no answers were less than 5% of the total in each subgroup).

TABLE 17.10

Length of Time in Current Job, for Employed Patients Enrolled in the NYC MMTP on December 31, 1974, by Length of Time in Treatment

Months in Current Job	Percent Employed in Current Job Specified Number of Months					
		Months in Treatment as of December 31, 1974				
	Total	1–6	7–12	13–24	25–36	37–48
Number of employed patients	4622 (100%)	667 (100%)	662 (100%)	1222 (100%)	1277 (100%)	794 (100%)
1–3	18.9	39.7	21.7	15.5	15.6	10.6
4–6	16.3	22.8	21.9	16.2	13.9	10.6
7–9	12.4	5.5	21.7	15.3	11.0	8.0
10–12	10.9	6.2	12.2	12.5	11.9	9.5
Over 12	41.6	25.9	22.4	40.5	47.5	61.2

TABLE 17.11

Welfare Status during November and December, 1974 by Length of Time in Treatment and by Demographic Characteristics of Patients Enrolled in the NYC MMTP on December 31, 1974

	Percent of Patients Receiving Welfare during Report Period[a]				
		Months in Treatment as of December 31, 1974			
Group	Total	1–12	13–24	25–36	37–48
All patients	44.3	32.4	44.6	56.4	45.0
Sex					
Men	35.8	24.4	35.3	47.8	38.2
Women	68.6	56.8	70.8	77.6	69.3
Ethnic					
White	26.4	19.3	27.3	33.2	29.4
Black	51.6	39.4	49.2	62.8	55.7
Hispanic	48.3	34.4	48.6	60.5	56.1
Age (years)					
18–20	27.6	25.1	26.6	43.5	—
21–25	38.8	30.7	41.2	49.6	34.4
26–30	43.4	31.7	43.5	55.4	41.7
31–40	52.0	39.6	52.5	60.9	50.7
Over 40	62.9	48.2	58.6	70.1	63.9

[a] Percentages are based on those patients for whom welfare status was reported on the Patient Progress Report for this time period (no answers were less than 5% of the total in each subgroup).

TABLE 17.12

Arrests during November and December, 1974 by Length of Time in Treatment and by Demographic Characteristics of Patients Enrolled in the NYC MMTP on December 31, 1974

	Percent of Patients Arrested during Report Period[a]				
		Months in Treatment as of December 31, 1974			
Group	Total	1–12	13–24	25–36	37–48
All patients	2.7	3.7	2.7	2.0	1.8
Sex					
Men	2.9	4.0	3.0	2.0	1.9
Women	2.1	2.8	1.7	1.9	1.4
Ethnic					
White	2.2	3.0	2.1	1.6	1.9
Black	3.2	4.5	2.8	2.6	2.4
Hispanic	2.3	3.3	2.9	1.3	1.0
Age (years)					
18–20	2.8	2.4	4.0	1.4	—
21–25	3.0	3.9	2.4	2.6	1.9
26–30	2.6	3.7	3.2	2.1	0.8
31–40	2.7	3.6	2.8	1.8	3.2
Over 40	1.5	5.0	0.8	0.7	1.5

[a] Percentages are based on those patients for whom the Patient Progress Report legal status section was answered for this time period (no answers were less than 3% of the total in each subgroup).

TABLE 17.13

Arrests during November and December, 1974 of Patients Enrolled in the NYC MMTP on December 31, 1974 by Length of Time in Treatment, and by Drug Abuse and Employment Status During Reporting Period

	Percent of Patients Arrested During Report Period			
		Months in Treatment as of Dec. 31, 1974		
Status	Total	1–12	13–24	Over 24
All patients	2.7	3.7	2.7	1.9
Drug abuse[a]				
None	2.4	3.0	2.6	1.8
Heroin	4.7	5.7	4.5	3.7
Barbiturates	3.7	6.1	3.8	2.0
Amphetamines	3.0	3.5	1.8	3.4
Cocaine	3.5	8.0	3.2	0.7
Excessive alcohol	3.2	6.9	1.1	2.8
Employment				
Employed	1.4	1.5	1.9	1.1
Unemployed	3.6	5.1	3.2	2.6

[a] Drug abuse categories are not mutually exclusive.

18

Retention and Termination of Patients in the Maintenance Program

INTRODUCTION

There are numerous factors which must be considered in attempting to assess the effectiveness of addiction treatment programs. One of the most important is the ability of a program to attract and retain patients in treatment. The New York City Methadone Maintenance Treatment Program (NYC MMTP) is in a unique position to analyze data related to retention and termination; from its inception in November, 1970 through the end of 1974, 20,653 individuals entered treatment. This large number of patients, treated in clinics operating under uniform policies and procedures which are established and monitored by a central office, permits meaningful analysis of retention for subgroups defined by demographic characteristics, preadmission social and drug-use history, year of admission, year of termination, and reason for termination.

METHODOLOGY

Source of Data

Centralized computer records, containing all data used in this study, are maintained by the Program on every admission. The control system precludes the medication of patients without Central Office being advised. Similarly, all terminations are processed by the central staff; the capability for identifying patients who have not received any medication for 2 consecutive months ensures that "inactive" patients will not continue to be maintained on the active census.

The data analyzed in this study include all first admissions from the inception of the Program through December, 1974 and all terminations through March, 1975, thus providing at least three months of observation for all patients.

Definitions

An "admission" is defined as any individual who has received even one dose of methadone in a Program clinic; the date of admission is the day methadone is first administered. Criteria for eligibility of applicants are consistent with the Food and Drug Administration regulations governing methadone treatment, and include a history of at least 2 years of heroin use and a minimum age of 18; in addition, since the Program is largely supported by New York City tax funds, residence in the City is required.

Reasons for termination are assigned as follows:

- Voluntary withdrawal
- Failure to report for 30 consecutive days (without detoxification)
- Incarceration for more than 6 weeks (includes involuntary transfers mandated by the criminal justice system to drug-free and State commitment programs)
- Administrative cause (disruptive behavior, failure to comply with Program rules, or persistent, serious drug abuse)
- Transfer to other addiction treatment programs
- Hospitalization for more than 6 weeks
- Death

The Program's orientation precludes a discharge category of "treatment completed."

Termination may be delayed for a maximum of 3 months following voluntary detoxification, to permit patients continued access to all Program services. The date of termination, however, is in all cases the last date for which methadone was dispensed, regardless of the interval between the last medication received by the patient and actual completion of discharge.

Analysis

The retention rate, defined as the proportion of patients who have remained in continuous active treatment in the Program for a specified length of time since admission, was calculated using standard life-table methods in order to include the full experience of all patients ever admitted (216,217).

Separate life tables were constructed to compare retention rates for various subgroups.

Corresponding to each reason for termination, the termination rate was computed for successive intervals following admission to the Program, based on the number of patients in active treatment at the start of the specified time period. The rates were obtained for cohorts defined by calendar year of admission, and plotted against length of time in treatment.

In addition, termination rates were computed for calendar trimesters of termination. These rates were calculated for separate admission cohorts, as well as for specific reasons for termination.

The findings presented below are grouped into four major sections: the association of retention and termination rates with patient characteristics at the time of admission; the association of retention rates with the patient capacity of Program clinics; the association of retention and termination rates with the patients' preadmission reporting history to the New York City Narcotics Register; and the association of termination rates with patient status during treatment, with respect to gainful occupation and drug abuse. In the following chapter, which deals with readmissions to the NYC MMTP after initial termination, the retention experience of patients who reenter the Program will be presented.

RESULTS

The Association of Retention and Termination Rates with Patient Characteristics at the Time of Admission

Retention Rates

Retention Rates for All Patients. The overall retention in the Program for the 20,653 patients first admitted through December, 1974, is shown in Figure 18.1. The retention rate was 65.3% at the end of 1 year; 47.1% at the end of 2 years; and 35.3% at the end of 3 years. That is, approximately two-thirds of all patients admitted to the Program completed one year of treatment, while about three-quarters of those still active at the end of the first year completed the second year; similarly, about three-quarters of those remaining active 2 years after admission were still in treatment in the NYC MMTP at the end of the third year.

Retention Rates by Sex. The life-table analysis was performed for male and for female patients; the results are shown in Figure 18.2. Women were found to have consistently higher retention rates than men: at 1 year, the rate for women was 70.5%, and for men 63.8%; at 2 years, the rates were 50.6% and 46.0%, and at 3 years, 37.5% and 34.5%, respectively.

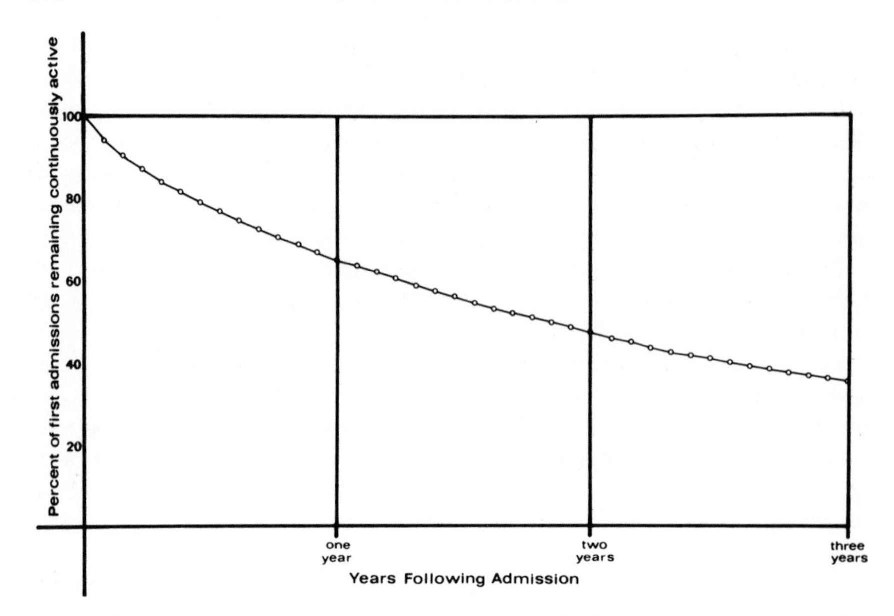

Figure 18.1. Retention in continuous active treatment following first admission to the NYC MMTP; all patients. $N = 20{,}653$.

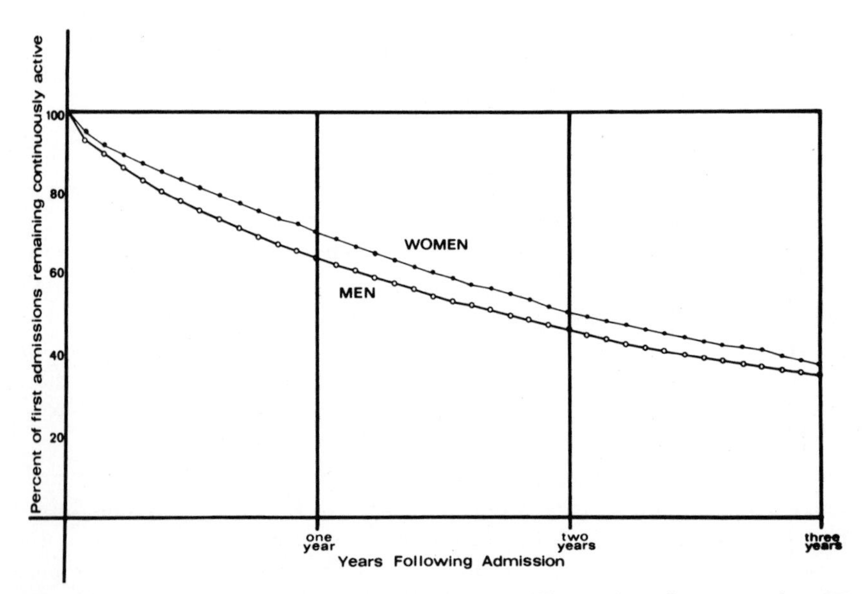

Figure 18.2. Retention in continuous active treatment following first admission to the NYC MMTP, by sex. Men, $N = 15{,}590$; Women, $N = 5063$.

Retention Rates by Ethnicity. More than 99% of all patients admitted to the NYC MMTP belonged to one of three ethnic groups: white, black, or Hispanic. The retention rates for each group are shown in Figure 18.3. Throughout the 3-year period of observation, the rates were almost identical. At 1 year they were 65.7, 64.7, and 65.2% for white, black, and Hispanic patients, respectively; at 2 years, the corresponding rates were 48.3, 45.8, and 47.6%; and at 3 years, 36.8, 34.3, and 35.5%.

Retention Rates by Age at Time of Admission. The retention rates were calculated for patients who, at the time of admission, were 18–20 years of age, 21–25, 26–30, 31–40, and over 40 (Figure 18.4). Table 18.1 shows the percent of patients in each age cohort remaining in continuous active treatment at 1, 2, and 3 years following admission.

There is very little difference in retention among the age groups through age 40. Patients over 40 had somewhat higher retention rates than other age groups. At the other extreme, however, patients 18–20 years old at the time of admission did not have the lowest rates; in fact, the retention rates of this youngest group consistently exceeded those for patients 21–25 and 26–30.

Retention Rates of Cohorts Admitted in Successive Years, 1971 through 1974. Figure 18.5 shows the retention rates for each of the four cohorts admitted to the NYC MMTP during 1971, 1972, 1973, and 1974 (104 admissions in November and December, 1970, are included with the 1971 cohort). Retention declined markedly for each succeeding year of admission from 1971 through 1973, but leveled off for patients admitted in 1974. The per-

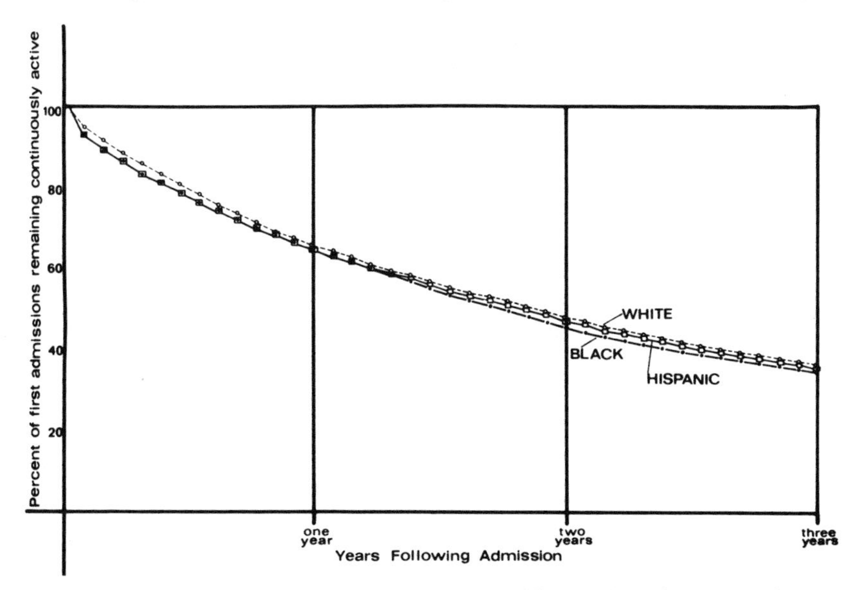

Figure 18.3. Retention in continuous active treatment following first admission to the NYC MMTP, by ethnicity. Blacks, $N = 9467$; whites, $N = 6246$; Hispanics, $N = 5813$.

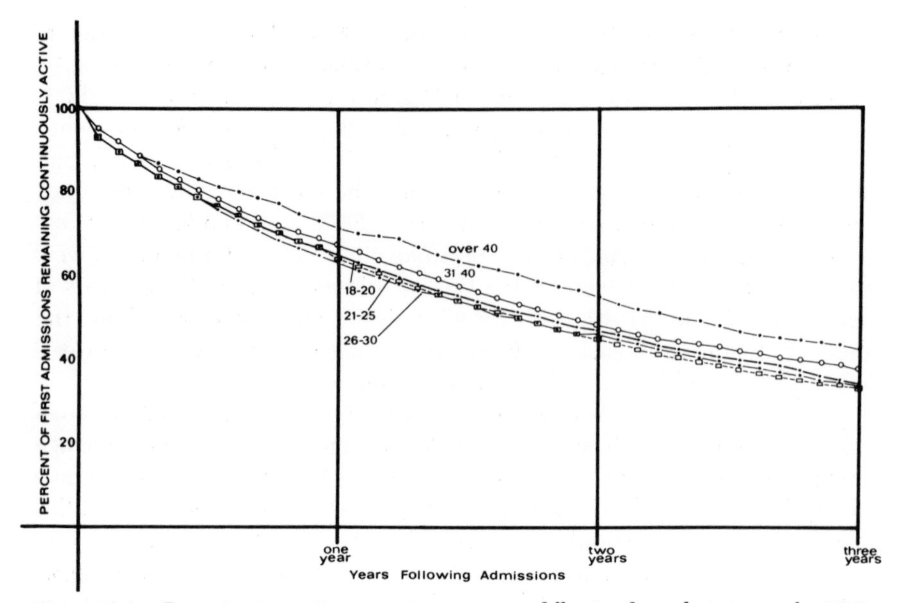

Figure 18.4. Retention in continuous active treatment following first admission to the NYC MMTP, by age at time of admission. Age group 18–20 years, $N = 3250$; age group 21–25 years, $N = 8350$; age group 26–30 years, $N = 4283$; age group 31–40 years, $N = 3516$; age group over 40 years, $N = 1254$.

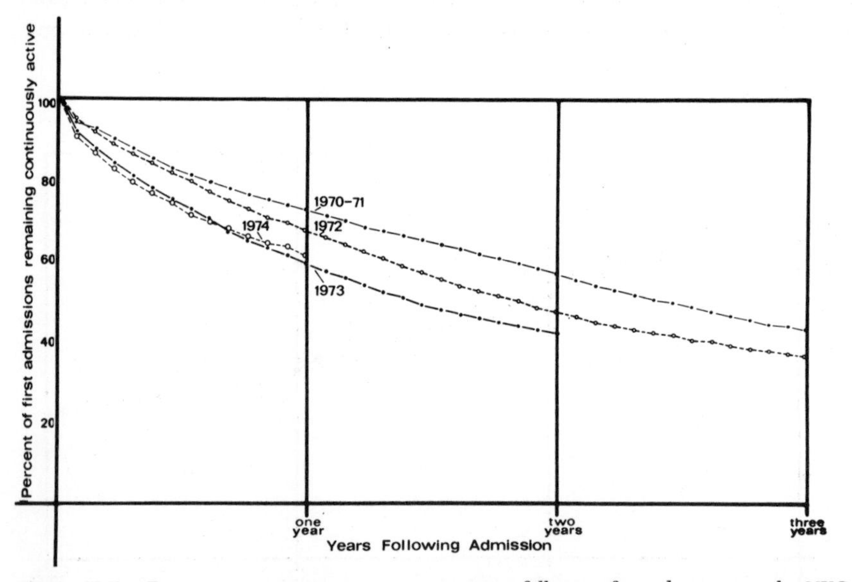

Figure 18.5. Retention in continuous active treatment following first admission to the NYC MMTP, by year of admission. First admissions in 1971, $N = 4377$ (includes 104 admissions in November and December, 1970); first admissions in 1972, $N = 7346$; first admissions in 1973, $N = 5340$; first admissions in 1974, $N = 3590$.

centages of patients in each cohort remaining in treatment after 1, 2, and 3 years following admission are shown in Table 18.2.

Termination Rates

Rates of Termination, for All Reasons, in Successive Intervals following Admission, for All Patients Admitted to NYC MMTP 1970 through 1974. The rates of termination, for all reasons, for each successive 12-week period after admission are shown in Figure 18.6. The highest rate, 13.2%, occurred during the first 12-week interval; the peak termination rate within this period was in the first 4 weeks after admission, when the rate was 6.4%, compared to 3.7% and 3.5% in the two following 4-week periods, respec-

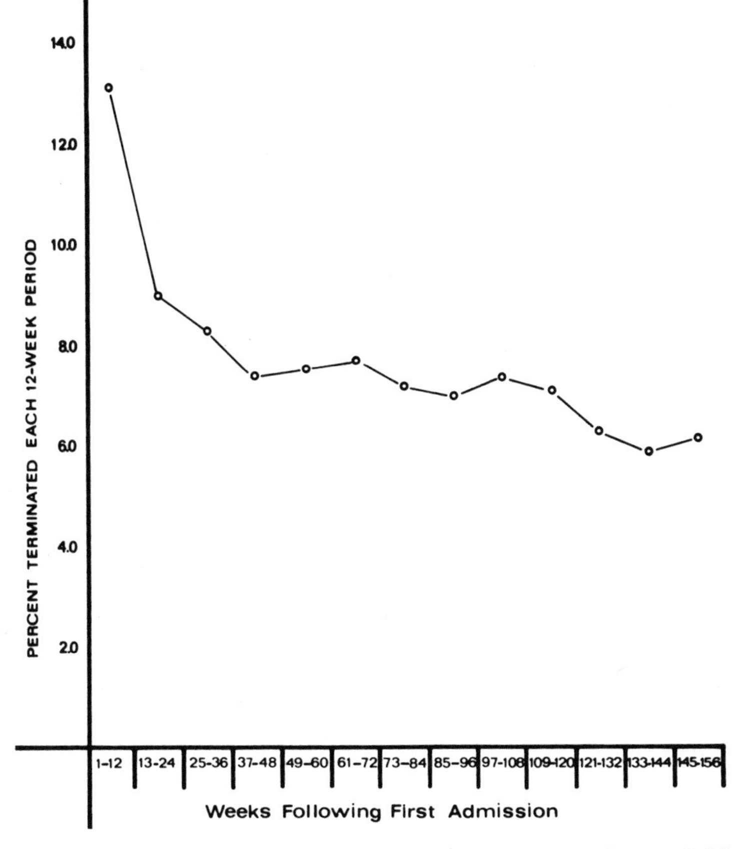

Figure 18.6. Rate of termination, for all causes, during successive 12-week intervals following first admission to the NYC MMTP. Rate based on patients surviving to the start of specified interval.

tively. The rate decreased sharply from 1–12 weeks to 13–24 weeks after admission, and thereafter continued to decline gradually through the end of the third year.

Rates of Termination, for Specific Reasons, in Successive Intervals following Admission, for All Patients Admitted to NYC MMTP 1970 through 1974. Figure 18.7 shows the termination rates in successive periods after admission for each of the specific reasons for discharge. While, in general, the rate of termination decreases with increasing time since admission, in the case of voluntary withdrawal the rate rises throughout the first 3 years. The strict

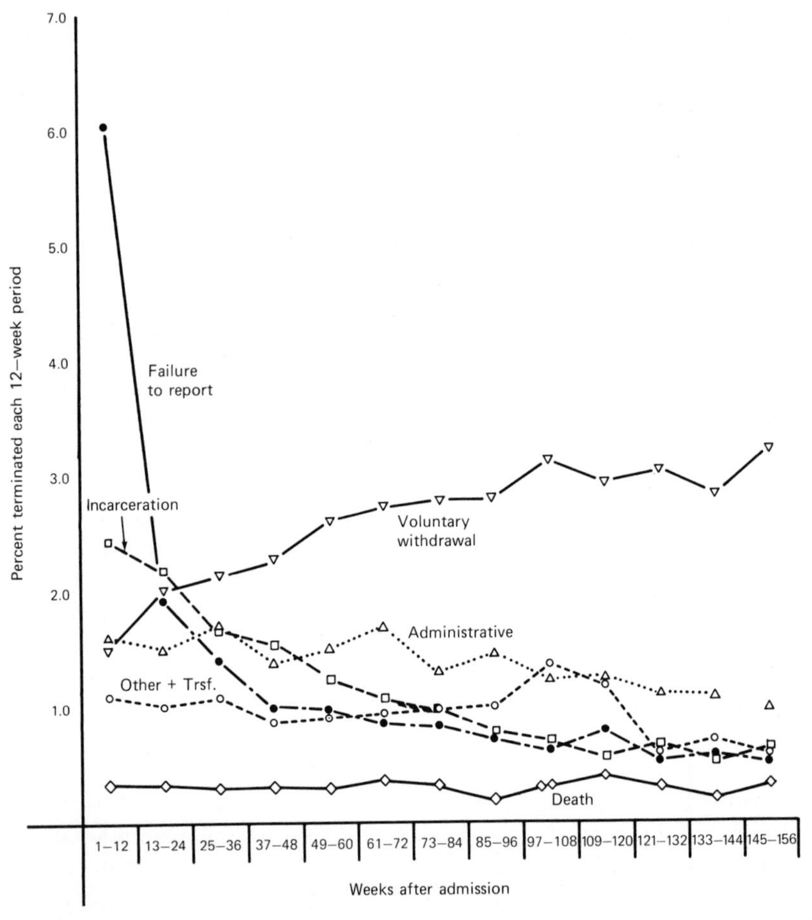

Figure 18.7. Rate of termination for specified causes, during successive 12-week intervals following first admission to the NYC MMTP. Rate based on patients surviving to the start of specified interval.

definition of admission, which includes every individual who received even a single dose of medication, is reflected in the high initial rate of termination due to failure to report.

Rates of Termination, for All Reasons, in Successive Intervals following Admission, for Patient Cohorts Defined by Year of Admission to NYC MMTP. The rates of termination in each 12-week period following admission, for each of the 4 admission-year cohorts, are shown in Table 18.3. The data indicate that the likelihood of termination increased in successive cohorts from 1971 to 1973. This increase was most marked in the earlier time periods; by 85–96 weeks following admission, there was no longer a consistent pattern.

Rates of Termination, for Specific Reasons, in Successive Intervals through the First 84 Weeks after Admission, for Patients Admitted to the NYC MMTP in 1971, 1972, and 1973. The data were analyzed further to determine the specific reason(s) associated with the consistent increase in overall termination rates during the first 84 weeks after admission for successive admission-year cohorts from 1971 through 1973. The rates for each cohort were calculated separately for failure to report, voluntary withdrawal, incarceration and administrative cause (no more than 1% of patients were terminated in any 12-week period for each of the remaining causes, i.e., transfer to other programs, long-term hospitalization, and death). Figure 18.8 shows that the increasing rate of termination for successive cohorts is largely the reflection of an increase in terminations initiated by the patients, i.e., failure to report and voluntary withdrawal. Of these, failure to report is the predominant factor during the initial interval, 1–12 weeks after admission; and voluntary withdrawal is the major factor in later periods.

Termination Rates, by Calendar Trimester, for Semiannual Admission Cohorts Entering the NYC MMTP in 1971 and 1972. For each of the first 4 semiannual admission cohorts, termination rates were computed based on the calendar trimesters in which the terminations occurred. (The data are limited to patients admitted in 1971 and 1972, to permit trend analysis over a period of at least 2 full years for each group.)

The patterns for the four cohorts are similar (Figure 18.9): subsequent to a general downward trend in the rate of termination, there is a reversal in all groups. The upswing, which begins in the first half of 1973, reaches a peak in the third quarter of the year and is followed by a drop in the fourth quarter; in the middle of 1974 there is a secondary peak noted for each of the cohorts.

Similar graphs were drawn depicting the rates of termination for specific reasons. The only reason which showed a sharp increase beginning in early 1973 was voluntary withdrawal (Figure 18.10). A similar increase was not evident in the termination rates for any of the other reasons; examples are provided by the graphs illustrating terminations for failure to report, incarceration and administrative cause (Figures 18.11–18.3, respectively).

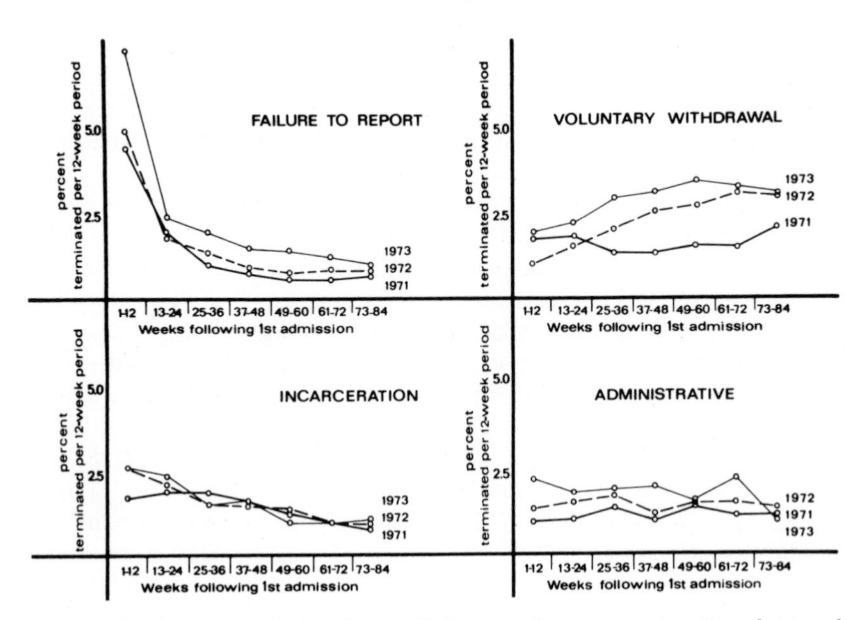

Figure 18.8. Rate of termination, for specified causes, during successive 12-week intervals following first admission to the NYC MMTP, by year of admission. Rate based on patients surviving to the start of specified interval.

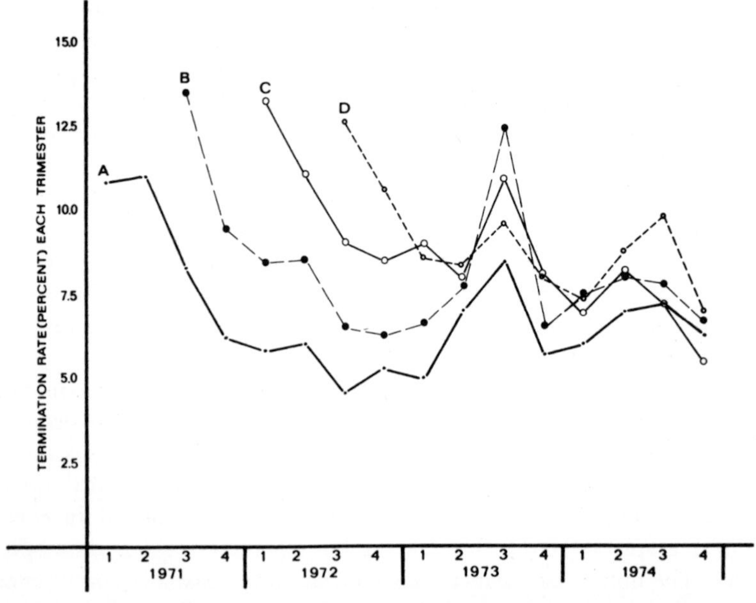

Figure 18.9. Rate of termination for all causes, by trimester of termination, 1971–1974, for semiannual cohorts of admission to the NYC MMTP during 1971 and 1972. Rate based on patients surviving to the start of specified trimester. (A) First admissions to the NYC MMTP January–June, 1971. (B) First admissions to the NYC MMTP July–December, 1971. (C) First admissions to the NYC MMTP January–June, 1972. (D) First admissions to the NYC MMTP July–December, 1972.

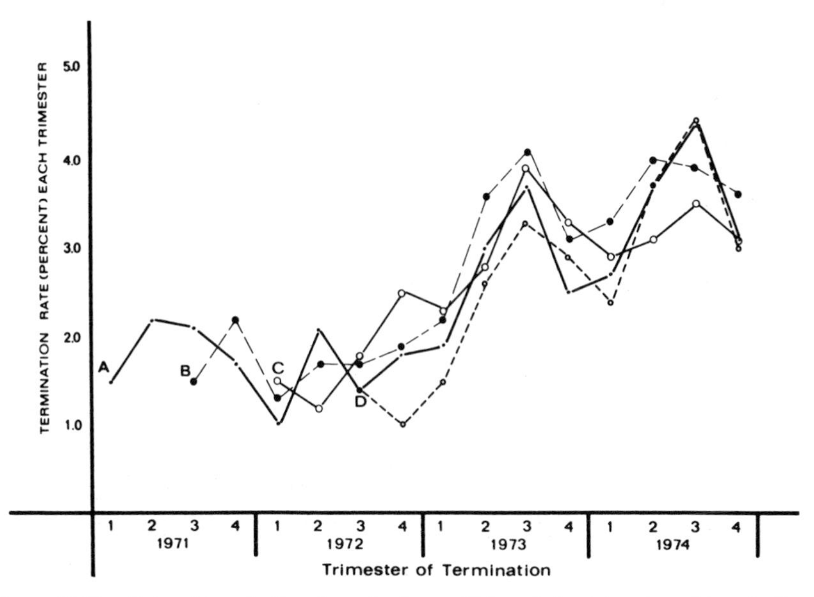

Figure 18.10. Rate of termination for voluntary withdrawal, by trimester of termination, 1971–1974, for semiannual cohorts of admission to the NYC MMTP during 1971 and 1972. Rate based on patients surviving to the start of specified trimester. (A) First admissions to the NYC MMTP January–June, 1971. (B) First admissions to the NYC MMTP July–December, 1971. (C) First admissions to the NYC MMTP January–June, 1972. (D) First admissions to the NYC MMTP July–December, 1972.

Termination Rates for Specific Reasons during the First 12 Months Following Admission, by Selected Social and Drug Use History Variables Reported at Time of Enrollment by Patients First Admitted to the NYC MMTP in 1973. At the time of admission to the NYC MMTP, an "Admission Screening Form" is completed for all patients (Appendix IV). Each item is completed by a clinic staff member, based on information reported by the patient; no attempt is made to confirm the responses with outside sources.

The current form was introduced at the end of 1972, and is considerably different in content and format from the admission questionnaire used during the initial 2 years of the Program's operation. Consequently, 1973 is the first year for which the revised data are available. In order to have a full year of observation following enrollment in the Program for all subjects, 1974 admissions were excluded from the analysis presented here. For the sake of consistency with other retention-termination analyses reported in this chapter, only individuals admitted to the NYC MTP *for the first time* in 1973 are included.

Since several variables, such as marital status, household composition, employment and welfare status, do not remain constant, the initial categorization of the cohorts could change during the course of the twelve months of

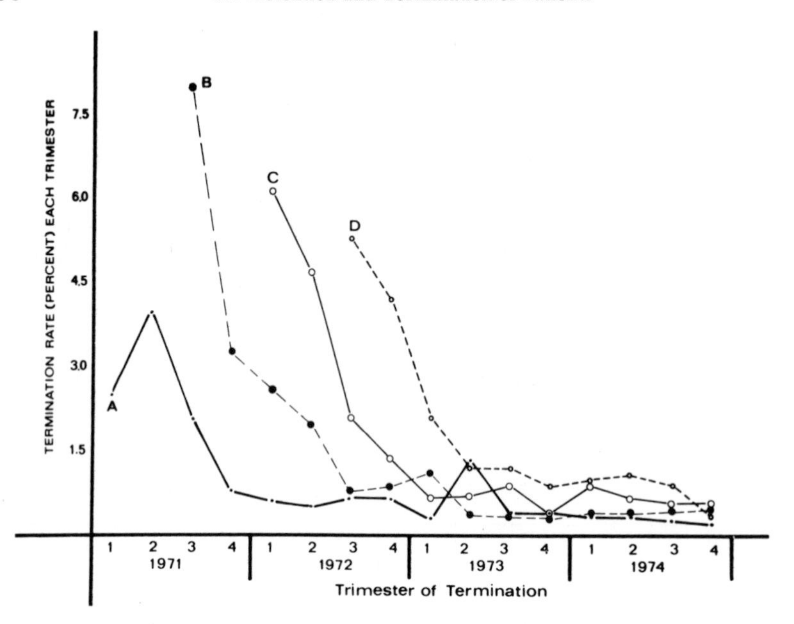

Figure 18.11. Rate of termination for failure to report, by trimester of termination, 1971–1974, for semiannual cohorts of admission to the NYC MMTP during 1971 and 1972. Rate based on patients surviving to the start of the specified trimester. (A) First admissions to the NYC MMTP January–June, 1971. (B) First admissions to the NYC MMTP July–December, 1971. (C) First admissions to the NYC MMTP January–June, 1972. (D) First admissions to the NYC MMTP July–December, 1972.

observation reflected by the data. This limitation must be kept in mind in considering the results.

Marital Status. The association of marital status at the time of admission with subsequent termination history during the first year of treatment is shown in Table 18.4. The results suggest that patients who are legally married when they enter the Program have a somewhat greater likelihood of voluntary withdrawal, and a lower likelihood of termination resulting from incarceration.

Household Composition. Since multiple responses are permitted with respect to the household composition item, the groups are not mutually exclusive.

In general, patients living with parents, spouse, or children at the time of admission have a lower rate of termination for all causes combined (Table 18.5). They are more likely than others to terminate voluntarily, but less likely to be discharged because of failure to report or incarceration.

Religion. As shown in Table 18.6, patients specifying any religion have a somewhat lower overall rate of termination than those specifying no religious preference (39.2% compared to 44.6%). The major differences for specific

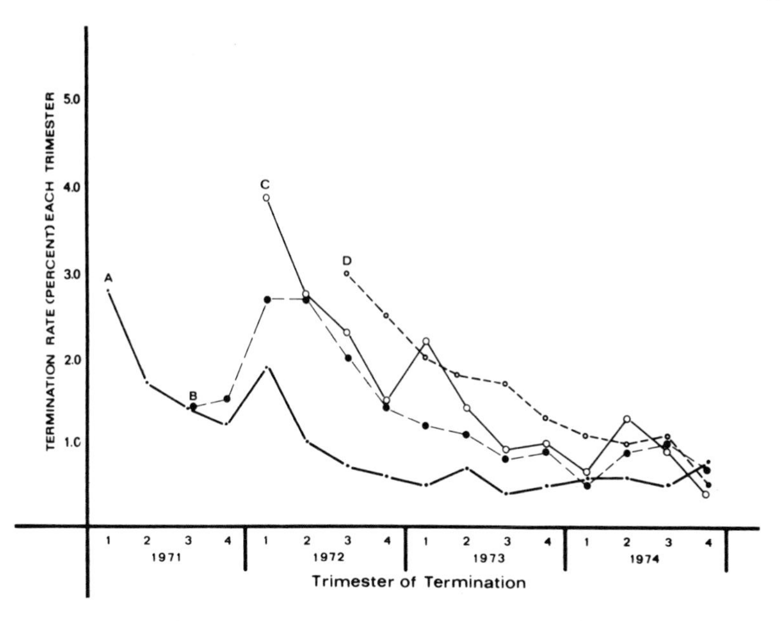

Figure 18.12. Rate of termination for incarceration, by trimester of termination, 1971–1974, for semiannual cohorts of admission to the NYC MMTP during 1971 and 1972. Rate based on patients surviving to the start of the specified trimester. (A) First admissions to the NYC MMTP January–June, 1971. (B) First admissions to the NYC MMTP July–December, 1971. (C) First admissions to the NYC MMTP January–June, 1972. (D) First admissions to the NYC MMTP July–December, 1972.

reasons for termination are with respect to voluntary withdrawal and incarceration; in both instances, those without religious preference have a considerably higher likelihood of termination.

Although the experience of Jewish and "other non-Christian" patients appears to be somewhat different from other religious groups, the small cohort sizes preclude any firm conclusions.

Educational Level. Although the overall likelihood of termination for all causes did not differ appreciably with the level of education, high school graduates had a slightly higher rate of voluntary withdrawal, and fewer were terminated for incarceration than those who had completed less than 12 grades (Table 18.7).

Employment Status at Time of Admission. As shown in Table 18.8, individuals who were employed at the time of admission had a lower overall termination rate during the first 12 months after entering the NYC MMTP, and in particular were less likely to be terminated for administrative cause, for failure to report, and for incarceration. The difference was most marked with respect to incarceration.

Prior Employment History. In contrast to the differences in termination

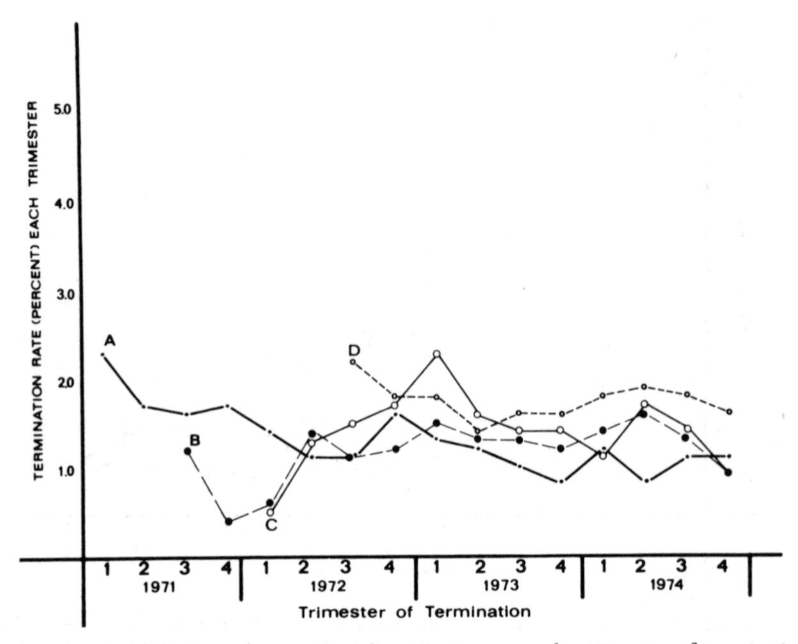

Figure 18.13. Rate of termination for administrative cause, by trimester of termination, 1971–1974, for semiannual cohorts of admission to the NYC MMTP during 1971 and 1972. Rate based on patients surviving to the start of the specified trimester. (A) First admissions to the NYC MMTP January–June, 1971. (B) First admissions to the NYC MMTP July–December, 1971. (C) First admissions to the NYC MMTP January–June, 1972. (D) First admissions to the NYC MMTP July–December, 1972.

experience noted with respect to employment status at the time of admission, the differences were minimal between patients who had *never* worked prior to entering the Program, and those with previous employment experience (Table 18.9). Patients with a more stable prior work history, however, as indicated by increasing length of time in any one job, had a lower overall rate of termination during the first year; they were less likely to be terminated for administrative cause, for incarceration, and for voluntary withdrawal.

Welfare Status at Time of Admission. About one-third of all patients admitted in 1973 were receiving public assistance at the time of enrollment. These patients had a somewhat higher rate of termination for administrative cause, but otherwise their experience was similar to that of other patients (Table 18.10).

Medical Problems. At the time of admission, 835 patients indicated a current medical problem, not further specified. Table 18.11 suggests that there is little association between the self-reported presence of medical problems at the time of enrollment and the likelihood of termination during the subsequent 12-month period.

Veteran Status (Men Only). Of the 3981 men admitted to the NYC MMTP for the first time in 1973, 747 (18.8%) stated that they were veterans. Table 18.12 indicates that there is little difference in termination experience between the veteran and nonveteran male cohorts.

Calendar Year of First Heroin Use. The data in Table 18.13 suggest that more recent onset of heroin use is associated with a somewhat greater likelihood of voluntary withdrawal during the first year after admission. There are no other major differences.

Age of First Heroin Use. As shown in Table 18.14, there is an inverse relationship between age of reported onset of heroin use and overall likelihood of termination for all causes, and the rates of termination for administrative cause and incarceration in particular.

Average Daily Cost of Heroin. There were 1390 patients (26.0%) who did not respond to the item on the admission questionnaire regarding average daily cost of heroin prior to entering treatment. For the remainder, the higher the self-reported cost of the illicit, preadmission heroin habit, the greater the overall likelihood of termination within one year, and the greater the likelihood of termination resulting from incarceration (Table 18.15).

Previous Addiction Treatment. Among the 2377 patients who indicated any prior treatment for addiction, 1316 reported methadone maintenance treatment only, 678 drug-free treatment only, and 383 both chemotherapeutic and drug-free program enrollment prior to entering the NYC MMTP. Table 18.16 shows the termination experience of these subgroups during the first 12 months following admission.

Patients with any prior treatment history were less likely to be terminated for failure to report, but had almost twice the rate of transfer to other addiction programs than did the patients for whom the NYC MMTP was allegedly the first treatment experience. Those patients who previously had methadone treatment, either alone or in addition to prior drug-free treatment, were found to be less likely than others to terminate for all reasons, for voluntary withdrawal, for failure to report and for incarceration. On the other hand, they were more likely to be terminated for administrative cause.

Longest Period of Voluntary Abstinence since Onset of Addiction. Patients who indicated a period of voluntary (i.e., noninstitutional) abstinence of more than 12 months since onset of addiction had a considerably higher likelihood of voluntary withdrawal from treatment than other patients; they were also the least likely to be terminated because of incarceration. Among the remaining cohorts there are no consistent differences (Table 18.17).

Excessive Alcohol Use prior to Admission. Excessive alcohol use prior to admission, as self-reported by patients, was associated with a higher likelihood of termination overall, and most notably for administrative cause (which includes persistent, serious drug and/or alcohol abuse). The data are shown in Table 18.18.

Preadmission Arrest History. Of the 5340 patients admitted to the NYC MMTP for the first time in 1973, 4004 (75.0%) stated that they had been arrested one or more times prior to entering treatment (the nature of the charges was not recorded). As shown in Table 18.19, these patients were more likely to be terminated for all causes during the first twelve months after admission. With respect to incarceration, patients with any arrests prior to admission had a discharge rate four times as great as those with no reported arrest history (8.9 and 2.2%, respectively). They were also more likely to be terminated for administrative cause. On the other hand, patients with prior arrests were less likely to withdraw voluntarily from treatment.

There was a fairly consistent association between likelihood of termination for incarceration and number of preadmission arrests. Thus, of patients with only one prior arrest, 4.2% were terminated for incarceration compared with 13.2% of those with more than 10 arrests. The likelihood was inversely related to age at time of first arrest; while 11.1% of those first arrested under 18 years of age were terminated for incarceration, only 3.1% of those first arrested after age 30 were terminated for this reason.

Preadmission Conviction History. The data shown in Table 18.20 indicate a pattern with respect to self-reported convictions which is similar to that observed for preadmission arrest history: patients reporting one or more convictions prior to enrollment in the NYC MMTP were more likely to terminate because of incarceration and administrative cause, and less likely to withdraw voluntarily, than other patients.

The Association of Retention Rates with Patient Capacity of NYC MMTP Clinics

The 44 treatment units which comprise the NYC MMTP were classified into three groups, according to the average patient census from the time of opening through the end of 1974. There were 16 clinics with an average census of 250 patients or less; 23 clinics with a census of 251–400 patients; and 5 clinics with an average of over 400 patients.

Using life-table methods, it was found that the retention curves for the three clinic groups were very similar (Figure 18.14). At the end of 52 weeks, the retention rates were 66.1%, 66.0%, and 62.9% for small, medium, and large clinics, respectively.

The Association of Retention and Termination Rates with the Patients' Preadmission Reporting History to the New York City Narcotics Register

In cooperation with the New York City Narcotics Register, an analysis was made of the retention and termination experience of patients, as related to

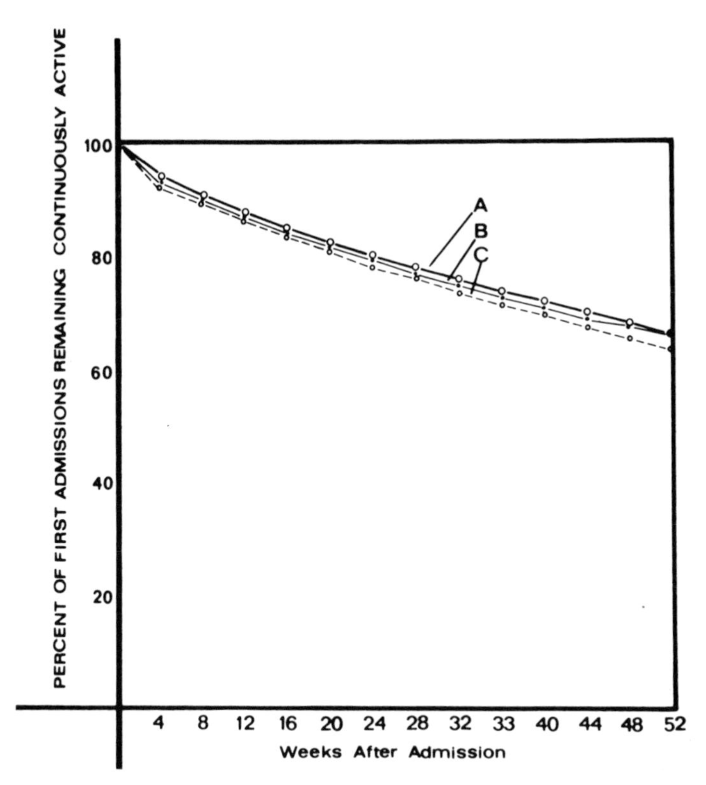

Figure 18.14. Retention in continuous active treatment following first admission to the NYC MMTP, by size of clinic to which admitted. (A) Clinics with average census 250 or less. (B) Clinics with average census 251–400. (C) Clinics with average census over 400.

their preadmission history of reports to the Register.* Patients were grouped into those who had been reported to the Register prior to admission to the NYC MMTP, and those who had not. The patients comprising the first group were further categorized according to the time interval between the most recent preadmission report to the Register and the date of enrollment in the NYC MMTP, as well as according to the type of agency submitting the report.

To permit 2 full years of observation for all patients, only those admitted to the Program prior to 1973 were included. Only first admissions to the NYC MMTP were analyzed.

Reports to the Narcotics Register from Any Agency

Of the 11,723 first admissions to the NYC MMTP from the Program's inception in November, 1970 through the end of 1972, 9902 (84.5%) had

*The operation of the New York City Narcotics Register is described in Chapter 20.

one or more reports to the Narcotics Register prior to enrollment. Of those known to the Register, over half (54.5%) had been reported most recently during the 6 months immediately preceding admission, while at the other extreme, 12.0% had not been reported for over 2 years prior to entering the NYC MMTP.

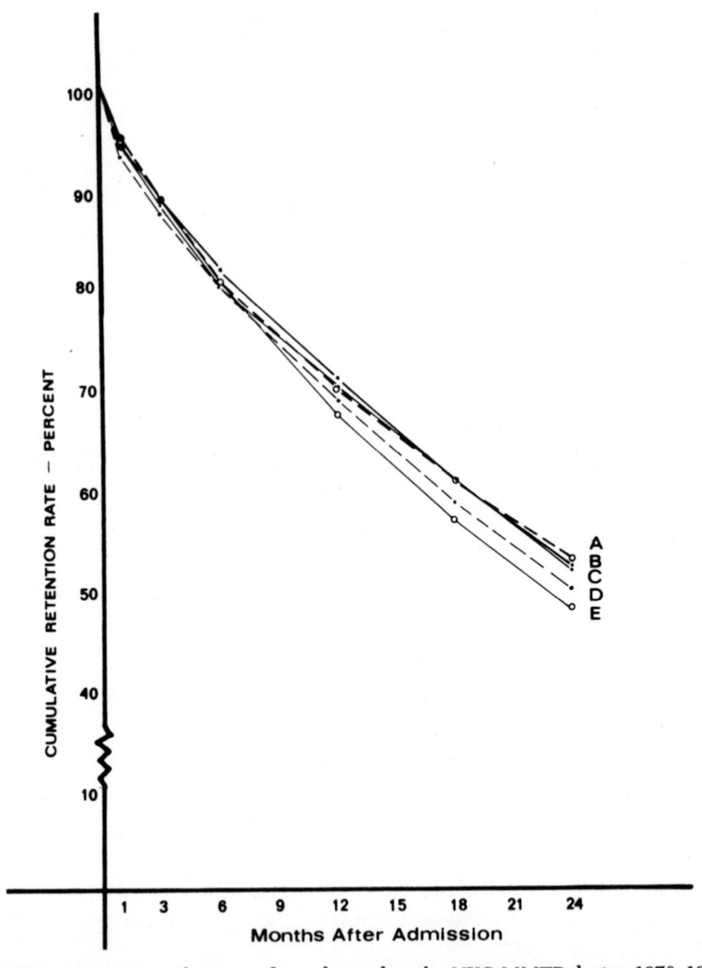

Figure 18.15. Retention of patients first admitted to the NYC MMTP during 1970–1972, by preadmission reporting history to the NYC Narcotics Register from any agency. (A) Never reported to Register before admission: $N = 1821$. (B) Most recent report to Register more than 24 months before admission; $N = 1193$. (C) Most recent report to Register 13–24 months before admission; $N = 1469$. (D) Most recent report to Register 7–12 months before admission; $N = 1847$. (E) Most recent report to Register 1–6 months before admission; $N = 5393$.

Figure 18.15 shows the retention curves for cohorts defined by the length of time between the most recent Narcotics Register report (if any), and admission to the Program. Although the differences are slight, those patients who had been reported most recently 1–6 and 7–12 months before entering treatment had a somewhat lower retention rate at the end of 2 years than did those who had never been reported at all, or whose most recent report was more than one year before enrollment.

*Reports to the Narcotics Register from Criminal Justice System Agencies**

There were 7167 patients, 61.1% of those admitted during the first 2 years of the Program's operation, who had previously been reported to the Narcotics Register from criminal justice system (CJS) agencies. Only about 25% of these patients had been reported most recently from the CJS within 6 months prior to entering treatment in the NYC MMTP, while 34.2% had not been reported for over 2 years prior to admission.

As shown in Figure 18.16, the retention in treatment varied considerably with the reporting history from CJS agencies. At the end of 2 years, the retention was 42.5% for patients whose most recent report was within 6 months of admission, 45.9% for those with the latest report 7–12 months before admission, and 49.4% for those whose most recent report was 13–24 months prior to entering the Program. The highest retention rate, 53.0%, was observed for patients who had never had a report to the Narcotics Register from a CJS agency, as well as for those whose most recent report was more than 2 years before enrollment.

Table 18.21 shows the rates of termination for each of the cohorts during specified intervals following admission, based on patients surviving to the start of each time period. The disparity in termination rates was most marked in the 7–12-month interval after enrollment.

The Association of Termination Rates with Patient Status during Treatment, with Respect to Gainful Occupation and Drug Abuse

Once every 2 months, NYC MMTP clinics submit a "patient progress report" on every patient enrolled (Appendix V). Using the reports submitted for November–December, 1973, as a base, all patients admitted to the Program from its inception in November, 1970 through the end of October, 1973 and still active on December 31, 1973 were divided into cohorts

*Criminal justice system agencies are defined as police, corrections, parole, and probation departments.

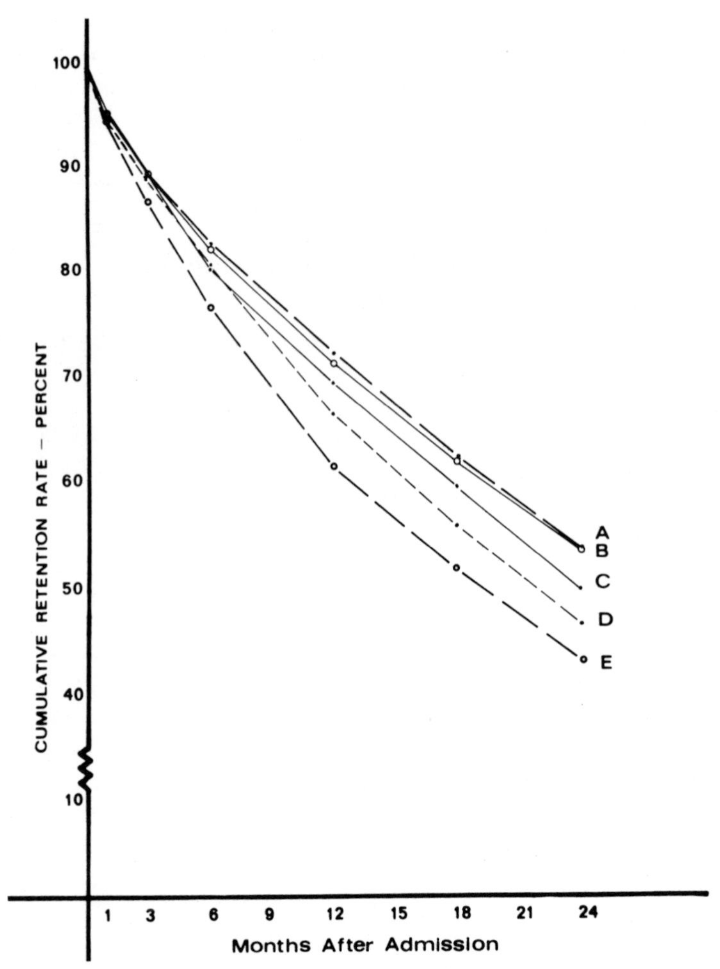

Figure 18.16. Retention of patients first admitted to the NYC MMTP during 1970–1972, by preadmission reporting history to the NYC Narcotics Register from criminal justice agencies. Criminal justice agencies are defined as police, corrections, parole and probation departments. (A) Never reported to Register from criminal justice agencies before admission; $N = 4556$. (B) Most recent report to Register from criminal justice agency more than 24 months before admission; $N = 2451$. (C) Most recent report to Register from criminal justice agency 13–24 months before admission; $N = 1644$. (D) Most recent report to Register from criminal justice agency 7–12 months before admission; $N = 1177$. (E) Most recent report to Register from criminal justice agency 1–6 months before admission; $N = 1895$.

according to the number of months in continuous active treatment. These cohorts were then subdivided according to gainfully occupied status and drug abuse pattern during the 2-month reporting period.* For each of these subgroups, the rate of termination during the following six months (i.e., from January 1 through June 30, 1974) was determined for all reasons combined, as well as for voluntary withdrawal and administrative cause in particular.

Since neither gainful occupation nor drug abuse remain constant over time, changes will occur for an indeterminate proportion of patients during the six months which comprise the period of observation in this analysis. This limitation must be considered in interpreting the results.

Association of Gainfully Occupied Status and Likelihood of Termination within Six Months

Patients reported as gainfully occupied had a considerably lower overall termination rate in the following 6 months of observation (Table 18.22). While the gainfully occupied patients had a slightly higher rate of voluntary withdrawal, they were far less likely to be terminated during this period for administrative cause.

As shown in Table 18.23, these associations were observed for both sexes, and for cohorts in treatment for varying lengths of time.

Association of Drug Abuse and Likelihood of Termination within Six Months

Patients who had no drugs of abuse indicated for the 2-month reporting period ending December 31, 1973 had a markedly lower rate of termination for all causes, and for administrative discharge in particular, than did those with one or more reported drugs of abuse (Table 18.24). On the other hand, the rate of voluntary withdrawal was essentially the same for both groups.

With respect to the specific drugs of abuse mentioned, patients with amphetamine and cocaine use had the lowest overall termination rates during the 6-month period, and were the least likely to be terminated for administrative cause. Patients with excessive alcohol use were the most likely to be terminated for administrative cause and for all reasons combined. The results with respect to voluntary withdrawal differed only slightly for the specific drug categories.

When comparisons between patients using one or more drugs and those using none are made for subgroups defined by length of time in treatment (Table 18.25), the same pattern emerges. In every instance, those with no reported drugs of abuse have a lower overall termination rate, and a lower

*Gainfully occupied is defined as employed and/or in school and/or homemaker; determination is based primarily on self-reporting by the patients. Responses by the clinic staff to questions regarding drug abuse are based on clinical observation and urinalysis results.

rate of administrative discharge; except for patients in treatment 2–6 months, patients without drug use were more likely to terminate by voluntary withdrawal, but the differences are slight.

DISCUSSION

Comparability of the NYC MMTP Data with Those of Other Programs

The reported experience of addiction treatment programs employing a wide variety of approaches suggests that increasing time in treatment is associated with greater benefits to patients and the community (218–224). Hence, while there are many parameters which are relevant to the evaluation of treatment efforts, a program's ability to retain patients is one important measure of its effectiveness.

The marked differences in patient retention reported by addiction programs are in large part a consequence of the lack of consistency in defining "admission" and "termination," as well as in analyzing the data. In addition, however, disparities reflect programmatic differences. For instance, some therapeutic communities consider it important that applicants first complete a period of orientation and detoxification in an ambulatory facility before being afforded patient status; it might be anticipated that such a procedure would result in a significantly lower early drop-out rate than that experienced by programs which accept applicants directly from the street. At the other end of the treatment spectrum, program goals and philosophy will determine whether, when and why patients are to be discharged; those methadone treatment programs which view a drug-free state as the ultimate therapeutic objective will generally maintain patients on the active census following detoxification, while other programs will terminate patients promptly after withdrawal is complete.

It is neither feasible nor desirable to compromise treatment philosophy and practices in order to achieve comparability of research and evaluation data. The consequence, however, is that great care must be exercised in interpreting and comparing results of different programs. Above all, it is essential that the presentation of findings be accompanied by a detailed description of the policies and procedures which govern both the delivery of treatment and the collection and analysis of data.

Retention Experience of All Patients in the NYC MMTP

The NYC MMTP was successful in retaining over 65% of patients for at least 12 months of continuous treatment. This experience is especially significant for several reasons.

The program admitted into treatment 95% of all applicants who reported for treatment and who met the basic criteria of age, duration of addiction, and residence. It has been suggested that the high retention rates reported for some methadone maintenance programs may reflect stringent eligibility criteria which ensure that only the most highly motivated applicants are accepted (225–227). This was clearly not a factor in the NYC MMTP experience.

Every patient who received even one dose of methadone was included in the study, and life-table methods ensured that the full experience of all patients would be incorporated. In some large studies of retention it has been considered necessary to omit from the analysis over 20% of all patients because of insufficient data, withdrawal immediately after enrollment, and other reasons (228).

Treatment in the NYC MMTP is voluntary. Patients at all times retain the option of discontinuing treatment.

Patients are promptly terminated when methadone treatment is discontinued for any reason, and the date of termination used in calculating retention rates is the last day for which medication was dispensed. Retention, as defined in this study, signifies continued, active participation.

Retention of Different Patient Subgroups

Many conflicting reports are found in the literature regarding the suitability of methadone maintenance treatment for specific segments of the addict population (229–237). The large number of patients upon which the current study is based permits a meaningful comparison to be made of separate cohorts defined by demographic, social, and drug-use characteristics. While differences are noted in some cases, the most striking finding is the remarkable consistency in retention which is observed for the various subgroups.

With respect to demographic characteristics, the three major ethnic groups had almost identical retention curves over the course of 3 years following admission. A slightly greater proportion of women than men remained in treatment, but the difference was never greater than 7 percentage points, and even this discrepancy steadily diminished with increasing time since admission. Among the different age groups, there was no consistent pattern except that patients over 40 at the time of enrollment had a somewhat higher retention rate; here too, however, the spread among the various groups was small, never exceeding 10 percentage points over the course of 3 years of observation.

The proportion of patients terminated for any reason during the first 12 months after admission did not exceed 50% for any subgroup defined by marital status, household composition, religion, educational level, employment status, prior work history, welfare status, drug use pattern, or criminal history prior to entering the Program. These findings suggest that, as measured by patient retention in treatment, methadone maintenance is equally well suited to all segments of the narcotic addict population.

The Effect of Clinic Size on Patient Retention

It has been suggested that clinic size and quality of treatment services are inversely related (238,239). The difficulty of quantifying treatment outcome makes such an association difficult to prove or disprove. With respect to patient retention, however, no appreciable difference was noted among NYC MMTP clinics grouped according to the number of patients served.

Declining Retention Rates of Successive Admission Cohorts

The retention rates of patients entering treatment in successive years from 1971 through 1973 declined markedly, before leveling off in the case of the 1974 admissions. The data indicate that this trend was primarily a result of the increase in terminations initiated by the patients. Most striking was the sharp rise in the termination rate due to voluntary withdrawal during the second and third trimesters of 1973, which cannot be explained as a function of length of time in treatment. A similar pattern was not observed for any other reason for termination.

The downward trend in retention which has been noted is undoubtedly a consequence of a multiplicity of factors, including a progressive shortening of the preadmission waiting period from many months to a few weeks or days; the implementation of restrictive and inflexible Federal and State regulations governing methadone treatment programs; and increased skepticism and hostility directed at programs and patients by the general community. Perhaps the greatest influence, however, has been exerted by the growing focus on achieving a drug-free state for every patient, an objective currently imposed on all methadone programs, and on their patients, by the Food and Drug Administration.

In the chapters which follow, data will be presented regarding two indicators of the posttermination adjustment of patients who left the NYC MMTP: the rate of readmission to the Program, and the reporting history to the New York City Narcotics Register subsequent to discharge.

TABLE 18.1

Retention Rates in the NYC MMTP at One, Two, and Three Years after Admission, by Age at Time of Admission

Age at Admission (Years)	Number Admitted	Retention Rate (Percent)		
		1 Year after Admission	2 Years after Admission	3 Years after Admission
18–20	3339	65.1	47.3	34.5
21–25	8324	64.4	45.3	34.0
26–30	4257	63.3	46.4	33.9
31–40	3505	67.6	48.5	37.8
Over 40	1248	71.6	55.2	42.7

TABLE 18.2

Retention Rates in the NYC MMTP at One, Two, and Three Years after Admission, by Year of First Admission

Year of Admission	Number Admitted	Retention Rate (Percent)		
		1 Year after Admission	2 Years after Admission	3 Years after Admission
1971	4377[a]	72.8	56.7	42.9
1972	7346	67.5	47.3	36.3
1973	5340	59.4	42.3	*b*
1974	3590	61.5	*b*	*b*

[a] Includes 104 admissions in November and December, 1970.
[b] Data not available due to recency.

TABLE 18.3

First Termination Rates[a] Each 12-Week Interval Following Admission to NYC MMTP, by Year of Admission

Year of Admission	First Termination Rate (Percent) during Specified Interval (Weeks)												
	1–12	13–24	25–36	37–48	49–60	61–72	73–84	85–96	97–108	109–120	121–132	133–144	145–156
1971[b]	10.2	7.9	6.7	5.3	5.7	5.2	5.6	6.6	7.3	7.2	6.5	6.3	6.3
1972	11.0	8.0	8.2	7.5	7.6	8.6	7.9	7.5	7.6	7.0	6.2	4.8	5.6
1973	15.6	10.7	9.9	9.5	9.0	8.9	8.1	6.0	5.7	*c*	*c*	*c*	*c*
1974	17.3	10.3	8.4	6.3	9.3	*c*	*c*	*c*	*c*	*c*	*c*	*c*	*c*

[a] Based on number of patients surviving to start of each time period.
[b] Includes 104 admissions in November and December, 1970.
[c] Data not available due to recency.

TABLE 18.4

Percent of Patients Terminated for Specific Causes during the First Twelve Months after Admission,[a] by Marital Status

Marital Status	Number Admitted	Rate of Termination (Percent) for Specified Cause						
		All Causes	Fail. to Report	Volunt. Withdr.	Incarceration	Adminis. Cause	Transfer	Medical[b]
Total	5340[c]	40.5	11.9	8.9	7.2	6.9	3.8	1.6
Single	2429	42.9	11.8	9.1	8.1	7.9	4.1	1.9
Married	960	38.5	10.8	10.1	5.7	6.8	3.5	1.6
Widowed	64	26.6	7.8	4.7	4.7	4.7	1.6	3.1
Separated	630	41.4	13.7	8.7	6.8	6.8	4.4	1.0
Divorced	174	42.5	12.6	8.0	6.9	9.2	2.9	2.9
Common-law	558	34.4	11.3	6.8	7.0	5.0	3.2	1.1

[a] First admissions to the NYC MMTP during 1973.
[b] "Medical" includes long-term hospitalization and death.
[c] Includes 525 (9.8%) "no answer."

TABLE 18.5

Percent of Patients Terminated for Specific Causes during the First Twelve Months after Admission,[a] by Household Composition

Household Composition[b]	Number Admitted	Rate of Termination (Percent) for Specified Cause						
		All Causes	Fail. to Report	Volunt. Withdr.	Incarceration	Adminis. Cause	Transfer	Medical[c]
Total	5340[d]	40.5	11.9	8.9	7.2	6.9	3.8	1.6
With parents	1542	40.3	11.4	10.0	6.9	7.5	3.0	1.5
With spouse	1394	36.0	10.2	9.1	6.1	5.5	3.6	1.4
With children	685	36.8	11.4	10.2	3.8	6.7	3.1	1.6
With other relatives	624	45.0	13.8	9.0	9.9	6.7	4.5	1.1
With friends	565	43.7	14.0	6.5	8.0	7.6	5.0	2.7
No stable arrangement	67	44.8	14.9	6.0	9.0	7.5	4.5	3.0
Alone	970	43.2	12.2	8.5	8.2	8.2	4.5	1.5

[a] First admissions to the NYC MMTP during 1973.
[b] Categories are not mutually exclusive.
[c] "Medical" includes long-term hospitalization and death.
[d] Includes 131 (2.5%) "no answer."

TABLE 18.6

Percent of Patients Terminated for Specific Causes during the First Twelve Months after Admission,[a] by Religious Preference

Specified Religion	Number Admitted	Rate of Termination (Percent) for Specified Cause						
		All Causes	Fail. to Report	Volunt. Withdr.	Incarceration	Adminis. Cause	Transfer	Medical[b]
Total	5340[c]	40.5	11.9	8.9	7.2	6.9	3.8	1.6
"None"	968	44.6	12.2	12.3	8.7	6.5	3.5	1.4
Any	3873	39.2	11.7	8.1	6.7	7.0	3.8	1.6
Catholic	2224	38.4	10.8	8.0	6.3	7.2	4.5	1.6
Other Christian	1462	39.8	13.9	7.9	7.0	6.7	2.8	1.5
Jewish	83	47.0	6.0	10.8	3.6	15.7	7.2	3.6
Other non-Christian	104	39.4	4.8	12.5	14.4	4.8	1.0	1.9

[a] First admissions to the NYC MMTP during 1973.
[b] "Medical" includes long-term hospitalization and death.
[c] Includes 499 (9.3%) "no answer."

TABLE 18.7

Percent of Patients Terminated for Specific Causes during the First Twelve Months after Admission,[a] by Educational Level

Educational Level	Number Admitted	Rate of Termination (Percent) for Specified Cause						
		All Causes	Fail. to Report	Volunt. Withdr.	Incarceration	Adminis. Cause	Transfer	Medical[b]
Total	5340[c]	40.5	11.9	8.9	7.2	6.9	3.8	1.6
Grade 9 or less	1098	41.0	11.9	7.3	8.7	7.7	3.3	2.0
Grade 10–12	2558	40.8	13.3	8.8	6.9	7.0	3.3	1.5
High School grad. or more	1551	39.9	9.2	10.5	6.6	7.0	5.0	1.5

[a] First admissions to the NYC MMTP during 1973.
[b] "Medical" includes long-term hospitalization and death.
[c] Includes 133 (2.5%) "no answer."

TABLE 18.8

Percent of Patients Terminated for Specific Causes during the First Twelve Months after Admission,[a] by Employment Status at Time of Admission

Employment Status at Admission	Number Admitted	Rate of Termination (Percent) for Specified Cause						
		All Causes	Fail. to Report	Volunt. Withdr.	Incarceration	Adminis. Cause	Transfer	Medical[b]
Total	5340	40.5	11.9	8.9	7.2	6.9	3.8	1.7
No/no answer	4200	42.2	12.6	8.6	8.0	7.7	3.6	1.6
Employed	1140	34.1	9.1	9.9	4.1	5.1	4.6	1.2

[a] First admissions to the NYC MMTP during 1973.
[b] "Medical" includes long-term hospitalization and death.

TABLE 18.9

Percent of Patients Terminated for Specific Causes during the First Twelve Months after Admission,[a] by Prior Employment History

Prior employment	Number Admitted	Rate of Termination (Percent) for Specified Cause						
		All Causes	Fail. to Report	Volunt. Withdr.	Incarceration	Adminis. Cause	Transfer	Medical[b]
Total	5340	40.5	11.9	8.9	7.2	6.9	3.8	1.6
No prev. job/ no answer	985	40.5	12.6	7.4	7.0	7.1	4.0	2.3
Any prev. job	4355	40.5	11.7	9.2	7.2	6.9	3.8	1.4
Longest time in 1 job (months)								
1–6	1122	45.6	13.5	10.8	8.5	8.0	3.7	1.1
7–12	1068	40.7	11.6	8.8	8.1	7.1	3.5	1.6
13–24	947	38.2	10.0	9.3	6.2	7.1	4.2	1.4
Over 24	1218	37.3	11.3	8.1	6.1	6.2	3.9	1.6

[a] First admissions to the NYC MMTP during 1973.

[b] "Medical" includes long-term hospitalization and death.

TABLE 18.10

Percent of Patients Terminated for Specific Causes during the First Twelve Months after Admission,[a] by Welfare Status at the Time of Admission

		Rate of Termination (Percent) for Specified Cause						
Receiving Publ. Assist.	Number Admitted	All Causes	Fail. to Report	Volunt. Withdr.	Incarceration	Adminis. Cause	Transfer	Medical[b]
Total	5340	40.5	11.9	8.9	7.2	6.9	3.8	1.6
No/no ans.	3679	40.6	12.2	8.7	7.7	6.1	4.2	1.4
Yes	1661	40.2	11.0	9.3	6.0	9.0	3.0	2.0

[a] First admissions to the NYC MMTP during 1973.

[b] "Medical" includes long-term hospitalization and death.

TABLE 18.11

Percent of Patients Terminated for Specific Causes during the First Twelve Months after Admission,[a] by Self-Reported Medical Problem at Time of Admission

		Rate of Termination (Percent) for Specified Cause						
Medical Problem	Number Admitted	All Causes	Fail. to Report	Volunt. Withdr.	Incarceration	Adminis. Cause	Transfer	Medical[b]
Total	5340[c]	40.5	11.9	8.9	7.2	6.9	3.8	1.6
Yes	835	43.5	12.7	9.7	6.8	8.7	3.5	2.0
No	4244	40.1	11.6	8.9	7.4	6.9	3.9	1.5

[a] First admissions to the NYC MMTP during 1973.
[b] "Medical" includes long-term hospitalization and death.
[c] Includes 261 (4.9%) "no answer."

TABLE 18.12

Percent of Male Patients Terminated for Specific Causes during the First Twelve Months after Admission,[a] by Veteran Status

Veteran Status	Number Admitted	Rate of Termination (Percent) for Specified Cause						
		All Causes	Fail. to Report	Volunt. Withdr.	Incarceration	Adminis. Cause	Transfer	Medical[b]
Total	3981[c]	41.3	11.7	8.7	8.2	6.6	3.8	1.4
Veteran	747	42.8	12.6	10.6	7.4	5.8	4.7	1.9
Nonvet.	3109	41.3	11.7	8.6	8.7	7.1	3.7	1.3

[a] First admissions to the NYC MMTP during 1973.
[b] "Medical" includes long-term hospitalization and death.
[c] Includes 125 (3.1%) "no answer."

TABLE 18.13

Percent of Patients Terminated for Specific Causes during the First Twelve Months after Admission,[a] by Calendar Year of First Heroin Use

		Rate of Termination (Percent) for Specified Cause						
Year of First Heroin Use	Number Admitted	All Causes	Fail. to Report	Volunt. Withdr.	Incarceration	Adminis. Cause	Transfer	Medical[b]
Total	5340[c]	40.5	11.9	8.9	7.2	6.9	3.8	1.6
1971	101	42.6	13.9	10.9	5.9	9.9	2.0	0
1970	344	39.5	11.3	10.8	5.2	7.6	3.5	1.2
1969	680	43.5	12.5	12.8	6.2	6.8	4.0	1.3
1968	806	39.6	10.5	9.4	7.8	6.9	3.5	1.4
1967	682	40.9	12.6	8.2	7.5	7.8	4.1	0.7
1966	435	42.8	12.2	11.3	6.0	5.1	6.2	2.1
1961–1965	1127	40.8	12.3	8.4	8.0	7.1	3.5	1.5
1956–1960	496	42.3	13.1	4.6	9.5	8.3	4.4	2.4
1951–1955	235	33.2	7.7	7.2	5.1	7.7	2.6	3.0
1950/before	281	34.9	11.0	4.6	6.8	6.8	2.8	2.8

[a] First admissions to the NYC MMTP during 1973.
[b] "Medical" includes long-term hospitalization and death.
[c] Includes 153 (2.9%) "no answer."

TABLE 18.14

Percent of Patients Terminated for Specific Causes during the First Twelve Months after Admission,[a] by Age of First Heroin Use

		Rate of Termination (Percent) for Specified Cause						
Age First Heroin Use	Number Admitted	All Causes	Fail. to Report	Volunt. Withdr.	Incarceration	Adminis. Cause	Transfer	Medical[b]
Total	5340[c]	40.5	11.9	8.9	7.2	6.9	3.8	1.6
Under 16	1255	42.2	12.4	8.4	8.0	8.0	4.0	1.4
16–17	1438	40.5	10.6	9.4	7.8	7.0	4.0	1.8
18–20	1327	41.1	12.3	9.2	6.7	7.9	3.7	1.4
21–25	776	38.5	10.7	10.1	6.8	5.9	3.5	1.5
26–30	250	36.0	16.4	4.8	5.6	4.4	2.0	2.8
Over 30	148	37.8	10.8	6.8	4.7	7.4	6.1	2.0

[a] First admissions to the NYC MMTP during 1973.
[b] "Medical" includes long-term hospitalization and death.
[c] Includes 146 (2.7%) "no answer."

TABLE 18.15

Percent of Patients Terminated for Specific Causes during the First Twelve Months after Admission,[a] by Average Daily Cost of Heroin Habit

Average Cost ($) of Heroin/Day	Number Admitted	Rate of Termination (Percent) for Specified Cause						
		All Causes	Fail. to Report	Volunt. Withdr.	Incarceration	Adminis. Cause	Transfer	Medical[b]
Total	5340[c]	40.5	11.9	8.9	7.2	6.9	3.8	1.6
1–25	844	39.1	11.5	9.4	6.8	6.2	3.8	1.5
26–50	1655	42.5	14.4	9.1	6.8	7.3	3.4	1.5
51–100	1184	42.9	13.0	8.4	9.3	7.5	3.0	1.6
Over 100	267	46.4	13.5	9.4	12.7	7.1	2.6	1.1

[a] First admissions to the NYC MMTP during 1973.
[b] "Medical" includes long-term hospitalization and death.
[c] Includes 1390 (26.0%) "no answer."

TABLE 18.16

Percent of Patients Terminated for Specific Causes during the First Twelve Months after Admission,[a] by Prior Addiction Treatment History

		Rate of Termination (Percent) for Specified Cause						
Prior Rx History	Number Admitted	All Causes	Fail. to Report	Volunt. Withdr.	Incarceration	Adminis. Cause	Transfer	Medical[b]
Total	5340	40.5	11.9	8.9	7.2	6.9	3.8	1.6
None/no ans.	2963	41.4	13.9	9.3	7.7	6.4	2.7	1.4
Any prior Rx	2377	39.3	9.3	8.3	6.6	7.8	5.3	1.9
MM only	1316	38.9	8.4	7.9	5.5	8.8	5.7	2.6
DF only	678	43.4	12.8	9.9	8.7	6.8	4.0	1.2
MM and DF	383	33.7	6.3	7.1	6.3	7.3	6.0	0.8

[a] First admissions to the NYC MMTP during 1973.
[b] "Medical" includes long-term hospitalization and death.

TABLE 18.17

Percent of Patients Terminated for Specific Causes during the First Twelve Months after Admission,[a] by Longest Period of Voluntary Abstinence

Longest Period Vol. Abstin. (Months)	Number Admitted	Rate of Termination (Percent) for Specified Cause						
		All Causes	Fail. to Report	Volunt. Withdr.	Incarceration	Adminis. Cause	Transfer	Medical[b]
Total	5340	40.5	11.9	8.9	7.2	6.9	3.8	1.6
None/no ans.	2076	40.5	13.3	8.2	6.7	6.8	4.3	1.3
1–3	1383	40.8	11.4	9.0	8.7	7.3	3.0	1.4
4–6	598	39.0	10.7	8.9	6.9	6.9	3.7	2.0
7–12	681	41.1	11.0	7.8	7.5	8.5	4.4	1.9
Over 12	602	40.4	10.1	12.5	5.3	6.6	3.7	2.2

[a] First admissions to the NYC MMTP during 1973.

[b] "Medical" includes long-term hospitalization and death.

TABLE 18.18

Percent of Patients Terminated for Specific Causes during the First Twelve Months after Admission,[a] by Excessive Alcohol Use Prior to Admission

Excessive Preadm. Alcohol Use	Number Admitted	Rate of Termination (Percent) for Specified Cause						
		All Causes	Fail. to Report	Volunt. Withdr.	Incarceration	Adminis. Cause	Transfer	Medical[b]
Total	5340[c]	40.5	11.9	8.9	7.2	6.9	3.8	1.6
No	4381	40.2	12.0	8.9	7.3	6.8	3.7	1.5
Yes	382	47.4	11.3	10.2	8.9	12.0	3.1	1.8

[a] First admissions to the NYC MMTP during 1973.
[b] "Medical" includes long-term hospitalization and death.
[c] Includes 577 (10.8%) "no answer."

TABLE 18.19

Percent of Patients Terminated for Specific Causes during the First Twelve Months after Admission,[a] by Preadmission Arrest History

Preadmission Arrest History	Number Admitted	Rate of Termination (Percent) for Specified Cause						
		All Causes	Fail. to Report	Volunt. Withdr.	Incarceration	Adminis. Cause	Transfer	Medical[b]
Total	5340	40.5	11.9	8.9	7.2	6.9	3.8	1.6
No arrest/no answer	1336	35.9	12.1	11.9	2.2	4.6	3.7	1.4
One or more arrests	4004	42.0	11.8	7.9	8.9	7.8	3.9	1.6

Number of arrests								
1	759	41.0	14.2	10.7	4.2	6.7	3.2	2.0
2	602	38.2	11.3	7.3	6.8	8.3	3.3	1.2
3	543	42.5	13.4	7.2	9.2	6.3	4.6	1.8
4	347	38.9	9.8	7.5	8.9	8.6	3.2	0.9
5	322	43.5	11.2	8.4	9.3	8.7	5.0	0.9
6–10	785	45.1	10.7	8.9	11.0	8.7	4.5	1.4
Over 10	646	43.5	10.5	4.5	13.2	9.0	3.7	2.6
Age at first arrest[c]								
Under 16	581	43.9	11.5	6.7	10.8	9.1	4.6	1.0
16–17	1175	44.8	11.3	8.9	11.3	7.5	4.3	1.5
18–20	1068	40.6	12.2	8.1	7.2	8.1	3.2	1.9
21–25	708	39.5	10.2	7.1	7.9	8.3	4.5	1.6
26–30	225	37.8	12.9	9.3	5.8	4.0	2.2	3.6
Over 30	97	40.2	16.5	8.2	3.1	7.2	4.1	1.0

[a] First admissions to the NYC MMTP during 1973.
[b] "Medical" includes long-term hospitalization and death.
[c] Age at time of arrest was not specified for 150 patients, 3.7% of those with one or more preadmission arrests.

TABLE 18.20

Percent of Patients Terminated for Specific Causes during the First Twelve Months after Admission,[a] by Preadmission Conviction History

Preadmission Conviction History	Number Admitted	Rate of Termination (Percent) for Specified Cause						
		All Causes	Fail. to Report	Volunt. Withdr.	Incarceration	Adminis. Cause	Transfer	Medical[b]
Total	5340	40.5	11.9	8.9	7.2	6.9	3.8	1.6
No convict./ no answer	2546	37.6	12.2	10.7	3.6	5.7	3.7	1.8
One or more convictions	2794	43.1	11.6	7.2	10.5	8.3	4.0	1.4
Number of convictions								
1	937	43.1	11.6	8.9	9.1	8.1	4.2	1.3
2	513	41.9	11.9	8.0	9.4	7.0	4.5	1.2
3	388	46.6	13.7	6.7	11.1	10.1	3.4	1.8
4	196	46.4	12.8	9.2	10.2	7.7	5.6	1.0
5	151	39.1	9.9	4.6	12.6	7.9	4.0	0
6–10	365	42.2	10.1	4.4	12.1	9.9	3.6	2.2
Over 10	244	40.3	9.1	4.1	13.6	8.6	2.9	2.1

[a] First admissions to the NYC MMTP during 1973.
[b] "Medical" includes long-term hospitalization and death.

TABLE 18.21

First Termination Rates during Specified Time Periods after Admission to NYC MMTP, 1970–1972, by Preadmission Reporting History to the New York City Narcotics Register from Criminal Justice System Agencies

Most Recent Preadmission Report to the Register from CJS Agencies	Number Admitted	Percent Terminated during Specified Interval after Admission					
		Less Than 1 Month	1–3 Months	4–6 Months	7–12 Months	13–18 Months	19–24 Months
		Length of Interval (Months)					
		1	2	3	6	6	6
Total	11,723	5.3	6.3	8.8	14.8	14.6	15.0
No CJS report	4,556	5.5	5.7	7.4	12.9	14.3	14.2
Over 24 months preadmission	2,451	4.7	6.5	8.0	13.6	13.3	13.8
13–24 months preadmission	1,644	5.4	5.9	10.0	13.7	14.6	16.5
7–12 months preadmission	1,177	5.7	5.9	9.4	17.7	16.6	16.9
1–6 months preadmission	1,895	5.6	8.4	11.6	20.3	16.2	16.8

TABLE 18.22

Termination Rates within Six Months for Patients First Admitted to NYC MMTP November, 1970–October, 1973, and Still Active on December 31, 1973; by Gainfully Occupied Status as of December 31, 1973

Gainfully Occupied[a] as of 12/31/73	Number of Patients	Termination Rate (%) within 6 Months for		
		All Reasons	Voluntary Withdrawal	Administ. Cause
Total	9376[b]	14.9	5.9	2.9
Yes	5428	12.3	6.4	1.5
No	3948	18.5	5.2	4.8

[a] Gainfully occupied is defined as employed and/or in school and/or homemaker.

[b] Excludes 323 patients for whom gainfully occupied status is not known.

TABLE 18.23

Termination Rates within Six Months for Men and for Women First Admitted to NYC MMTP November, 1970–October, 1973 and Still Active on December 31, 1973; by Length of Time in Treatment and Gainfully Occupied Status as of December 31, 1973

Months in Treatment as of 12/31/73	Sex	Gainfully Occupied[a] as of 12/31/73	Number of Patients[b]	Termination Rate (%) within 6 Months for		
				All Reasons	Voluntary Withdrawal	Administ. Cause
All	Men	Yes	4073	12.7	6.5	1.6
		No	2793	19.3	5.5	4.5
	Women	Yes	1355	11.1	6.1	1.0
		No	1155	16.5	4.3	5.6
2–6	Men	Yes	702	16.4	6.4	1.7
		No	552	24.3	4.5	5.8
	Women	Yes	219	11.0	4.1	1.4
		No	238	15.1	3.4	4.2
7–12	Men	Yes	846	14.2	7.2	2.2
		No	577	20.8	6.4	6.2
	Women	Yes	234	12.8	7.7	0.4
		No	256	20.7	5.5	7.4
13–18	Men	Yes	1028	11.9	6.6	1.5
		No	853	17.7	5.5	3.8
	Women	Yes	416	9.9	5.0	1.0
		No	383	16.2	3.7	6.5
19–24	Men	Yes	591	12.4	6.1	1.9
		No	371	17.3	4.6	4.0
	Women	Yes	222	12.2	7.2	0.9
		No	160	11.3	4.4	2.5
Over 24	Men	Yes	906	9.5	6.2	0.9
		No	440	15.9	6.4	2.7
	Women	Yes	264	10.6	6.8	1.5
		No	118	18.6	5.9	5.9

[a] Gainfully occupied is defined as employed and/or in school and/or homemaker.

[b] Excludes patients in treatment on December 31, 1973 for whom gainfully occupied status is not known: 3.4% of men; 3.6% of women.

TABLE 18.24

Termination Rates within Six Months for Patients First Admitted to NYC MMTP November, 1970–October, 1973 and Still Active on December 31, 1973; by Reported Drug Abuse as of December 31, 1973

Reported Drug Abuse in Nov/Dec, 1973	*N*[a]	Termination Rate (Percent) within 6 Months for		
		All Reasons	Voluntary Withdrawal	Administ. Cause
Total	9294	14.9	5.9	2.9
No drugs of abuse	7957	13.9	6.0	2.2
1 or more drugs used	1337[b]	20.9	5.5	7.0
Heroin	227	21.6	6.6	7.0
Barbit.	286	22.7	5.2	9.1
Amphet.	111	14.4	4.5	2.7
Cocaine	330	16.7	4.5	3.9
Excessive alcohol	454	25.3	4.6	10.6
Other	141	22.0	7.1	7.1

[a] Excludes 414 patients for whom no drug abuse information was reported.

[b] Does not equal sum of drug abuse categories, which are not mutually exclusive; approximately 2% of patients had more than one drug of abuse reported during this time period.

TABLE 18.25

Termination Rates within Six Months for Patients First Admitted to NYC MMTP November, 1970–October, 1973 and Still Active on December 31, 1973; by Length of Time in Treatment and Reported Drug Abuse as of December 31, 1973

Status as of 12/31/73		Number of Patients[a]	Termination Rate (%) within 6 Months for		
Months in Treatment	Drug(s) of Abuse		All Reasons	Vol. Withdrawal	Admin. Cause
All	None	7957	13.9	6.0	2.2
	One/more	1337	20.9	5.5	7.0
2–6	None	1485	16.8	4.9	3.0
	One/more	209	27.3	5.7	6.7
7–12	None	1613	15.7	7.0	3.1
	One/more	279	24.0	6.1	8.6
13–18	None	2217	12.9	5.7	1.9
	One/more	439	19.1	5.0	7.1
19–24	None	1153	13.3	6.0	2.1
	One/more	185	17.3	4.9	4.9
Over 24	None	1489	10.9	6.3	1.0
	One/more	225	17.8	5.8	7.1

[a] Excludes 414 patients for whom no drug abuse information was reported.

19

Readmission of Patients following Termination from the Maintenance Program

INTRODUCTION

Through the end of 1974, 10,401 patients were terminated for causes other than death, following their first admission to the New York City Methadone Maintenance Treatment Program (NYC MMTP). In this chapter, the subsequent readmission experience of these individuals will be presented.

The NYC MMTP has consistently encouraged patients to apply for readmission if they wish to resume treatment. Even in the initial years of the Program's operation, when long waiting lists existed, former patients were given highest priority for prompt readmission (see p. 62).

Since the NYC MMTP is only one of more than 40 programs providing methadone treatment in the metropolitan New York City area, the observed readmission rates presented here understate the extent to which methadone treatment was resumed by patients discharged from the Program. Data were not available to determine the participation rate of former patients in other methadone programs.

METHODOLOGY

Readmission data were available through June, 1975 providing a minimum of 6 months follow-up for all patients terminated through the end of 1974.

Using life-table methods, and excluding patients terminated because of death, cumulative first readmission rates were determined. The elapsed time (i.e., the "inactive period") was calculated from the date of last medication to the date methadone administration was resumed.

Separate readmission rates were calculated for subgroups of patients defined by length of time in treatment, reason for termination, and by year of termination. In addition, the retention rates following the second enrollment in the NYC MMTP were determined.

RESULTS

Readmission Rates

Of the 10,401 patients who were terminated for the first time on or before December 31, 1974, for any reason other than death, 1908, or 18.3%, were readmitted through June 30, 1975.

All First Readmissions

Figure 19.1 shows the cumulative percentage of patients readmitted during the first 24 months subsequent to termination. The first 12 months show a

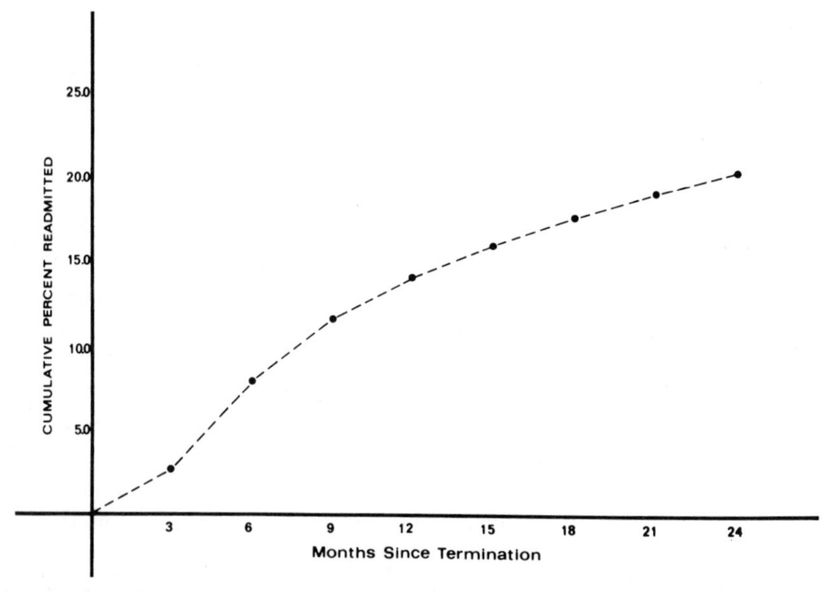

Figure 19.1. Cumulative percentage of patients readmitted to the NYC MMTP, by months since termination. Patients terminated, N = 10,401.

steep climb, with a cumulative rate of 13.9% at the end of one year. During the second year, readmissions continued to increase steadily, but somewhat more slowly, for a cumulative rate of 20.1% at the end of 24 months. The linear shape of the curve between 15 and 24 months gives no indication of when the readmission rate may be expected to taper off in subsequent intervals.

Readmission of Patients, by Length of Time in Treatment prior to Termination

Table 19.1 shows the cumulative readmission rates of patients terminated after less than 6 months, 7–12 months, 13–18 months, 19–24 months, and after more than 24 months following their initial admission to the NYC MMTP. There was no consistent association between length of time in treatment prior to termination and the likelihood of readmission. Those patients who terminated after more than 2 years in the Program had a cumulative readmission rate at 12 months which was similar to that of patients terminating within 6 months after their first admission.

Readmission of Patients, by Reason for First Termination

Separate life-table computations were performed for each of the four most frequent reasons for termination: voluntary withdrawal, failure to report, incarceration and administrative discharge. The results are presented in Table 19.2. Those who were terminated because of incarceration had the highest readmission rate; by 2 years after termination, over 25% had reentered the Program.

The voluntary withdrawal and failure-to-report cohorts exhibited similar readmission rates. It should be noted, however, that patients who simply drop out might be more likely than those voluntarily detoxifying to seek readmission in another program rather than return to the NYC MMTP. Similarly, patients discharged for administrative reasons, who had the lowest Program readmission rate of the four cohorts, might have a disproportionately high likelihood of applying for admission elsewhere.

Readmission by Year of Termination, for Patients Voluntarily Withdrawing from Treatment and for Those Terminated for All Other Reasons

The readmission experience of patients voluntarily withdrawing from treatment was studied for subgroups terminated in successive years from 1971 through 1974. The results are shown in Table 19.3.

Patients voluntarily leaving treatment in 1972 had a considerably lower readmission rate than did those who left for the same reason in 1971. From 1972 through 1974, however, there was a substantial increase in the

TABLE 19.1

Cumulative Readmission Rates following First Termination From NYC MMTP, by Duration of Initial Enrollment Prior to Termination

Months in Treatment during 1st Enrollment	Number of Terminations[a]	Cumulative Readmission Rate (Percent)	
		Within 12 Months	Within 24 Months
Total	10,401	13.9	20.1
1–6	4,726	13.9	19.7
7–12	2,223	15.3	21.8
13–18	1,580	12.1	19.3
19–24	1,095	12.1	*b*
Over 24	1,227	13.4	*b*

[a] Excludes terminations because of death.
[b] Not available due to insufficient period of observation following termination.

TABLE 19.2

Cumulative Readmission Rates following First Termination from NYC MMTP, by Specified Reason for First Termination

Reason for 1st Termination	Number of Terminations	Cumulative Readmission Rate (Percent)	
		Within 12 Months	Within 24 Months
Voluntary withdrawal	3049	14.5	20.1
Failure to report	2365	13.0	19.0
Incarceration	1856	19.0	27.3
Administrative cause	1874	8.8	14.4

readmission rates of the successive cohorts: within the first 12 months after termination, the readmission rate more than doubled, from 9% of those discharged in 1972, to 20% for those voluntarily withdrawing in 1974.

Table 19.4 shows the readmission rates for patients who terminated for reasons other than voluntary withdrawal (or death) in successive years from 1971 to 1974. While there was a drop in the 12-month readmission rate from 1971 to 1972, the marked increase in the readmission rate noted for patients voluntarily leaving treatment from 1972 to 1974 was not observed with respect to patients terminating for other reasons.

TABLE 19.3

Cumulative Readmission Rates following First Termination from NYC MMTP, for Voluntary Withdrawal Only, by Year of Termination

Year of 1st Termination	Number of Terminations	Cumulative Readmission Rate (Percent)	
		Within 12 Months	Within 24 Months
1971	151	15.9	21.2
1972	397	9.1	14.0
1973	1095	12.4	18.5
1974	1406	20.2	*a*

[a] Not available due to insufficient period of observation following termination.

TABLE 19.4

Cumulative Readmission Rates following First Termination from NYC MMTP, for All Reasons Except Voluntary Withdrawal and Death, by Year of Termination

Year of 1st Termination	Number of Terminations	Cumulative Readmission Rate (Percent)	
		Within 12 Months	Within 24 Months
1971	522	16.3	25.1
1972	1634	12.2	18.4
1973	2749	13.4	19.3
1974	2446	13.1	*a*

[a] Not available due to insufficient period of observation following termination.

TABLE 19.5

Cumulative Readmission Rates following First Termination from NYC MMTP, for Voluntary Withdrawal Only, by Duration of Initial Enrollment

Months in Treatment During 1st Enrollment	Number of Terminations	Cumulative Readmission Rate (Percent)	
		Within 12 Months	Within 24 Months
1–6	706	15.5	20.9
7–12	676	15.6	21.8
13–18	590	12.9	19.4
19–24	474	13.7	*a*
Over 24	603	13.7	*a*

[a] Not available due to insufficient period of observation following termination.

Readmission by Length of Time in Treatment prior to Termination for Voluntary Withdrawal Only

As shown in Table 19.5, there was very little difference in the readmission rates of patients who voluntarily withdrew from the NYC MMTP, regardless of length of time in treatment prior to termination.

Retention following First Readmission

The retention of patients following their first readmission to the NYC MMTP was determined using the methods described in the previous chapter. The data analyzed include all first readmissions through December, 1974, and the termination experience through March, 1975, thus providing at least 3 months of observation for all patients.

Figure 19.2 shows the retention in the Program of the 1528 patients readmitted following their first termination. For comparison, the retention curve for all first admissions is also shown. Readmissions were found to have considerably lower retention rates than first admissions throughout the

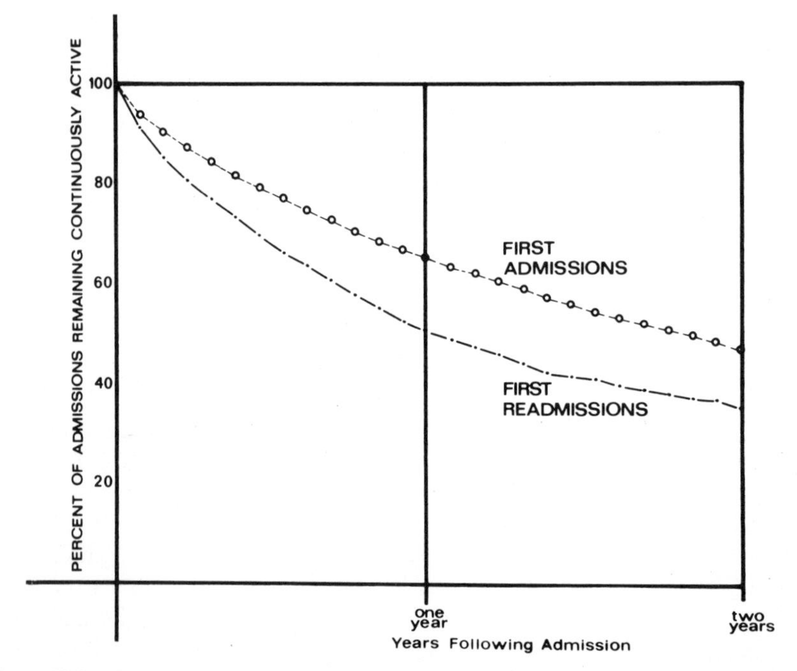

Figure 19.2. Retention in continuous active treatment in the NYC MMTP—First admissions and readmissions, 1971–1974. First admissions, $N = 20{,}653$ (includes 104 admissions during November and December, 1970); readmissions, $N = 1528$.

TABLE 19.6

One-Year Retention Rates following First Readmission to the NYC MMTP, 1971–1974, by Reason for First Termination

Reason for First Termination	Number of Readmissions	Retention (%) 1 Year after Readmission
Total	1528	50.5
Voluntary withdrawal	416	55.5
Incarceration	395	48.4
Failure to report	357	47.6
Administrative cause	193	46.9
Transfer to other program	167	54.1

TABLE 19.7

One-Year Retention Rates following First Readmission to the NYC MMTP, 1971–1974, by Length of Time in Treatment Prior to First Termination

Months in Treatment During 1st Enrollment	Number of Readmissions	Retention (%) 1 Year after Readmission
Total	1528	50.5
1–6	710	48.7
7–12	456	48.1
13–18	196	54.6
Over 18	166	60.1

2-year period of observation. At the end of one year following enrollment, the retention rate was 50.5% for readmissions, compared to 65.3% for first admissions; at the end of two years, the rates were 35.4% and 47.1%, respectively.

The 1-year retention rates* were calculated separately for patients readmitted following first termination for specific causes. As shown in Table 19.6, patients who initially withdrew from treatment voluntarily, and those transferred to other addiction programs, had the highest retention rates

*Because of the relatively small sizes of the cohorts, retention was not calculated beyond one year.

after readmission. The range among all subgroups, however, was less than 9 percentage points.

Retention rates one year after readmission were also determined for subgroups defined by length of time in treatment prior to first termination from the NYC MMTP. The results suggest a positive association between duration of treatment following first admission, and retention after readmission (Table 19.7).

DISCUSSION

Within 2 years following termination from the NYC MMTP, one out of five patients reentered the Program. This high readmission rate, especially in the face of the many alternative sources of methadone treatment currently available to patients in the metropolitan New York area, suggests that the treatment experience in the NYC MMTP is often perceived positively even among those who leave. This observation is particularly important since it applies not only to those who terminate voluntarily, but to those who presumably have a greater likelihood of relapse, i.e., patients terminated for incarceration and failure to report; even among patients terminated for administrative reasons, one out of seven was readmitted in less than 2 years.

Patients terminating in 1971 had a considerably higher readmission rate to the NYC MMTP than did those who left the Program in 1972. It is likely that in 1971, the last year in which long waiting lists for methadone treatment existed throughout the City, patients wishing to resume treatment had little option but to reapply to the NYC MMTP, which gave applicants for readmission top priority. By the end of 1972, many methadone programs, public as well as private, had exhausted their waiting lists and were offering immediate admission to all eligible applicants. It is probable that a substantial number of former patients availed themselves of these alternative sources of care in the last few years, and that the observed readmission rate of 20% is considerably lower than the actual frequency with which methadone treatment was resumed following discharge from the Program.

It is significant that the marked increase in readmissions in successive years from 1972 through 1974 was observed only for patients voluntarily withdrawing from treatment, while the experience of those leaving for other reasons remained relatively constant. Similarly, as has been noted (see Chapter 18), the rate of voluntary withdrawal increased considerably since 1972, while all other causes of termination showed no corresponding increase. It seems reasonable to conclude that these observations are related, and that new pressures are entering into the decision of patients to request detoxification. These pressures undoubtedly include the progressively more restrictive regulations imposed by Federal and State authorities on methadone programs and their patients, and the growing sentiment that the ultimate aim of addiction treatment must be a completely drug-free state.

In light of the findings presented here, it is imperative that the strong emphasis which detoxification from methadone maintenance receives today be reevaluated. Of the patients in the NYC MMTP who voluntarily withdrew from treatment, and who would presumably have the best prognosis after termination, one out of five returned to the Program within 2 years. Since the Federal Government has established an arbitrary goal of detoxification within 2 years for all patients, it is especially significant that those patients who had been enrolled in the NYC MMTP for at least 2 years before voluntarily discontinuing treatment had essentially the same readmission rate as those who left in less than 6 months.

Patients who resumed treatment in the NYC MMTP following termination had a lower retention rate than did first admissions to the Program. Nevertheless, half of all readmissions remained in treatment at least one year after their second enrollment. This suggests that many patients who reapply after discharge perceive a need for continued, long-term care. Furthermore, those patients who might have been expected to have the best prognosis after the first termination from the NYC MMTP, i.e., those voluntarily requesting detoxification and those with the longest initial treatment experience, had the highest retention rates upon readmission.

The number of patients resuming methadone maintenance treatment after termination attests to the complexity of the narcotic addiction problem, and serves as a reminder that the optimal duration of treatment has yet to be determined.

20

Reports to the New York City Narcotics Register before and after Admission to the Maintenance Program

INTRODUCTION AND METHODOLOGY

The Narcotics Register of the New York City Department of Health was established in 1964, and during the subsequent ten years received 800,000 reports from a wide variety of agencies and institutions having contact with addicts.* Each report (Appendix X) contains the name and other identifying data which are used to determine whether the individual is already "known" to the Register; for each person, a computerized "case file" is maintained which includes all reports which have been submitted, the source, and the date of contact. Accordingly, the Register lends itself to the study of the natural course of the addiction process, and the degree to which addiction treatment influences that course.

In the present study, the preadmission and postadmission Register reporting histories were compared for all patients entering the NYC MMTP, as well as for subgroups defined by duration of treatment in the Program. The reporting experience was determined separately with respect to criminal justice system (CJS) agencies,† and for all sources of reports. In addition, the

*Although the legal reporting requirement is not limited to narcotic addicts, fewer than 5% of all reports received through the end of 1974 specified drugs other than heroin. The operation of the Narcotics Register is described in more detail elsewhere (240–242).

†Criminal justice system agencies are defined as police, corrections, parole, and probation departments.

reporting history to the Register was analyzed for patients following termination from the Program for causes other than death.

RESULTS

Individuals Reported to the Narcotics Register in Each 6-Month Period during the 3 Years before and the 2 Years after Admission

The reporting history to the New York City Narcotics Register during the 3 years before and the 2 years after first admission to the NYC MMTP is shown in Figure 20.1. The analysis was limited to patients admitted to the Program in 1970–1972 (the Narcotics Register file used in this study was complete through June, 1975).

For all patients, the percentage reported prior to admission gradually increased during successive 6-month periods, reaching a peak in the half-year immediately preceding enrollment. Following admission, there was a steady decline in the reporting rate, and by 19–24 months after admission, the proportion reported was lower than at any time in the previous 4 years. These observations apply to reports from criminal justice system agencies as well as to reports from all sources.

The results varied considerably for patient subgroups defined by retention in the NYC MMTP. The greatest drop in postadmission reporting was experienced by those who remained in continuous treatment throughout the

TABLE 20.1

Reporting History to the NYC Narcotics Register prior to Termination from the NYC MMTP, by Retention in the Program[a]

		Percent of Active Patients Reported to the Register Each 6-Month Period after Admission					
		From All Agencies			From CJS Agencies		
Months in Treatment prior to Termination	Number of Patients	1–6 Months	7–12 Months	13–18 Months	1–6 Months	7–12 Months	13–18 Months
6 or less	2241	*b*	*b*	*b*	*b*	*b*	*b*
7–12	1399	35.9	*b*	*b*	18.5	*b*	*b*
13–18	1180	26.5	27.2	*b*	12.5	13.9	*b*
19–24	1037	23.9	19.8	22.1	10.3	10.9	11.9
Over 24	5866	18.7	13.5	12.0	7.9	6.2	5.4

[a] First NYC MMTP admissions in 1970–1972.

[b] Not applicable; cohort was not in active treatment throughout the 6-month period.

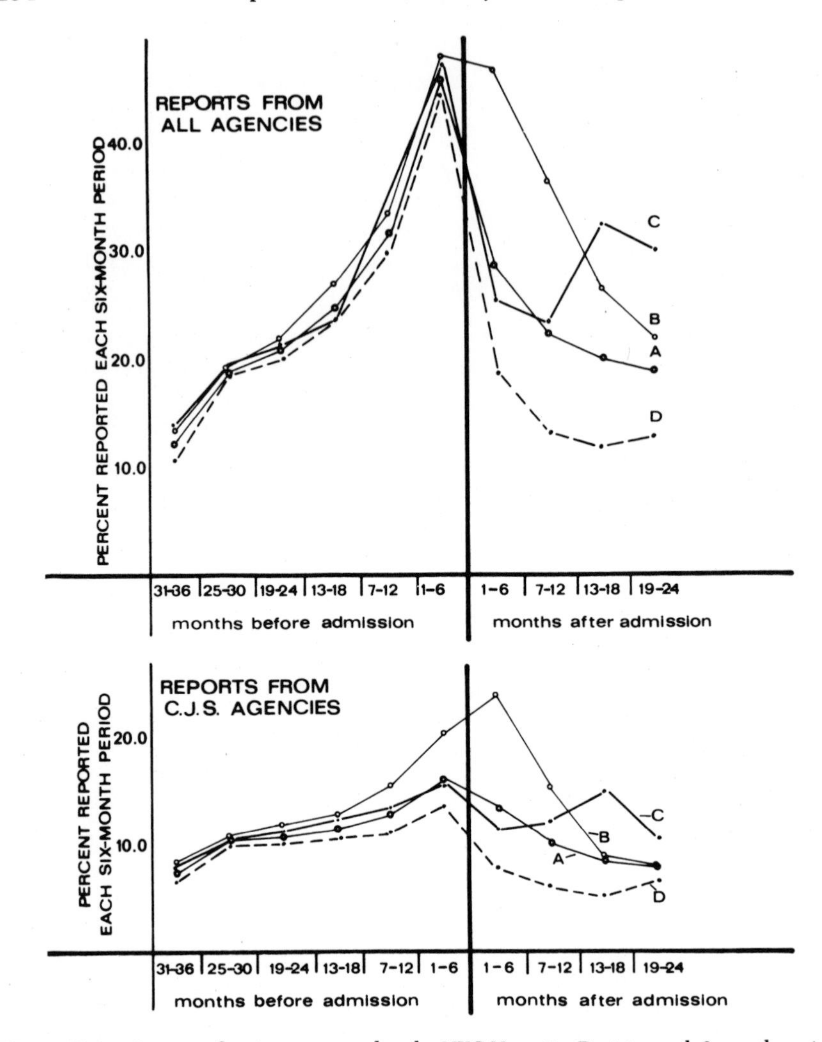

Figure 20.1. Percent of patients reported to the NYC Narcotics Register each 6-month period before and after admission to the NYC MMTP, by retention in the Program. First admissions to the NYC MMTP in 1970, 1971, and 1972. (A) All patients, $N = 11{,}723$; (B) patients terminated 1–12 months after admission, $N = 3640$; (C) patients terminated 13–24 months after admission, $N = 2217$; (D) patients remaining in treatment more than 24 months, $N = 5866$.

2-year period of observation. With respect to patients who left treatment within one year after admission, the proportion reported from CJS agencies actually increased following admission. Those who were terminated during the second year of treatment showed an initial decline in the rate of reports from all agencies, and from CJS agencies in particular, followed by an increase in the two 6-month periods in which termination occurred.

The data presented above describe the experience of all subjects following admission to the NYC MMTP, and reflect both in-treatment and posttermination reporting history to the Narcotics Register. In Table 20.1, the data are limited to the experience of patients actively enrolled in the Program throughout the 6-month period of observation. Consistently, the earlier termination occurred, the higher the previous reporting rate, from all agencies as well as from CJS agencies in particular. The disparity among cohorts defined by retention was observed from the very first 6-month period after admission; thus, compared to patients who remained active for at least 2 years, those terminated 19–24 months after admission had a 28% greater likelihood of being reported to the Register from any agency (23.9 versus 18.7%), and a 30% greater likelihood of being reported from a CJS agency (10.3 versus 7.9%), during the first 6 months following enrollment.

Comparison of Reporting History during the 2-Year Period before and the 2-Year Period after Admission

Table 20.2 shows, by length of time in treatment, the proportion of patients reported to the Narcotics Register at least once during the 2 years before admission, and the proportion reported at least once during the 2 years after beginning treatment in the NYC MMTP. Among patients terminated within 12 months, there was very little change in the likelihood of

TABLE 20.2

Reporting History to the NYC Narcotics Register during the Two Years before and the Two Years after Admission to the NYC MMTP, by Retention in the Program[a]

		Percent of Patients Reported, and Change from Preadmission to Postadmission Period			
		From All Agencies		From CJS Agencies	
Months in Treatment Prior to Termination	Number of Patients	2 Years before Admission	2 Years after Admission	2 Years before Admission	2 Years after Admission
Total	11,723	74.3	56.5 (−24.0%)	40.2	31.4 (−21.9%)
12 or less	3,640	75.9	73.5 (−3.2%)	45.2	42.6 (−5.8%)
13–24	2,217	75.0	66.1 (−11.9%)	41.2	37.8 (−8.3%)
Over 24	5,866	73.0	42.3 (−42.1%)	36.7	22.1 (−39.8%)

[a] First NYC MMTP admissions in 1970–1972.

being reported to the Register before and after enrollment, from CJS agencies and from all sources. A decline of approximately 10% in CJS and in total reporting was noted for patients terminated during their second year of treatment, while the greatest decline, about 40%, was experienced by patients who remained in the Program continuously throughout the 2 years of observation. Among the latter group, almost 60% were never reported in the 24 months after treatment began, and approximately 80% were not reported from a criminal justice agency.

Reports to the Narcotics Register following Termination from the NYC MMTP

The analysis of posttermination reporting history to the New York City Narcotics Register was limited to patients leaving the NYC MMTP during the first 2 years after admission, since patients terminated more than 2 years following enrollment would not have had a sufficient period of observation after leaving the Program. For the same reason, only patients whose first NYC MMTP admission occurred prior to 1974 were included in the study. Patients terminated because of death were excluded from the base.

Using life-table methods, the cumulative percentage of patients having one or more reports to the Register after termination, from CJS agencies and from all sources, was determined. As shown in Figure 20.2, almost half of the 7708 former patients included in the study were reported at least once, from any agency, during the first 6 months after discharge; by the end of 36 months, the proportion exceeded 70%.

With respect to criminal justice system agencies, almost 25% of the patients were reported from police, corrections, parole, or probation departments during the initial 6 months after termination; by the end of the third year after discharge, over 40% had been reported by CJS agencies.

Table 20.3 shows the proportion of patients, grouped by length of time in treatment prior to discharge, who were reported to the Narcotics Register from all agencies, and from CJS agencies in particular, during the first 12 months following termination. For comparison, the reporting history of each subgroup during the 12 months immediately preceding enrollment in the Program is also shown.

Overall, the likelihood of being reported to the Narcotics Register during the year preceding admission and in the first 12 months after termination was very similar; this was true with respect to reports from all agencies as well as for reports from criminal justice system agencies in particular. Patients who remained in treatment for at least one year after admission, however, showed a reduction in likelihood of being reported from any source, and specifically from criminal justice system agencies.

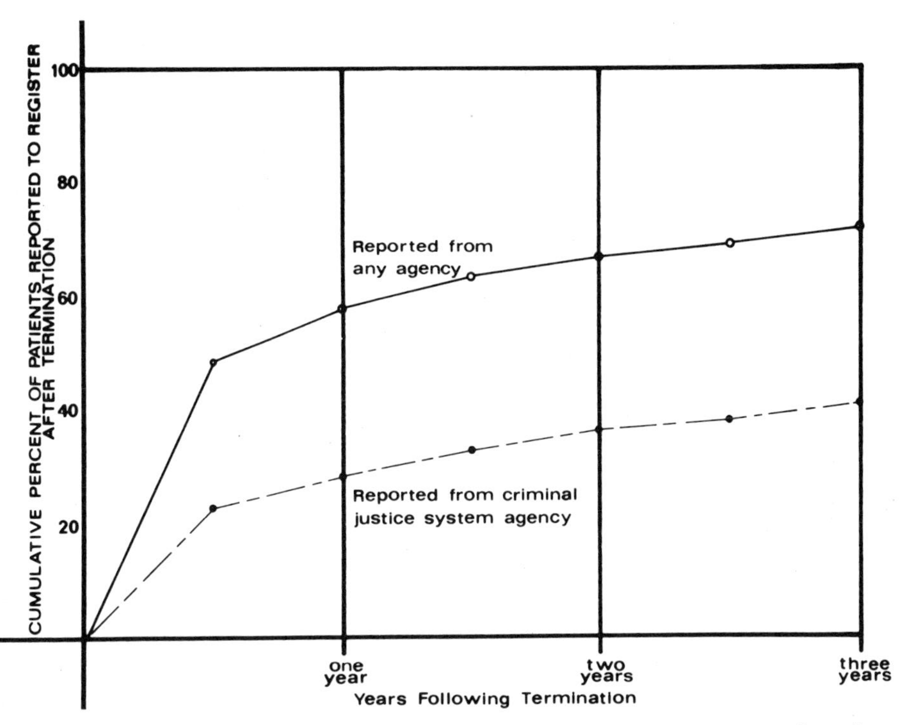

Figure 20.2. Cumulative percent of patients reported to the NYC Narcotics Register from all agencies and from criminal justice agencies, during the first three years following termination from the NYC MMTP. Criminal justice agencies are defined as police, corrections, parole and probation departments.

The posttermination reporting history differed markedly depending on the reason for termination from the NYC MMTP (Table 20.4). Patients who voluntarily withdrew from treatment were far less likely to be reported subsequently than were those who terminated for other reasons, and the differences were more marked the longer the initial period of treatment in the Program. This was especially true in the case of CJS reports: of those patients terminated within 6 months after admission, 19% of voluntary withdrawals were reported to the Register from CJS agencies in the following 12 months, compared to 34% of those leaving treatment for all other causes; in the case of patients terminated after 19–24 months, the corresponding percentages were 7% and 29%, respectively. The increasing discrepancy between the two groups reflects the fact that, for voluntary withdrawals only, longer duration of treatment was associated with a markedly lower likelihood of a subsequent report to the Narcotics Register.

TABLE 20.3

Percent of Patients Reported to the NYC Narcotics Register, from All Agencies and from Criminal Justice System Agencies, during the 12 Months Preceding Admission and 12 Months after Termination; by Length of Time in Treatment prior to Termination from the NYC MMTP

Months in Treatment prior to Termination	Number of Patients[a]	Percent of Patients Reported during Specified Interval			
		From All Agencies		From CJS Agencies	
		12 Months before Admission	12 Months after Termination	12 Months before Admission	12 Months after Termination
Total	7708	63.9	58.0	28.0	28.3
1–6	3497	64.7	61.3	28.1	31.3
7–12	2107	63.0	59.9	29.4	29.1
13–18	1111	64.7	51.6	26.8	23.7
19–24	993	61.9	46.8	26.2	19.2

[a] Patients first admitted to the NYC MMTP 1970–1973, and terminated within 24 months after enrollment.

TABLE 20.4

Percent of Terminated Patients Reported to the NYC Narcotics Register, from All Agencies and from Criminal Justice System Agencies, during the First 12 Months Following Termination for Voluntary Withdrawal and for All Other Causes; by Length of Time in Treatment in the NYC MMTP

Months in Treatment Prior to Termination	Reason for Termination	Number of Patients[a]	Percent of Patients Reported during First 12 Months after Termination	
			From All Agencies	From CJS Agencies
Total	Voluntary withdrawal	2041	41.8	13.6
	All other causes	5667	63.7	33.6
1–6	Voluntary withdrawal	574	50.3	19.0
	All other causes	2923	63.4	33.7
7–12	Voluntary withdrawal	636	44.0	13.6
	All other causes	1471	66.7	35.8
13–18	Voluntary withdrawal	403	32.5	11.0
	All other causes	708	62.4	30.9
19–24	Voluntary withdrawal	428	33.0	6.8
	All other causes	565	57.3	28.7

[a] Patients first admitted to the NYC MMTP 1970–1973, and terminated within 24 months after enrollment.

DISCUSSION

The reporting history to the New York City Narcotics Register is a readily quantifiable, independent parameter which is useful in assessing outcome of addiction treatment. For all patients admitted to the NYC MMTP in its first 2 years of operation, a considerable reduction in the frequency of Register reports followed enrollment in the Program. The decline, which was observed with respect to reports from CJS agencies as well as those from all sources, was especially noteworthy since it represented a sharp reversal in the preadmission reporting pattern. The peak reporting rate during the 6 months just prior to admission was the culmination of a trend which was apparent over the entire 3-year period preceding enrollment. Furthermore, the reduction in reporting history was not merely in relation to the immediate preadmission interval; in the 2 years after admission, 20–25% fewer patients were reported than in the same time period before admission. This improvement, therefore, is not an artifact of an unrepresentative experience just before entrance into the Program (243–245).

Many factors, extraneous to the treatment services per se, may have an impact on outcome measures. Priorities of law enforcement agencies can greatly influence arrests; the availability and quality of illicit narcotics may affect the natural course of the addiction process, and especially the decision to enter and remain in treatment; changing patterns of nonopiate drug usage by the addict and ex-addict population can be an important determinant of adjustment during and after admission to an addiction treatment program; and social and economic conditions in the general community will also inevitably play a role. These and other external factors do not explain the findings reported here, however. There is a striking association of decreased reporting, from criminal justice agencies and from all sources, with increasing exposure to treatment services. The postadmission reporting history of patients leaving treatment within one year, compared to the experience of the same cohort prior to admission, is almost unchanged. On the other hand, patients remaining for at least 2 full years of treatment show a marked reduction in likelihood of being reported to the Register, and those with only 13–24 months of treatment have results which fall between these 2 extremes.

Nevertheless, it is still not possible to unequivocally attribute to methadone maintenance treatment the improvement which is observed. Differences inherent in the patients themselves may play a major role in determining outcome. In this regard, it is important to note that patients in the study who were terminated had a considerably greater likelihood of being reported to the Register *while still in treatment* than those who were not subsequently discharged, and this disparity was observed long before termination occurred. This suggests that certain patients may have a poorer prognosis from the outset, and that treatment has only limited effectiveness in overcoming the factors which predispose to termination, and to contacts with criminal justice and other agencies which report to the Register. On the other hand, if such predisposing factors exist, it has not been possible to identify them, and they appear to have little, if any, impact on the *preadmission* course. In contrast to the marked differences in postadmission Narcotics Register reporting history associated with varying lengths of time in treatment, the experience before enrollment for the various cohorts generally was similar. In a previous chapter, it was noted that patient subgroups defined by demographic, social, and drug-use characteristics have remarkably similar retention rates. In addition, earlier studies have demonstrated that the preadmission trend with respect to increasing frequency of arrest continues in the interval between application for admission and initiation of treatment (246), suggesting that the motivation to seek treatment is not, by itself, enough to change an addict's course.

The precise determinants of successful treatment outcome, and their relative importance, remain a matter of speculation. Nevertheless, the data presented here provide strong support for the contention that methadone maintenance treatment is associated with major benefits to patients as well as to the general community, and that the extent of these benefits is directly related to the duration of treatment which the patients receive.

This conclusion receives added support from the findings with respect to Narcotics Register reporting history after discharge from the NYC MMTP. Although it is not possible to equate absence of a report to the Register with abstinence, the converse is valid: a report to the Register following termination from treatment is presumptive evidence of active drug use. For this reason, patients discharged from treatment can be examined for minimal frequency of recidivism, by using the reporting history to the Narcotics Register; similarly, comparisons of recidivism can be made between subgroups defined by length of time in treatment and reason for termination.

The findings presented here suggest that resumption of drug use is the rule, rather than the exception, following termination from methadone maintenance treatment. Within the first 6 months after medication was discontinued, almost 50% of all patients had been reported to the Register at least once, and by the end of 3 years the proportion had increased to 75%. Furthermore, these figures understate the actual rate of recidivism, since reporting is not complete from all agencies, some drug users will manage to avoid contact with a reporting source, and an unknown proportion of former patients will leave the New York City metropolitan area.

Voluntary withdrawals, who represent over 25% of all terminations from the NYC MMTP, have a strikingly different experience than patients discontinuing treatment for other reasons. In addition to a considerably lower overall likelihood of being reported to the Register after leaving the Program, patients who voluntarily request detoxification have a posttermination course which is highly correlated with the duration of treatment prior to discharge. Voluntary withdrawals with the longest duration of treatment have the most favorable outcomes, particularly as measured by reports from the criminal justice system.

It must be emphasized that voluntary withdrawals are a self-selected subgroup of the patient population. As external pressures, including arbitrary limits on the duration of treatment permitted by regulatory agencies, play an increasing role in determining retention, the relatively positive outcome of these patients, as suggested by their reporting history to the Narcotics Register, may be adversely affected. Additionally, it remains to be seen whether the lower reporting rates to the Register associated with voluntary termination and with increased duration of treatment persist when observation following discharge is extended beyond the period of follow-up presented here.

21

The Ambulatory Detoxification Program: Duration of Treatment and Referral to Long-Term Treatment Programs

INTRODUCTION AND METHODOLOGY

In this chapter the experience of the New York City Ambulatory Detoxification Program from its inception in July, 1971, through the end of 1974, is analyzed with respect to its primary objectives: to eliminate physical dependence on narcotics through the administration of decreasing doses of methadone; to provide a safe, legal and effective alternative to the physical need to self-administer illicit narcotics; and to motivate patients to seek long-term treatment for their narcotic addiction and provide referral services to long-term treatment programs.

Data regarding patient stay are derived from the daily methadone accounting forms (Appendix VII) of the individual Program clinics. For the purpose of this study, "referral" to long-term programs indicates that confirmation was received that patients actually entered treatment within 30 days after completion of detoxification, following referral by the NYC ADP. For the remainder, no distinction is made between those patients who were not referred, who failed to follow through or were rejected by the recipient program, and those who entered treatment more than 30 days after referral.

TABLE 21.1

Average Duration of Treatment and Percentage of Patients Completing the Prescribed Treatment Regimen in the New York City Ambulatory Detoxification Program, Each Six-Month Period July, 1971–December, 1974

		Six-Month Period of Admission						
		1971	1972		1973		1974	
	Total	Jul–Dec	Jan–Jun	Jul–Dec	Jan–Jun	Jul–Dec	Jan–Jun	Jul–Dec
Number of admissions	63,559	3,238	9,488	9,018	9,463	9,471	10,879	12,002
Average stay (days)[a]	6.0	5.4	5.3	5.9	6.0	6.4	6.3	6.2
Percent of patients completing prescribed detoxification regimen	43.2	46.7	45.9	38.8	41.1	45.2	40.7	46.1

[a] The maximum duration of treatment was increased from seven to fourteen days in the latter half of 1972.

RESULTS

Duration of Treatment and "Completion Rate"

Table 21.1 shows the average number of days that patients remained in treatment in the NYC ADP, and the percentage of patients who completed the detoxification course prescribed. The data are presented for each 6-month period through the end of 1974.

The average patient stay was 6 days. Although Program policy was modified during the latter half of 1972 to permit patients to remain for a maximum of 14 days (compared to the previous limit of 7 days), the average duration of treatment increased only slightly following the change.

Overall, slightly more than 40% of the patients entering the NYC ADP (i.e., those who received at least one dose of methadone) remained for the full detoxification course prescribed. There was little change in the "completion rate" in successive 6-month periods of observation.

Referrals to Long-Term Treatment Programs

Of the 63,559 admissions to the NYC ADP between July, 1971, and December, 1974, 9350 (15%) entered a long-term addiction treatment program within thirty days of referral. The proportion of completed referrals varied considerably (from 8% to 20% in different 6-month periods), but there was no consistent pattern over the 3.5 years of observation reported here (Table 21.2). More than 50% of the completed referrals were to ambulatory drug-free programs.

Although variations were observed in the proportion of patients in successive cohorts who entered different treatment modalities, an increase in completed referrals to one type of treatment program was generally not associated with a decrease in the proportion entering others. In other words, the fluctuations were not simply the result of inverse relationships between modalities.

Comparison of First Admissions and Readmissions to the NYC ADP (January–March, 1974)

The experience of first admissions and readmissions to the Program during the first 3 months of 1974 was compared with respect to average patient stay and likelihood of entering long-term treatment following detoxification. As shown in Table 21.3, the only major difference in the demographic characteristics of the two groups was that whites were relatively underrepresented

TABLE 21.2

Percent of NYC ADP Patients Entering Long-Term Treatment Programs Following Referral, Each Six-Month Period July, 1971–December, 1974

		Six-Month Period of Admission						
		1971	1972		1973		1974	
	Total	Jul–Dec	Jan–Jun	Jul–Dec	Jan–Jun	Jul–Dec	Jan–Jun	Jul–Dec
Total Admissions	63,559 (100%)	3,238 (100%)	9,488 (100%)	9,018 (100%)	9,463 (100%)	9,471 (100%)	10,879 (100%)	12,002 (100%)
Referrals to								
All modalities	14.7%	14.9%	8.2%	13.7%	17.2%	16.1%	19.8%	13.0%
Methadone maintenance[a]	4.2%	2.9%	0.9%	0.7%	5.8%	6.0%	6.7%	5.0%
"Methadone-to-abstinence"	1.0%	*b*	*b*	*b*	*b*	*b*	4.4%	1.5%
Ambulatory drug-free	7.7%	9.6%	6.2%	10.5%	7.5%	8.4%	7.9%	5.7%
Residential drug-free	1.7%	2.3%	1.0%	2.6%	3.9%	1.7%	0.9%	0.8%

[a] Includes admissions to the NYC MMTP as well as to unaffiliated programs.
[b] "Methadone-to-abstinence" programs were established in New York City in February, 1974.

TABLE 21.3

Age, Sex, and Ethnic Distributions of First Admissions and Readmissions to the NYC ADP, January–March, 1974

Demographic Characteristic	Total Admissions	First Admissions	Readmissions
Number of Admissions	5102 (100%)	2296 (100%)	2806 (100%)
Age (years)			
Under 18	0.2%	0.4%	0.1%
18–20	11.0%	11.2%	10.9%
21–25	41.5%	39.5%	42.5%
26–30	24.1%	25.0%	23.6%
Over 30	23.3%	23.9%	22.9%
Sex			
Men	80.4%	80.8%	80.1%
Women	19.6%	19.2%	19.9%
Ethnic			
White	10.4%	14.1%	7.4%
Black	58.8%	56.4%	60.8%
Hispanic	26.8%	25.9%	27.6%
Other	3.9%	3.6%	4.2%

among the readmissions (7%, compared to 14% of those entering the NYC ADP for the first time).

With regard to patient stay and the overall likelihood of entering long-term treatment within thirty days of referral, the results of first admissions and readmissions were almost identical (Table 21.4). The proportion of patients in each group who entered each of the long-term treatment modalities varied only slightly, with relatively fewer readmissions entering methadone maintenance treatment, and more enrolling in ambulatory drug-free programs.

DISCUSSION

As measured by the objectives of the Program, the New York City Ambulatory Detoxification Program achieved a high level of success during its first 3.5 years of operation:

From July, 1971 through the end of 1974, the Program provided almost 375,000 patient-days of treatment

Over 40% of the 63,500 admissions completed the full course of treatment prescribed

TABLE 21.4

Average Patient Stay and Referral Experience of First Admissions and Readmissions to the NYC ADP, January–March, 1974

Treatment Outcome	Total Admissions	First Admissions	Readmissions
Number of Admissions	5102 (100%)	2296 (100%)	2806 (100%)
Average stay (days)	6.4	6.5	6.4
Referrals to			
All modalities	19.4%	19.3%	19.4%
Methadone maintenance[a]	7.1%	8.1%	6.3%
"Methadone-to-abstinence"[b]	0.6%	0.5%	0.6%
Ambulatory drug-free	10.7%	9.3%	11.8%
Residential drug-free	0.9%	1.4%	0.7%

[a] Includes admissions to the NYC MMTP as well as to unaffiliated programs.
[b] "Methadone-to-abstinence" programs were established in February, 1974.

More than 9000 addicts (15% of all admissions) entered long-term treatment programs as a result of referral by the NYC ADP staff

The precise reasons for this success are not clear. Since the treatment regimen lasts no more than 2 weeks, there are no supportive services in areas such as employment, housing, or legal assistance to explain the attractiveness of the Program, or its ability to retain patients after enrollment. Similarly, the demand for treatment and the average patient stay were quite constant, and cannot be explained as a consequence of a reduction in heroin availability in New York City, or of varying degrees of pressure from law enforcement activities. The acknowledged black market in methadone would appear to rule out the possibility that addicts were simply seeking to "supplement" their narcotic consumption; the price of 30 or 40 mg of illicit methadone (the maximum dose administered by the Program) has never been more than about $5.00, and it is most improbable that a Program operated by the City of New York could compete with the street seller if medication were the only attraction.

Whatever the underlying reasons, the extraordinary demand for admission clearly reflects the widespread motivation among the addict population to eliminate, or at least to reduce markedly, physical dependence on illicit narcotics. The adequacy of a 1-week ambulatory detoxification regimen, as perceived by the patients themselves, is indicated by the average patient stay of approximately 6 days. Very few patients availed themselves of the option to remain for a second week when the Program policy regarding duration of treatment was changed in the latter half of 1972 (this experience is further evidence that patients generally were not attracted merely by the prospect of receiving "free narcotics").

The NYC ADP has never required a commitment to enter long-term addiction treatment following detoxification as a condition of enrollment. Since maintenance and drug-free treatment programs were readily available to all addicts in New York City by 1973, those addicts who sought admission to the Ambulatory Detoxification Program were obviously not willing, at the outset, to accept ongoing treatment to achieve rehabilitation and abstinence from illicit drug use. The fact that 15% of all admissions to the NYC ADP not only agreed to referral, but followed through and actually began treatment in a long-term program, is a remarkable achievement.

The similarity of patients entering the NYC ADP for the first time to those who had previously been enrolled is striking. The two groups in the sample that was studied were essentially indistinguishable, both demographically and in terms of treatment outcome; they did not vary with respect to average stay, or likelihood of referral to long-term treatment programs after detoxification. Since there is no identifiable subgroup of addicts "using" the Ambulatory Detoxification Program as a substitute for maintenance or drug-free treatment, the policy of encouraging readmission of those patients who initially do not accept referral should be continued.

It is noteworthy that the percentages of patients entering the different types of programs varied independently of one another. From 1972 (the last year in which waiting lists for methadone maintenance existed) to 1973, the proportion of NYC ADP admissions entering maintenance programs after detoxification increased from 0.8% to 5.9%; the total ambulatory and residential drug-free referrals, however, remained essentially unchanged (10.1% and 10.8% in 1972 and 1973, respectively). This suggests that the motivation to seek long-term treatment is selective, and supports the premise that the widest possible diversity of treatment options should be made available.

APPENDIXES I—X

Appendix I

Organization of the New York City Methadone Maintenance Treatment Program*

I. General

Each clinic is an integral component of the overall Program, and must adhere to the policies and procedures stipulated by the Program Director and the Central Office staff. The New York City Methadone Maintenance Treatment Program is *not* a funding agency which supports numerous individual, autonomous units.

The Program is *service* oriented and not experimental. Modifications in the operation of clinics which pose a risk to the patients will not be permitted. Final decisions regarding deviation from procedures specified by Central Office will rest with the Program Director.

Back-up supportive services to all clinics in the areas of staff training, patient vocational services, legal assistance, general social welfare resources, and educational information will be provided by the NYC MMTP Central Office.

II. The Two Principal Treatment Components of the Program Are:

A. *Contract Units*

These clinics are administered under 1-year renewal contracts between the New York City Department of Health and voluntary hospitals, the Health and Hospitals Corporation, or other nonprofit service organizations. The capacity of individual clinics varies from 150 to 600 patients.

The staffing pattern for a treatment unit of 300 patients is†:

*From the New York City Department of Health Methadone Maintenance Treatment Program Policy and Procedures Manual, January, 1974, Section A.

†Modifications in the staffing pattern are permitted, with prior approval of the Program Director.

Medical Director (M.D.)
Unit Supervisor
Assistant Unit Supervisor, or Senior Counselor
Head Nurse
Staff Nurses (3)
Counselors (6)
Assistant Counselors (2)
Secretaries (2)

Treatment units operated under contract are staffed by personnel hired by the contract agency. Central Office assists contract agencies in recruiting candidates for unit staff positions if requested to do so.

Approval by the Program Director of his (her) designee must be obtained by the agency *prior* to the appointment of candidates for the following positions:

Medical Director
Unit Supervisor
Assistant Unit Supervisor
Assistant Counselor

All contracts specify that the Program Director has the authority to require the termination of any staff member of the clinic who fails to comply with the standards and procedures of the Program.

B. *Central Units*

These clinics are staffed by personnel hired by Central Office, subject to the policies of the New York City Department of Personnel.

Staffing patterns are the same as for contract units.

III. Job Specifications and Qualifications for Staff of Treatment Units

A. *General policy*

It is the unequivocal policy of the NYC MMTP that discrimination against job applicants on the basis of sex,age, ethnicity, or sexual preference is not permitted.

No applicant for any position at a treatment unit can be employed by a unit at which he or she has been a patient within the past year.

B. *Medical Director*

General statement of duties and responsibilities: under the direction of the Director of the NYC MMTP and the head of the contract agency's supervising department, will have ultimate responsibility for all aspects of the clinic operation.

Qualifications. Must be currently licensed to practice medicine in New York State. Specialty training and certification in internal medicine or psychiatry is desirable but not essential. Also desirable is some background, association or experience with problems of addiction and/or community medicine; a sensitivity to and understanding of the general life style, emotional and behavioral patterns often associated with narcotics addiction.

Job Description. The Medical Director will have the ultimate responsibility for the operation of the clinic. He (she) will also provide the initial and annual medical examination of patients, and ongoing medical evaluation and treatment. This responsibility will be met by the physician either through services rendered directly or through appropriate referral as specified in the contract and the Program's Procedure Manual.

The Medical Director will work closely with the Unit Supervisor and counselors in assessing the overall progress of patients, participate in regularly scheduled staff meetings, and encourage the joint effort of all staff for maximum effectiveness of the clinic and achievement of Program goals.

C. *Unit Supervisor*

General statement of duties and responsibilities: has general administrative responsibility for the clinic's operation and ensures that all policies and procedures of the NYC MMTP are complied with.

Qualifications. Baccalaureate Degree and four years of full-time, paid experience in health care delivery, social work, rehabilitation, counseling, community or addiction services, public health, social research, public administration, or related fields; or a satisfactory equivalent combination of education and experience, generally with relevant experience substituting for education on a year-for-year basis. In either case, candidates must have a minimum of one year of experience in a managerial and/or supervisory capacity.

Job Description. Provides administrative supervision for the staff, holds regularly scheduled supervisory conferences, and conducts staff meetings; initiates ongoing training programs on matters of policy, procedures, and overall treatment goals; maintains administrative liaison with the Central Office staff and is responsible for submitting all reports as required by the Program Director; supervises and coordinates all staff activities of the unit.

D. *Assistant Supervisor/Senior Counselor*

General statement of duties and responsibilities: under the direction of the Unit Supervisor, assumes delegated responsibility for clinic administration.

Qualifications. A Baccalaureate Degree and 2 years of full-time, paid experience in health care delivery, social work, rehabilitation, counseling, community or addiction services, public health, social research, public administration, or related fields, or a satisfactory equivalent combination of education and experience.

Job Description: Supervises and provides ongoing training for the counseling staff, and coordinates staff activities. Assists Unit Supervisor in maintaining administrative liaison with the Central Office staff. Assumes the responsibilities of the Unit Supervisor in his (her) absence.

E. *Counselor*

General statement of duties and responsibilities: under the supervision of the Unit Supervisor or Assistant Unit Supervisor/Senior Counselor, performs full range of duties in counseling patients under treatment.

Qualifications. Baccalaureate Degree plus a minimum of one year of full-time, paid experience in social work, community or addiction services, rehabilitation, counseling, or related fields. Relevant full-time paid experience may be substituted for the educational requirement on a year-for-year basis. Candidates for this position must have a High School diploma.

Job Description: the counselor will be supportive to all patients on his (her) assigned caseload. This support will include, but not be limited to:

Guiding the patient in dealing with personal problems
Aiding the patient in outside adjustment by effecting referrals to relevant social service agencies
Aiding the patient in obtaining vocational, occupational and educational assistance
Where appropriate, acting as advocate and mediator in assisting the patient in contacts with the courts and various service agencies
Maintaining for each patient in his (her) caseload appropriate records as stipulated by Program policy

F. Assistant Counselor

General statement of duties and responsibilities: under the direction of the Unit Supervisor or Assistant Supervisor/Senior Counselor, assists in the care and management of patients in the clinic.

Qualifications. High School diploma or High School Equivalency diploma. Assistant Counselors must themselves be methadone patients or former methadone patients who have been in treatment in a program approved by the NYC MMTP Director for at least one year. An applicant must have at least 6 months of paid working experience within the past year, and can not be hired by a clinic in which he (she) has been a patient within the last year.

Job Description. Acts as liaison between the patient and the counselor, nurse, and doctor. Assists patients in their daily activities. Responds to questions and concerns about the medication, side effects and adjustment problems and, when necessary, refers such problems to appropriate medical or nursing staff members. Under the supervision of the Unit Supervisor or Assistant Unit Supervisor/Senior Counselor, may provide ongoing counseling support to a small caseload of patients.

Requirements for Promotion. Consideration may be given to promotion of the Assistant Counselor to the position of Counselor after one year of employment with the Program.

G. Head Nurse

General statement of duties and responsibilities: supervises activities of the nursing staff and ensures that all policies and procedures of the NYC MMTP regarding medical records are complied with.

Qualifications. Registered Nurse, licensed in New York State, with at least 2 years of paid nursing experience.

Job Description. Under the supervision of the Unit Supervisor, shares responsibility for the management of patients and for the functioning of the clinic in fulfilling the objectives of the Program.

Under the direction of the physician, and in consultation with the Unit Supervisor, has responsibility for the coordination of medical services for patients, including referrals for medical and psychiatric diagnostic and/or therapeutic care. Organizes and coordinates the service of nursing personnel with other hospital departments. Is responsible for maintaining accurate medical records in accordance with NYC MMTP and regulatory agency requirements.

Supervises the nursing staff.

H. Staff Nurse

General statement of duties and responsibilities: under the direction of the Head Nurse, carries out nursing functions, medical record keeping and contributes to the overall care of patients.

Qualifications. Registered Nurse, licensed in New York State, with at least one year of nursing experience.

Job description. The Staff Nurse administers medication prescribed by the physician, and maintains all required records. With the approval of the Unit Supervisor, the nurse is strongly encouraged to assume responsibility for individual and group counseling of patients. Depending on the training and interests of the nursing staff, this need not be limited directly to health-related areas. The nurse also assists in making referrals for health care, and ensuring that follow-up information is received.

IV. Central Office Management Analyst

Under the direct supervision of the Director of Treatment Units, the Central Office Management Analyst is responsible for the support and monitoring of assigned clinics which operate under contract with the NYC MMTP.

The Management Analyst's primary responsibilities are to ensure that the clinics are operated in accordance with all contractual agreements and in conformity to NYC MMTP policies and procedures. This includes: quality of care, planning, coordination of services, acquisition of resources, fiscal accountability, compliance with regulatory agency requirements, and community relations.

Each Management Analyst is assigned responsibility for five to seven clinics, with an overall patient capacity of approximately 1800. Specific duties include:

- Assessment of quality of care by direct clinic visits, audit of patient records, analysis of program performance reports, and attendance at clinic staff meetings
- Planning for expansion, enhancement of services, problem-solving and training needs
- Coordination and integration of Central Office and extra-agency support services, e.g., employment, education, medical, legal and social welfare services
- Assists in recruitment and selection of clinic staff
- Assists in preparing clinic budgets, and in the ongoing monitoring of expenditures, voucher submission and reimbursement
- Ensures compliance with regulatory agency requirements, and participates, as the representative of the Program Director, in any discussions held with regulatory agency personnel regarding assigned clinics
- Provides information and guidance on implementation of new policies, procedures and regulatory agency requirements
- Ensures good relations with neighborhood communities through communications with appropriate local organizations
- Provides evaluations and recommendations to the Program Director regarding clinic performance

V. Orientation and Training of Clinic Personnel

All new personnel in contract and centrally operated clinics must participate in the orientation program conducted by Central Office as soon as possible after employment begins. In addition, all personnel are strongly encouraged to participate in the in-service training programs conducted by Central Office.

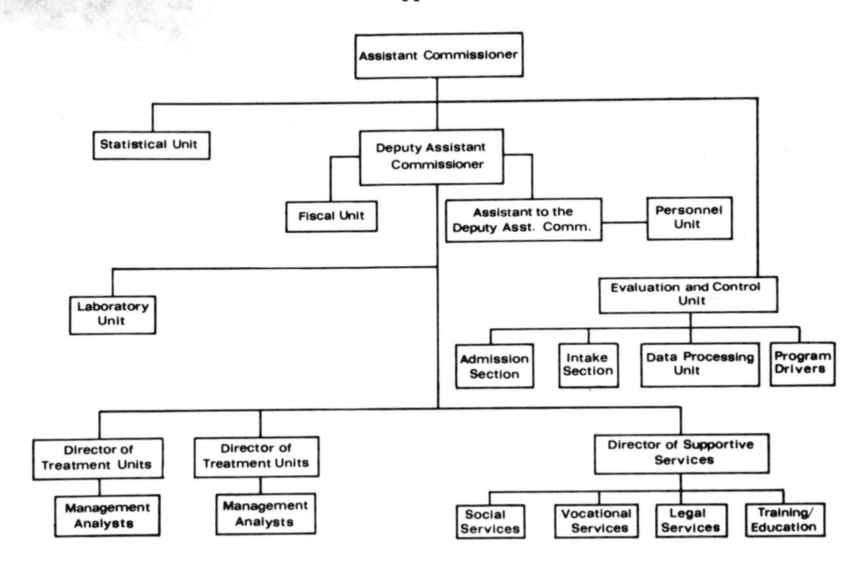

New York City Department of Health Methadone Maintenance Treatment Program Central Office—table of organization

Appendix II

UNIT 64 WEEK BEGINNING MONDAY 01/07/74 (65-70)

NYC HSA METHADONE MAINTENANCE PROGRAM
METHADONE DOSAGE AND PICKUP SCHEDULE

PAGE NO 1 (79-80 = "58")

PATIENT NAME MEDICAID NO./EXP. DATE	I.D. NO.	MONDAY	TUESDAY	WEDNESDAY	THURSDAY	FRIDAY	SATURDAY	SUNDAY	Subsequent Methadone Orders Recorded: DOSE	DURATION	P/U CODE	COMMENTS
		DOSE × DAYS = TOTAL RN	DOSE × DAYS = TOTAL RN	DOSE × DAYS = TOTAL RN	DOSE × DAYS = TOTAL RN	DOSE × DAYS = TOTAL RN	DOSE × DAYS = TOTAL RN	DOSE × DAYS = TOTAL RN				
	3-7	9-11 12 13-15 16	17-19 20 21-23 24	25-27 28 29-31 32	33-35 36 37-39 40	41-43 44 45-47 48	49-51 52 53-55 56	57-59 60 61-63 64				
B---, Herbert	01298	80x3=240			80x4=320				80	99	I	
H-------, Aaron	37728	60x2=120		60x2=120		60x3=180			70 80	10 99	4 4	
K-----, Spiro	12345	40x1=40	40x1=40	40x1=40	50x1=50	50x1=50	50x2=100		60 70 80	03 07 99	= = =	
L----, Franklin	53426	100x2=200	100x2=200	100x2=200		100x3=300			100	99	4	
R----------, Rosa	62101		70x2=140		70x2=140		70x3=210		60 50 40	07 07 99	N N N	
W---------, George	54321	60x1=60	60x2=120		60x2=120		60x2=120		60	99	F	

Appendix III

DO NOT WRITE IN THIS SECTION

CAL 1-5

THE NEW YORK CITY METHADONE MAINTENANCE TREATMENT PROGRAM APPLICATION FORM

(LAST NAME) 6-23

(FIRST AND MIDDLE NAMES) 24-41

ALIAS ____

(MOTHER'S FIRST NAME AND MAIDEN NAME) 42-62

(SOCIAL SECURITY NUMBER) 63-71

BIRTH DATE Month Day Year 72-77

SEX: 78 M F

ETHNIC GROUP (Circle One) 79
1. White 3. Puerto Rican
2. Black 4. Oriental
5 Other (specify) ____

PERMANENT MAILING ADDRESS: (Where mail can always reach you)

NUMBER AND STREET 6-35

APARTMENT 36-38

ZIP CODE 39-43

IN CARE OF 44-63

BOROUGH (Circle One) 64
1. Manhattan 2. The Bronx 3. Brooklyn 4. Queens 5. Staten Island 6. Other (specify): ____

TELEPHONE NUMBER 65-71

SOURCE OF REFERRAL (Circle One) 72
1. Inst./Agencies
2. Welfare
3. Hospital
4. Court/Police
5. Detox. Program
6. Other Drug Treatment Prog.
7. Drug Referral Program
8. Self
9. Family/Friends

U.S. VETERAN 73 YES NO

IF VETERAN YEAR OF DISCHARGE 74-75 1 9

DID HEROIN USE BEGIN IN SERVICE 76 YES NO

DID YOU SERVE IN SOUTHEAST ASIA 77 YES NO

NOW ON WELFARE 78 YES NO

NOW EMPLOYED 79 YES NO

TOTAL NUMBER OF ARRESTS 6-7

TOTAL NUMBER OF CONVICTIONS 8-9

NOW IN PRISON 10 YES NO

IF SENTENCED, EXPECTED RELEASE DATE 11-16 Month Day Year

AGE FIRST USED HEROIN 17-18

NUMBER YEARS DAILY HEROIN USE 19-20

DO NOT WRITE IN THIS SECTION 78-79

PRESENT HEROIN USE: COST PER DAY $ 21-23

NUMBER BAGS PER DAY 24-25

PRIMARY DRUG NOW USED ____

PREVIOUS ADDICTION TREATMENT 26 YES NO

IF PREVIOUS ADDICTION TREATMENT

METHADONE MAINTENANCE 27 YES NO

DRUG FREE PROGRAM 28 YES NO

NUMBER TIMES DETOXIFIED 29-30

DATE OF APPLICATION Month Day Year 31-36

NUMBER YEARS LIVING IN NEW YORK CITY 48-49

RETURN THIS FORM TO
DEPT. OF HEALTH – MMTP
377 Bway., 5th Floor
New York, N.Y. 10013
ATT.: Intake Director

WHERE APPLIED ____ 37 47

SIGNATURE OF APPLICANT ____

MMTP 2
50M - 521035(74)

Appendix IV

NEW YORK CITY METHADONE MAINTENANCE TREATMENT PROGRAM ADMISSION SCREENING FORM

APPLICANT'S NAME ______ ADDRESS ______

Phone No. ______ Applic. No. ______ Unit No. ______

Date of Birth [ ] Soc. Sec. No. [ ] Medicaid No. [ ]

Medicaid Expiration Date [ ] **ACTIVE MEMBER OF** *(circle one)* Protestant Catholic Other Christian Jewish Islam Other Non-Christian None

ETHNIC GROUP *(circle one)* Wh Bl P.R. Other Hisp. Orient Other

CURRENT MARITAL STATUS *(circle one)* Never Married Married Widowed Separated Divorced Common-law

US VETERAN [ ] Y [ ] N If yes, Southeast Asia [ ] Y [ ] N Date separated / discharged [ ] MO. YR.

Type discharge *(circle one)* Honorable Dishonorable Bad Conduct Undesirable General Other

HOUSEHOLD COMPOSITION *(circle all applicable)* 1) Alone 2) With parents 3) With spouse 4) With children 5) With other relatives 6) With friends 7) No Stable Arrangement

EDUCATION *(circle only one)* 1) None 2) Grade 1-6 3) Grade 7-9 4) Grade 10-12 5) H.S. Grad 6) Some college 7) College graduate

PRESENT ACTIVITY *(circle all applicable)* JOB TRAINING full-time part-time SCHOOLING full-time part-time. EMPLOYMENT full-time part-time *Other Constructively Occupied*

EMPLOYMENT *(circle only one)*
1) Never worked 2) Worked in past

SKILLS OR SPECIAL ABILITIES: ______

If worked in past, longest period in one job [ ] months

Most recent job ______ From [ ] MO. DY. YR. To [ ] MO. DY. YR.

WELFARE *(check only one)* 1) Currently on 2) Not now but within past 2 years 3) Never on

If now on welfare, which Center ______

HISTORY OF DRUG USE

Year first used heroin 19 [ ] Age started daily use heroin [ ]

How heroin was taken *(check all applicable)* 1) mainlining 2) skin-popping 3) Snorting Present daily drug habit: [ ] bags = $ [ ]

Date last used heroin [ ] MO. YR.

Since onset daily heroin use, what was longest period of voluntary abstinence [ ] months

COMPLETE ALL APPLICABLE

Age first used	Drug	Use in Last 3 Months Daily	Use in Last 3 Months Less than Daily
	Heroin		
	Methadone		
	Codeine		
	Other narcotic		
	Cocaine		
	Barbituates		
	Amphetamines		
	Marijuana/Hashish		
	Other Hallucinogens		
	Other		

Previous methadone maintenance [ ] Y [ ] N First treatment (where) ______ From [ ] MO. YR. To [ ] MO. YR.

Most recent treatment (where) ______ From [ ] MO. YR. To [ ] MO. YR. Total No. Months in treatment [ ]

Previous drug free [ ] Y [ ] N First treatment (where) ______ From [ ] MO. YR. To [ ] MO. YR.

Most recent treatment (where) ______ From [ ] MO. YR. To [ ] MO. YR. Total No. months in treatment [ ]

Times medically detoxified [ ] Excessive alcohol use [ ] Y [ ] N If yes, how many yrs. heavy use [ ]

LEGAL HISTORY Number of Arrests [ ] Number of Convictions [ ] Age first arrested [ ]

Current case pending *(circle)* Yes No If yes, what is charge ______

What county (or state or federal) ______ Criminal or Supreme Court? ______

Place and date of next court appearance ______ Attorney's name ______

Warrants now outstanding *(circle)* Yes No If yes, when was warrant issued? ______

Warrant issued by whom (eg NACC, State Parole, Probation, Court) ______

If issued by court, what was underlying charge? ______ Name of attorney ______

Now on parole? *(circle)* Yes No If yes, name of officer ______ Where paroled ______

Months remaining ______

Now on probation? *(circle)* Yes No yes, name of officer ______ Where ______

Months remaining ______

ACUTE OR CHRONIC MEDICAL PROBLEMS *(circle)* YES NO If yes, specify ______

If yes, presently under treatment? ______ If under treatment, where ______ Dr. ______

ACUTE OR CHRONIC PSYCHIATRIC PROBLEMS *(circle)* YES NO If yes, specify ______

Presently under treatment? ______ If under treatment, where ______ Dr. ______

Ever hospitalized for psychiatric care? ______ If yes, where? ______ When ______

WHY DID YOU APPLY FOR METHDAONE MAINTENANCE? ______

WHAT ARE YOUR GOALS FOR THE FUTURE? ______

COMMENTS:

Interviewer's signature ______

NYCMMTP Form 105 (Rev. 7/72)
30M sets-1102067(74)

Date ______ **IF ADMITTED, HSA ID NO.** [ ]

Appendix V*

NYC HSA METHADONE MAINTENANCE TREATMENT PROGRAM
REPORT OF INDIVIDUAL'S PROGRESS

****

PERIOD OF REPORT (8-9) (10-11)

I. MEDICAL/PSYCHIATRIC PROBLEMS *(not including abuse of drugs/alcohol)*

A. *(Circle all applicable code numbers)*
(12) 1) None (13) 2) Acute (14) 3) Chronic (15) 4) Pregnancy ____/____/____ (due date)

B. If acute and/or chronic, specify ______________________

C. If problem was acute or chronic, was it attributed to methadone? (16) 1) Yes 2) No

D. Total days hospitalized this period due to all of the above (17-18) [|] (number of days)
(Please enter two digits, even if first is a zero, eg. 02)

II. SELF-ADMINISTERED DRUGS OF ABUSE

A. *(Circle applicable code numbers)*
(19) 1) None (20) 2) Heroin (21) 3) Barbiturates (22) 4) Amphetamines (23) 5) Cocaine
(24) 6) Excessive alcohol (25) 7) Other ______________________ (Specify)

B. Total days hospitalized this period due to drug abuse (26-27) [|] (number of days)
(Please enter two digits, even if first is a zero)

III. — CLINIC BEHAVIOR THIS PERIOD 1) Satisfactory 2) Disruptive
(Circle applicable code number) (28)

IV. TREATMENT STATUS AT END OF THIS PERIOD
(Circle applicable code number)
1) Buildup 2) Stabilized Maintenance
3) Being detoxified from Methadone
4) Completely detoxified from Methadone but still being seen regularly. (29)

V. LEGAL STATUS THIS PERIOD

A. CIVIL CASES PENDING END OF PERIOD *(Exclude parole/probation cases)*
NUMBER OF SUCH CASES PENDING (30-31) [|]
(Please enter two digits, even if first is a zero)

B. CRIMINAL CASES
1. If no criminal problems this period, Check here (32) [ ]
2. If criminal problems this period, specify below by checking, for each applicable item, whether felony or misdemeanor.

		FEL. (1)	MISDMR. (2)	DATE OF ALLEGED OFFENSE MONTH DAY (47-48)	YEAR (49-50)
(33)	ARRESTED (40)			/	/
(34)	CONVICTED (41)			(51-52) /	(53-54) /
(35)	CASE PENDING (1) (42)			(55-56) /	(57-58) /
(36)	CASE PENDING (2) (43)			(59-60) /	(61-62) /
(37)	CASE PENDING (3) (44)			(63-64) /	(65-66) /

		FEL. (1)	MISDMR. (2)	DATE OF ALLEGED OFFENSE MONTH DAY	YEAR
(38)	PAROLE (45)			(67-68) /	(69-70) /
(39)	PROBATION (46)			(71-72) /	(73-74) /

3. TOTAL DAYS SPENT IN JAIL THIS PERIOD (75-76) [|]
(Please enter two digits, even if first is a zero)

VI. EMPLOYMENT THIS PERIOD *(Circle one applicable code number)* (77)

A. 1) No job this period 2) Homemaker 3) Any job this period 4) Both homemaker AND Job

B. If *any* job this period, complete a. and/or b.;
(78) a. FULL-TIME JOB: 1) Any time this period 2) Entire period
(79) b. PART-TIME JOB: 1) Any time this period 2) Entire period

80:1

C. How long on present job? 1) Less than 1 month 2) More than 1 month: specify [|] months.–
(9) (8-9) *(Please enter two digits, even if first is a zero)*

CARD 2

VII. OTHER MEANS OF SUPPORT THIS PERIOD
(Circle applicable code numbers)
(10) 1) None (11) 2) Welfare (12) 3) Unemployment insurance (13) 4) Pension (14) 5) Training stipend
(15) 6) Family/friends (16) 7) Other source of income (specify) ______________________

VIII. SCHOOLING THIS PERIOD *(Circle applicable code numbers)*
(17) A. 1) None 2) Full-time school 3) Part-time school
B. If any school this period specify kind: (18) 1) Job training (19) 2) High School (20) 3) College

---

IX. LIVES WITH *(Circle applicable code numbers)*
(21) 1) Alone (22) 2) Parents (23) 3) Spouse and/or children (24) 4) Other relatives (25) 5) Friends
(26) 6) In this facility (27) 7) Other institution (28) 8) No permanent residence (29) 9) Other

80:2

COMMENTS:

____/____/____
date completed

RETURN TO CENTRAL OFFICE

HSA MMTP-UDR-6/73

____
signature staff member completing report

*Appendix V, reproduced here on pp. 261 and 262, is a single form, with the "Report of Individual's Progress" appearing on p. 261 and the "Bi-monthly Patient Profile" on p. 262.

BI-MONTHLY PATIENT PROFILE

NYCMMTP CLINIC (1-2)
PATIENT NAME
PATIENT ID (3-7)
MONTHS IN PROGRAM

AGE
SEX
ETHNICITY

*LEGEND
C = CLINIC VISIT
T = TAKE HOME
M = MISSED

DATE	DAY	DOSAGE/ AMT.	ATT. HISTORY *	URINE PROFILE

Appendix VI

PATIENT I.D. NUMBER
Yr. | Clinic | Cycle | Number
1

APPLICATION FORM
AMBULATORY DETOXIFICATION PROGRAM
The City of New York–Department of Health

11 (9 10)

INTERVIEW DATE: Mo. 11 | Day | Yr.

APPLICANT'S NAME: Last Name 17 | First Name 32 | M.I. 42

TELEPHONE NO. 43
SOCIAL SECURITY NO. 50
MEDICAID NO. 59
suffix 66
BIRTHDATE: Month 67 | Day | Year
PARENTAL CONSENT OBTAINED ? Yes 73 No 74

12 (9 10)

MOTHER'S MAIDEN NAME 11
MOTHER'S FIRST NAME 25

PRESENT ADDRESS: House No. 35 | Street No. 41

56 BOROUGH (Circle One): 1. Man. 2. Bx. 3. Bklyn. 4. Qns 5. Rich. 6. Other

ZIP CODE 57
APT. 62

13 (9 10)

PRESENTLY EMPLOYED? Yes 11 No 12
NOW ON WELFARE ? Yes 13 No 14
SEX M 15 F 16

17 ETHNIC GROUP (circle one): 1. Black 2. Hisp. 3. White 4. Other

SKILLS OR SPECIAL ABLILITIES ______

18 EDUCATION (circle one)
1. None 2. Grade 1–6 3. Grade 7–9 4. Grade 10–12 5. H.S. Grad. 6. Some College 7. College Grad.

19 MARITAL STATUS (circle one)
1. Married 2. Separated 3. Divorced 4. Widowed 5. Single, Never Married

20 CURRENT LIVING ARRANGEMENTS (circle one)
1. Alone 2. With Spouse (no children) 3. With Spouse & Children 4. With Children 5. With Friends 6. With Parents 7. With Other Relatives 8. Theraputic Community/Institution 9. Undomiciled

21 SOURCE OF REFERRAL (circle one)
1. Agency/Institution 2. Family/Friends 3. Self (walk in) 4. Advertisements (Posters, etc.) 5. Other 6. ASA Van

IF AGENCY REFERRAL, SPECIFY ______

22 PRIMARY DRUG USED (circle one)
1. Heroin 2. Methadone 3. Other

23 SECONDARY DRUG USED (circle one)
1. Heroin 2. Methadone 3. Amphetamines 4. Barbiturates 5. Marijuana/Hashish 6. Other Halucinogens 7. Doriden 8. Cocaine 9. Other

Age First Used Heroin 24
Years Addicted To Heroin 26
Average Cost/Day 28
Veteran? Yes 31 No 32
Onset of Addiction In Service? Yes 33 No 34
If Yes, Year Addicted In Service 35

No of Arrests. 37
No. Of Convictions 39
Is This Your First Treatment For Addiction? Yes 41 No 42

IF PREVIOUS ADDICTION TREATMENT:
Methadone Maintenance Yes 43 No 44
Drug Free Program Yes 45 No 46
Number Of Times Detoxified 47

______ Counselor's Signature

IDENTIFICATION USED
Type ______
Number ______

SUBSTANTIATION USED
Type ______
Number ______

CONTROL CHECK

14 (9 10)

Presently In Treatment Elsewhere? Yes 11 No 12
Treated Within 28 Days? Yes 13 No 14

MEDICAL SECTION check where applicable

Rejected For Serious Multiple Addiction? Yes 15 No 16
If Yes, What Kind of Multiple Addiction? Barbiturates 17 Other 18 Specify ______

Serious Medical Problem? Yes 19 No 20 Specify ______
Accepted for Treatment? Yes 21 No 22
If Not Accepted, Referred To Another Program/Hospital Specify ______

MEDICAL TESTS ORDERED: Check Where Applicable.

Serology 23 Tine 24 CBC 25 Sickle Cell Prep. 26 Chest X-Ray 27 Pap. Smear 28 G–C Smear 29 Preg. Test 30 Other 31 ______ Specify

Number of Days Recommended for Treatment. 32
Dosage of Methadone Prescribed First Day. 34
Date of Physical: Month 36 | Day | Year 41

______ Physician's Signature

COMMENTS ______

40M-702126(77) AD-1 (REV.9/73)

Appendix VII

THE CITY OF NEW YORK – DEPARTMENT OF HEALTH
AMBULATORY DETOXIFICATION PROGRAM
PATIENT MEDICATION ROSTER

(PLEASE TYPE)			DATE															
				DAY 1	DAY 2	DAY 3	DAY 4	DAY 5	DAY 6	DAY 7	DAY 8	DAY 9	DAY 10	DAY 11	DAY 12	DAY 13	DAY 14	DO NOT WRITE IN THIS SPACE
LAST NAME	FIRST NAME	PATIENT I.D. cc. 1-8	9 - 10	11	13	15	17	19	21	23	25	27	29	31	33	35	37	39
			4 1															
		Yr. Clinic Cycle Number	4 1															
			4 1															
			4 1															
			4 1															
			4 1															
			4 1															
			4 1															
			4 1															
			4 1															
			4 1															
			4 1															
			4 1															
			4 1															
			4 1															
			4 1															
			4 1															
			4 1															
			4 1															
NUMBER OF PATIENTS TREATED																		
TOTAL Mg. METHADONE ADMINISTERED																		

AD-9-5M-503049(74)

Appendix VIII

THE CITY OF NEW YORK – DEPARTMENT OF HEALTH
AMBULATORY DETOXIFICATION PROGRAM

PATIENT STATUS AND DISCHARGE REPORT

PATIENT I.D. NO.

Yr.	Clinic	Cycle	No.	
1				3 1

TERMINATION DATE

Mo.	Day	Year
11		

PATIENT'S NAME

Last Name 17 | First Name 32 | Middle Initial 42

REASON FOR DISCHARGE 43 (Circle One)

BEGAN TREATMENT

1. Never Received Medication
2. Completed Detox
3. Medical Discharge
4. Missed Appointments
5. Disruptive Behavior, specify ________
6. Arrest
7. Other, specify ________

MEDICAL PROBLEMS DURING TREATMENT (Check where applicable)

MEDICAL PROBLEMS BELIEVED RELATED TO DETOX TREATMENT

NONE [44] GASTRO-INTESTINAL [45] INSOMNIA [46] PERSISTANT DROWSINESS [47] OTHER [48] SPECIFY ________

MEDICAL PROBLEMS BELIEVED RELATED TO ADDICTION

NONE [49] SKIN [50] HEPATITIS [51] CARDIO VASCULAR [52] OTHER [53] SPECIFY ________

GENERAL MEDICAL PROBLEMS DIAGNOSED OR SUSPECTED

NONE [54] VENEREAL [55] SICKLE CELL ANEMIA [56] OTHER ANEMIA [57] CARDIO-VASCULAR [58] OTHER [59] SPECIFY ________

LONG TERM REFERRAL ADDICTION TREATMENT

1ST REFERRAL ________

2ND REFERRAL ________

USE CODE ON CODE SHEET [60] [63]

MEDICAL TREATMENT REFERRAL
66 (Circle One)

0–NONE
1–INPATIENT TREATMENT
2–OUTPATIENT TREATMENT

IF REFERRED, DID PATIENT ENTER A LONG TERM ADDICTION TREATMENT PROGRAM?

Y 71 N

SOCIAL AGENCY REFERRAL Y N

1ST REFERRAL ________

2ND REFERRAL ________

REPORTER'S SIGNATURE ________

ADDITIONAL COMMENTS ________

45M-DPM 225032(75) AD–11 (REV. 1/73)

Demographic Characteristics of the 20,653

Sex	Ethnicity: / Year of Admission / Age at Admission	All 1970–1971	All 1972	All 1973	All 1974	White 1970–1971	White 1972	White 1973	White 1974
Both	All:	4377	7346	5340	3590	1760	1513	1036	937
Men	All:	3497	5377	3984	2732	1406	1160	792	723
Women	All:	880	1969	1356	858	354	353	244	214
Both	18–20 years	617	1131	924	578	343	309	226	155
	21–25 years	1699	2818	2211	1622	741	704	493	469
	26–30 years	919	1465	1102	797	376	280	200	203
	31–35 years	516	839	532	327	156	123	62	70
	36–40 years	328	548	282	144	77	57	31	21
	41–50 years	245	450	224	97	44	29	18	17
	51–60 years	35	71	39	14	12	5	3	2
	Over 60 years	18	24	26	11	11	6	3	0
Men	18–20 years	459	753	638	393	260	221	150	94
	21–25 years	1350	2033	1600	1209	595	544	371	369
	26–30 years	752	1108	854	646	307	222	173	174
	31–35 years	426	653	427	270	135	101	54	56
	36–40 years	272	404	223	110	64	45	26	17
	41–50 years	196	350	183	82	30	22	14	12
	51–60 years	28	59	36	11	8	2	2	1
	Over 60 years	14	17	23	11	7	3	2	0
Women	18–20 years	158	378	286	185	83	88	76	61
	21–25 years	349	785	611	413	146	160	122	100
	26–30 years	167	357	248	151	69	58	27	29
	31–35 years	90	186	105	57	21	22	8	14
	36–40 years	56	14	59	34	13	12	5	4
	41–50 years	49	100	41	15	14	7	4	5
	51–60 years	7	12	3	3	4	3	1	1
	Over 60 years	4	7	3	0	4	3	1	0

Appendix IX

Individuals Admitted to the NYC MMTP, 1970–1974

Black				Hispanic				Other			
1970–1971	1972	1973	1974	1970–1971	1972	1973	1974	1970–1971	1972	1973	1974
1545	3827	2515	1580	1029	1983	1746	1055	43	23	43	18
1197	2618	1738	1106	855	1578	1416	885	39	21	38	18
348	1209	777	474	174	405	330	170	4	2	5	0
158	494	392	215	114	319	302	206	2	9	4	2
533	1383	1008	702	409	729	708	451	16	2	2	0
307	739	516	363	232	447	384	229	4	1	2	2
204	471	272	147	151	244	196	110	5	1	2	0
167	341	151	85	78	149	98	37	6	1	2	1
159	337	151	60	40	83	49	18	2	1	6	2
15	54	20	8	4	10	7	3	4	2	9	1
2	8	5	0	1	2	2	1	4	6	16	10
113	292	249	133	84	232	235	164	2	8	4	2
407	903	665	462	333	584	562	378	15	2	2	0
243	512	355	274	198	373	324	196	4	1	2	2
154	350	212	115	133	201	160	99	4	1	1	0
135	246	112	64	68	112	84	28	5	1	1	1
129	261	122	51	35	66	42	17	2	2	5	2
14	47	19	7	3	8	7	2	3	2	8	1
2	7	4	0	1	2	2	1	4	5	15	10
45	202	143	82	30	87	67	42	0	1	0	0
126	480	343	240	76	145	146	73	1	0	0	0
64	227	161	89	34	74	60	33	0	0	0	0
50	121	60	32	18	43	36	11	1	0	1	0
32	95	39	21	10	37	14	9	1	0	1	0
30	76	29	9	5	17	7	1	0	0	1	0
1	7	1	1	1	2	0	1	1	0	1	0
0	1	1	0	0	0	0	0	0	1	1	0

Appendix X

CONFIDENTIAL REPORT OF DRUG ABUSE IN NEW YORK CITY

HEALTH DEPARTMENT STATISTICAL REPORT

CONTACT DATE
7 MO DAY YR 12

CARD 1
REG. No. 2-6

LAST NAME 13 32

FIRST NAME 33 47

MIDDLE NAME 48 57

ALIAS 58 77

CARD 2
DUP. No. 2-6

SOCIAL SECURITY NUMBER 7 15

CLIENT'S MAIDEN NAME 16 35

ADDRESS 36 53

ZIP CODE 54 58

BOROUGH 59 1. Manhattan 2. Bronx 3. Brooklyn 4. Queens 5. Staten Island 6. Other (Specify)

BIRTHDATE 60 MO DAY YR 65

PLACE OF BIRTH 66 1. New York City 2. Other New York State 3. Puerto Rico 4. Other USA 5. Other (Specify)

ETHNIC GROUP (Circle one) 67 1 White 3. Hispanic 2 Black 4. Oriental 5 Other(Specify)

SEX 68 M F

CARD 3
DUP. No. 2-6

MOTHER'S MAIDEN OR FIRST NAME 7 26

CURRENT PRIMARY DRUG OF ABUSE (Circle one) 27
1. Heroin 2. Methadone 3. Other Narcotic 4. Barbiturate 5. Amphetamine 6. Cocaine 7. Marijuana 8. None 9. Other (Specify)

Age First Used 36 37

SECONDARY DRUG OF ABUSE (Circle one or all) 38-46
1. Heroin 2. Methadone 3. Other Narcotic 4. Barbiturate 5. Amphetamine 6 Cocaine 7. Marijuana 8. None 9. Other (Specify)

MEDICAL COMPLICATIONS (Circle one or all) 47-54
1. Skin Infections 2. Hepatitis 3. T.B. 4. Venereal Disease 5. Birth/Pregnancy 6. Cardiovascular 7. Trauma 8. Other (Specify)

REPORTING SOURCE

(Leave Blank) 55 58

Name

Address

BOROUGH (Circle one) 59 1. Manhattan 2. Bronx 3. Brooklyn 4. Queens 5. Staten Island 6. Other (Specify)

TO BE COMPLETED ONLY BY ADDICTION TREATMENT AGENCIES

TYPE OF CONTACT (Circle one) 60
1. Application
2. Admission

MODALITY (Circle one) 61
1. Chemotherapy
2. Drug Free

IF CHEMOTHERAPY (Circle one) 62
1. Detoxification
2. Maintenance

FACILITY (Circle one) 63
1. Hospital
2. Residential
3. Ambulatory

(Do not write below this line)

RECEIVE DATE 64-69

CASE NUMBER 70 76

ACTION CODE 77
1 2 3 4 5

RETURN FORM TO

NR2(Rev. 2/73)-100M-811063(75) 346

Bibliography

1. Nixon, R., State of the Union Message. *Congr. Q.* **118,** 506 (1972).
2. King, R., "The Drug Hangup," pp. 25–28. Norton, New York, 1972.
3. King, R., "The Drug Hangup," p. 39. Norton, New York, 1972.
4. King, R., "The Drug Hangup," p. 38. Norton, New York, 1972.
5. Berg, R. H., New hope for drug addicts. *Look* **29**(24), 23–25 (1965).
6. Jaffe, J. H., Multimodality approaches to the treatment and prevention of opiate addiction. *In* "Opiate Addiction: Origins and Treatment" (S. Fisher and A. M. Freedman, eds.), p. 133. V. H. Winston, Washington, D.C., 1973.
7. Dogoloff, L. I., Priorities and plans for services to the drug dependent. *In* "Developments in the Field of Drug Abuse" (E. Senay, V. Shorty, and H. Alksne, eds.), p. 43. Schenkman, Cambridge, Massachusetts, 1975.
8. New York State Drug Abuse Control Commission, "The New York State Drug Abuse Program—Current Activities and Plans," p. 26. Drug Abuse Control Commission, Albany, New York, 1973.
9. Newman, R. G., and Kagen, J. G., The New York City Methadone Maintenance Treatment Program after two years—an overview. *In* "Proceedings of the Fifth National Conference on Methadone Treatment," p. 795. National Association for the Prevention of Addiction to Narcotics, New York, 1973.
10. Domestic Council Drug Abuse Task Force, "White Paper on Drug Abuse," p. 20. US Gov. Printing Office, Washington, D.C., 1975.
11. Domestic Council Drug Abuse Task Force, "White Paper on Drug Abuse." US Govt. Printing Office, Washington, D.C., 1975.
12. Robinson, L., Hospitals here to treat addicts. *N.Y. Times* June 5, p. 29 (1959).
13. Advisory Council on Narcotic Addiction, Preliminary report to Mayor Robert Wagner. Quoted in David, S. M., "A History of the Narcotic Addiction Political Arena in New York City: 1954–August 1, 1971," mimeo., p. 11. Institute for Social Research of the Fordham University, New York, 1971.
14. Bennett, C., War on narcotics mapped for city. *N.Y. Times* Jan. 30, p. 31 (1962).
15. "Dorland's Illustrated Medical Dictionary," 23rd ed. (L. Arey, W. Burrows, J. P., Greenhill, and R. Hewitt, eds.), p. 1440. Saunders, Philadephia, Pennsylvania, 1957.
16. Dole, V. P., Pharmacological treatment of drug addiction. *Mod. Med. (Minneapolis)* **40,** 19–21 (1972).
17. Lennard, H. L., Epstein, L. J., Bernstein, A., and Ransom, D. C., "Mystification and Drug Abuse," p. 95. Jossey-Bass, San Francisco, California, 1971.

18. Dole, V. P., and Nyswander, M. E., A medical treatment for diacetylmorphine (heroin) addiction. *J. Am. Med. Assoc.* **193,** 146–150 (1965).
19. Brown, J. W., Mazze, R., and Glaser, D., "Narcotics Knowledge and Nonsense—Program Disaster Versus a Scientific Model," p. 49. Ballinger, Cambridge, Massachusetts, 1974.
20. Brown, J. W., Mazze, R., and Glaser, D., "Narcotics Knowledge and Nonsense—Program Disaster Versus a Scientific Model," p. 51. Ballinger, Cambridge, Massachusetts, 1974.
21. David, S. M., "A History of the Narcotic Addiction Political Arena in New York City 1954–August 1, 1972," mimeo., p. 36. Institute for Social Research of the Fordham University, New York, 1971.
22. Brown, J. W., Mazze, R., and Glaser, D., "Narcotics Knowledge and Nonsense—Program Disaster Versus a Scientific Model," p. 52. Ballinger, Cambridge, Massachusetts, 1974.
23. Johnson, R. J. H., City plans to treat addicts. *N.Y. Times* May 30, p. 1 (1969).
24. Lukoff, I., Issues in the evaluation of heroin treatment. *In* "Drug Use—Epidemiological and Sociological Approaches" (E. Josephson and E. E. Carroll, eds.), p. 26. Hemisphere, Washington, D.C., 1974.
25. Moore, M., "A Case Study—The New York City Methadone Maintenance Treatment Program," mimeo., p. 21. Harvard Business School, Cambridge, Massachusetts, 1974.
26. Brown, J. W., Mazze, R., and Glaser, D., "Narcotics Knowledge and Nonsense—Program Disaster Versus a Scientific Model," p. 81. Ballinger, Cambridge, 1974.
27. Sibley, J., New health aide is under attack. *N.Y. Times* Dec. 10, p. 30 (1969).
28. Sibley, J., New health chief stirs anxiety. *N.Y. Times* Dec. 11, p. 29 (1969).
29. Chase, G., personal communication (1975).
30. Langrod, J., Brill, L., Lowinson, J., and Joseph, H. Methadone maintenance—from research to treatment. *In* "Major Modalities in the Treatment of Drug Abuse" (L. Brill and L. Lieberman, eds.), p. 140. Behavioral Publications, New York, 1972.
31. New York City Addiction Services Agency. "Comprehensive Plan for the Control of Drug Abuse and Addiction," p. 50. 1972.
32. Finney, G. S., "Drugs: Administering Catastrophe," p. 35. Drug Abuse Council, Washington, D.C., 1975.
33. New York City Health Services Administration, Memo to Budget Director Frederick O'R. Hayes, June 22, 1970.
34. No author, Protest Pelham Plan—City Island residents oppose project of drug hospital. *N.Y. Times* Aug. 5, p. 9 (1919).
35. No author, No addict hospital in Pelham Bay Park. *N.Y. Times* Aug. 6, p. 28 (1919).
36. No author, Drug addicts undesired—Staten Island residents against housing them in Sea View. *N.Y. Times* Aug. 10, p. 3 (1919).
37. No author, Director Copeland abandons plan to use Sea View. *N.Y. Times* Aug. 26, p. 5 (1919).
38. No author, Staten Island to treat young addicts. *N.Y. Times* Apr. 22, p. 53 (1962).
39. New York City Council, Intro. Bill No. 569 (1974).
40. No author, Villagers protest methadone boat. *N.Y. Post* Aug. 15, p. 6 (1972).
41. Weitz, A., Villagers march—'The Boat Must Go.' *Village Voice* Aug. 17, p. 59 (1972).
42. Dole, V. P., Nyswander, M. E., and Warner, A., Successful treatment of 750 criminal addicts. *J. Am. Med. Assoc.* **206,** 2708–2711 (1968).
43. Dole, V. P., and Nyswander, M. E., Heroin addiction—a metabolic disease. *Arch. Intern. Med.* **120,** 19–24, (1967).
44. Dole, V. P., Methadone maintenance treatment for 25,000 heroin addicts. *J. Am. Med. Assoc.* **215,** 1131–1134 (1971).

45. "Webster's New World Dictionary of the American Language," p. 1636. World, Cleveland, Ohio, 1964.
46. Department of Health, Education and Welfare, Confidentiality of alcohol and drug abuse patient records. *Fed. Regis.* **40**(127), Part IV, Sect. 2.39(c), p. 27814 (1975).
47. Edwards, C. N., "Drug Dependence," p. 93. Jason Aronson, New York, 1974.
48. Morgenthau, R. M., quoted in *N.Y. Times* Mar. 21, p. 70 (1970).
49. Civil commitment of heroin addicts—a panel discussion. *Contemp. Drug Probl.* **1,** 561–592 (1972).
50. American Medical Association Council on Mental Health, Report on narcotic addiction. *J. Am. Med. Assoc.* **165,** 1712 (1957).
51. Einstein, S., and Garitano, W., Treating the drug abuser: Problems, factors and alternatives. *Int. J. Addict.* **7,** 321–331 (1972).
52. Chambers, C., Hinesley, R. K., and Moldestad, M., Narcotic addiction in females: A race comparison. *Int. J. Addict.* **5,** 257–278 (1970).
53. *Fuller v. People,* 24NY2d 292, 300 N.Y.S. 2d 102 (1969).
54. Brill, L., and Lieberman, L., "Authority and Addiction," p. 57. Little, Brown, Boston, Massachusetts, 1969.
55. Lazare, A., Eisenthal, S., and Wasserman, L., The customer approach to patienthood. *Arch. Gen. Psychiatry* **32,** 553–558 (1975).
56. Moffet, A. D., Adler, F., Glaser, F. B., and Horvitz, D., "Medical Lollypop, Junkie Insulin, or What?," pp. 43 and 45. Dorrance, Philadelphia, Pennsylvania, 1974.
57. Moffet, A. D., Adler, F., Glaser, F. B., and Horvitz, D., "Medical Lollypop, Junkie Insulin, or What?," p. 47. Dorrance, Philadelphia, Pennsylvania, 1974.
58. Lukoff, I., Issues in the evaluation of heroin treatment. *In* "Drug Use—Epidemiological and Sociological Approaches" (E. Josephson and E. E. Carroll, eds.), p. 130. Hemisphere, Washington, D.C., 1974.
59. Kittrie, N., "The Right to Be Different," p. 246. Johns Hopkins Press, Baltimore, Maryland, 1971.
60. DeLong, J., Treatment and rehabilitation. *In* "Dealing with Drug Abuse—A Report to the Ford Foundation," p. 186. Praeger, New York, 1972.
61. President's Commission on Law Enforcement and the Administration of Justice, "Task Force Report: Narcotics and Drug Abuse," p. 17. US Govt. Printing Office, Washington, D.C., 1967.
62. Japan Ministry of Health and Welfare, "A Brief Account of Narcotics Abuse and Countermeasures in Japan," mimeo., p. 7, 1970.
63. Leone, S., quoted in *N.Y. Times* Dec. 12, p. 27 (1971).
64. *People v. Newman,* 32 NY 2d 379, 345 N.Y.S. 2d 502, 298 N.E. 2d 651 (1973); cert. denied sub. nom. *New York v. Newman* 414 U.S. 1163, 94 S. Ct. 927, 39 L. Ed. 2d 116 (1974).
65. *People v. Newman,* Court of Appeals, State of New York, "Brief for Appellant Robert Newman, MD," p. 18 (1973).
66. Department of Health, Education and Welfare, *Fed. Regist.* **40**(127), Part IV, Sect. 217(b), p. 27808 (1975).
67. *People v. Newman,* "Memorandum of Law in Support of Motion to Quash the Subpoena Duces Tecum," p. 5. Supreme Court, State of New York, (1973).
68. Department of Health, Education and Welfare, "Conditions for investigational use of methadone for maintenance programs for narcotic addicts" (proposed). *Fed. Regis.* **37**(67), 6943 (1972).
69. New York State C.P.L.R., Sect. 4504(a).
70. No author, Stay contempt term of methadone doctor. *N.Y. Daily News* July 27, p. 24 (1972).

71. Fosburgh, L., Methadone clinic head sentenced for contempt. *N.Y. Times* July 26, p. 74 (1972).
72. No author (editorial), Dr. Newman's fight. *N.Y. Post* July 26, p. 40 (1972).
73. New York City Charter, Sect. 395.
74. Crews, G., General Counsel, Special Action Office for Drug Abuse Prevention, Letter to Robert Newman, MD, July 22, 1972.
75. Steering Committee, National Association of Methadone Program Directors, Letter to Robert Newman, MD, July 22, 1972.
76. Hutt, P. B., Assistant General Counsel, Food and Drug Administration, Telegram to Robert Newman, MD, July 25, 1972.
77. New York State Appellate Division, decision entered October 2, 1972.
78. Ingersoll, J. E., Director, Bureau of Narcotics and Dangerous Drugs, Letter to Robert Newman, MD, November 8, 1972.
79. "Drug Abuse Office and Treatment Act of 1972," 21 U.S.C., 1175, Sect. 408 (1972).
80. *People v. Newman*, Court of Appeals, State of New York, "Respondent's Brief," p. 43 (1973).
81. Department of Health, Education and Welfare and Special Action Office for Drug Abuse Prevention, 21 C.F.R. 401, Sect. 401.62 (b) (2), *Fed. Regist.* **37**, p. 24636 (1972).
82. Court of Appeals, State of New York, decision entered May 31, 1973.
83. Department of Health, Education and Welfare, "Confidentiality of alcohol and drug abuse patient records." *Fed. Regist.* **40**(127), Sect. 265-1(d), p. 27821 (1975).
84. Department of Health, Education and Welfare, *Fed. Regist.* **40**, Sect. 2.65(e), p. 27820 (1975).
85. Pomeroy, W. A., "Police Chiefs Discuss Drug Abuse," p. 39. Drug Abuse Council, Washington, D.C., 1974.
86. Pomeroy, W. A., "Police Chiefs Discuss Drug Abuse," p. 42. Drug Abuse Council, Washington, D.C., 1974.
87. Goldstein, A., "Methadone in the Treatment of Heroin Addiction. Procedure Manual of the Santa Clara County Methadone Program," pp. 27–29. Santa Clara County, California, 1972 (unpublished).
88. Bloom, W. A., and Sudderth, E. W., Methadone in New Orleans—patients, problems and police. *In* "Methadone Maintenance" (S. Einstein, ed.), p. 125. Dekker, New York, 1971.
89. New York City Department of Health, "Methadone Maintenance Treatment Program Policy and Procedures Manual," p. F-1. New York City Department of Health, New York, 1974 (unpublished).
90. Committee on Conference of the Drug Abuse Office and Treatment Act of 1972, P.L. 92-255, 21 U.S.C., 1101–1191 (1972).
91. Special Action Office for Drug Abuse Prevention, Confidentiality of drug abuse patient records. *Fed. Regist.* **37**(223), 24636 (1972).
92. Campbell, B., Baby beating stirs call for added methadone care. *N.Y. Times* May 6, p. 24 (1973).
93. New York City Health Code, Sect. 11.07, as amended April 10 (1973).
94. Department of Health, Education and Welfare, Confidentiality of alcohol and drug abuse patient records. *Fed. Regist.* **40**(127), Sect. 2.39 (c), p. 27814 (1975).
95. New York City Department of Health, "Methadone Maintenance Treatment Program Policy and Procedures Manual," p. F-4. New York City Department of Health, New York, 1974 (unpublished).
96. Feinberg, L., Footprints 'identify' methadone patients. *Washington Post* Oct. 28, p. 18 (1973).

97. New York City Department of Social Services and Department of Health, Memo to Physicians of Methadone Maintenance Programs, September 11, 1972.
98. New York State Drug Abuse Control Commission, "Requirements for Operating a Methadone Program," p. 2. 1974.
99. Department of Health, Education and Welfare, 310, Multiple enrollment prevention. *Fed. Regist.* **39**(206), 21 C.F.R. Part 310, p. 37636 (1974).
100. Fallon, J. W., Regional Director, Drug Enforcement Agency, Letter to Robert Newman, MD, November 8, 1974.
101. Department of Health, Education and Welfare, Confidentiality of alcohol and drug abuse patient records. *Fed. Regist.* **40**(127), Part IV, Sect. 2.56, p. 27819 (1975).
102. New York City Health Code, Sect. 11.05, as amended January 1 (1963).
103. New York City Health Code, Sect. 11.07, as amended April 10 (1973).
104. Capazzalo, J., Contract Manager, Drug Abuse Control Commission, Letter to Bernard Bihari, MD, February 18, 1975.
105. Department of Health, Education and Welfare and Special Action Office for Drug Abuse Prevention, Confidentiality of alcohol and drug abuse patient records. *Fed. Regist.* **40**(91), 20538 (1975).
106. Department of Health, Education and Welfare and Special Action Office for Drug Abuse Prevention, Confidentiality of alcohol and drug abuse patient records, *Fed. Regist.* **40**(91), Sect. 2.53(c), p. 20537 (1975).
107. Department of Health, Education and Welfare, Confidentiality of alcohol and drug abuse patient records. *Fed. Regist.* **40**(127), Part IV, Sect. 2.52-1(p), p. 27816 (1975).
108. Department of Health, Education and Welfare and Special Action Office for Drug Abuse Prevention, Confidentiality of alcohol and drug abuse patient records. *Fed. Regist.* **40**(91), 20530 (1975).
109. Department of Health, Education and Welfare, Confidentiality of alcohol and drug abuse patient records. *Fed. Regist.* **40**(127), Part IV, Sect. 2.64(d), p. 27820 (1975).
110. Garbutt, G. D., and Goldstein, A., Blind comparisons of three methadone maintenance dosages in 180 patients. *In* "Proceedings of the Fourth National Conference on Methadone Treatment," pp. 411–414. National Association for the Prevention of Addiction to Narcotics, New York, 1972.
111. Nelkin, D., "Methadone Maintenance: A Technological Fix," p. 128. Braziller, New York, 1973.
112. Goldstein, A., Hansteen, R. W., Horns, W. H., and Rado, M., Control of methadone dosage by patients. *In* "Developments in the Field of Drug Abuse" (E. Senay, V. Shorty, and H. Alksne, eds.), pp. 373–381. Cambridge, Massachusetts, 1975.
113. Department of Health, Education and Welfare, Listing of methadone with special requirements for use. *Fed. Regist.* **37**(242), Sect. 130.44(d) (6), p. 26797 (1972).
114. New York City Chief Medical Examiner's Office, "Summary Tally: Deaths Caused Directly by Narcotism in the City of New York," mimeo. 1974.
115. New York City Department of Health, "Methadone Maintenance Treatment Program Policy and Procedures Manual," p. H-4. New York City Department of Health, New York, 1974 (unpublished).
116. Rucker, T. D., Drug use—data, sources and limitations. *J. Am. Med. Assoc.* **230,** 888–890 (1974).
117. Cushman, P., Detoxification of rehabilitated methadone patients: Frequency and predictors of long-term success. *Am. J. Drug Alc. Use* **1,** 393–408 (1974).
118. Stimmel, B., and Rabin, J., The ability to remain abstinent upon leaving methadone maintenance: A prospective study. *Am. J. Drug Alc. Use* **1,** 379–391 (1974).
119. Lowinson, J., Langrod, J., and Berle, B., Detoxification of long-term methadone patients.

In "Developments in the Field of Drug Abuse" (E. Senay, V. Shorty, and H. Alksne, eds.), pp. 336–343. Schenkman, Cambridge, Massachusetts, 1975.

120. Dole, V. P., and Nyswander, M. E., A medical treatment for diacetylmorphine (heroin) addiction. *J. Am. Med. Assoc.* **193,** 146–150 (1965).
121. Dole, V. P., In the course of professional practice. *N.Y. State J. Med.* **65,** 927–931 (1965).
122. Nyswander, M. E., and Dole, V. P., The present status of methadone blockade treatment. *Am. J. Psychiatry* **123,** 1441–1442 (1967).
123. Dole, V. P., Blockade with methadone. *In* "Narcotic Drugs: Biochemical Pharmacology" (D. Clouet, ed.), p. 480. Plenum, New York, 1971.
124. Dole, V. P., and Nyswander, M. E., Rehabilitation of patients on methadone programs. *In* "Proceedings of the Fifth National Conference on Methadone Treatment," pp. 1–7. National Association for the Prevention of Addiction to Narcotics, New York, 1973.
125. Department of Health, Education and Welfare, Listing of methadone with special requirements for use. *Fed. Regist.* **37**(242), Sect. 130.44 (d) (5), p. 26797 (1972).
126. Moffet, A. D., Adler, F., Glaser, F. B., and Horvitz, D., "Medical Lollypop, Junkie Insulin, Or What?," p. 17. Dorrance, Philadelphia, Pennsylvania, 1974.
127. Dole, V. P., and Nyswander, M. E., Heroin addiction—a metabolic disease. *Arch. Intern. Med.* **120,** 19–24 (1967).
128. Szasz, T., The ethics of addiction. *Harper's Mag.* April, pp. 74–79 (1972).
129. Szasz, T., "The Myth of Mental Illness." Delta, New York, 1967.
130. Department of Health, Education and Welfare, Listing of methadone with special requirements for use. *Fed. Regist.* **37**(242), 26798 (1972).
131. New York State Mental Hygiene Law, Artic. 81.03 (b)4, effective September 1, 1973.
132. Temporary State Commission to Evaluate the Drug Laws, "Employing the Rehabilitated Addict," N.Y. State Legislative Doc. No. 10, p. 49 (1973).
133. No author, Postal service lifts ban on ex-addicts. *N.Y. Times* Nov. 26, p. 45 (1974).
134. Rockefeller, N., Annual message of the Governor. *In* "McKinney's Session Laws of New York," p. 2318. 1973.
135. *Spady v. Mount Vernon Housing Authority*, 41, App. Div. 762, 2d Dep't. (1973).
136. Dobbs, W., Methadone treatment of heroin addicts. *J. Am. Med. Assoc.* **218,** 1536–1541 (1971).
137. Moffet, A. D., Adler, F., Glaser, F. B., and Horvitz, D., "Medical Lollypop, Junkie Insulin, or What?," p. 53. Dorrance, Philadelphia, Pennsylvania, 1974.
138. Jaffe, J. H., Drug addiction and drug abuse. *In* "The Pharmacological Basis of Therapeutics" (L. S. Goodman and A. Gilman, eds.), 4th ed., p. 277. Macmillan, New York, 1970.
139. Stimmel, B., "Heroin Dependency," p. 88. Stratton, New York, 1975.
140. "Webster's Third New International Dictionary (Unabridged)," p. 24. Merriam, Springfield, Massachusetts, 1969.
141. World Health Organization, Expert Committee on Mental Health, Addiction-producing drugs: 7th report, 1957. *W.H.O., Tech. Rep. Ser.* **116** (1957).
142. Maurer, D. W., and Vogel, V. H., "Narcotics and Narcotic Addiction," p. 29. Thomas, Springfield, Illinois, 1962.
143. Smart, R. G., Addiction, dependency, abuse or use: Which are we studying with epidemiology? *In* "Drug Use—Epidemiological and Sociological Approaches" (E. Josephson and E. E. Carroll, eds.), p. 26. Hemisphere, Washington, D.C., 1974.
144. New York City Department of Personnel, "Personnel Policy and Procedure Bulletin," Issue 4–72. 1972.
145. Krongel, B., Job development: A tool to fight discrimination. *In* "Proceedings of the Fifth National Conference on Methadone Treatment," pp. 63–66. National Association for the Prevention of Addiction to Narcotics, New York, 1973.

146. Nelkin, D., "Methadone Maintenance: A Technological Fix," p. 117. Braziller; New York, 1973.
147. New York City Commission on Human Rights, "Employment and the Rehabilitated Addict: Employment Experience and Recent Research Findings," p. xii. Drug Abuse Council, Washington, D.C., 1971.
148. Krongel, B., Job development: A tool to fight discrimination. *In* "Proceedings of the Fifth National Conference on Methadone Treatment," pp. 63–66. National Association for the Prevention of Addiction to Narcotics, New York, 1973.
149. Dole, V. P., and Nyswander, M. E., Study of methadone as an adjunct in rehabilitation of heroin addicts. *Ill. Med. J.* **139,** 487–489 (1966).
150. American Medical Association Committee on Narcotic Drugs, Minutes of the House of Delegates. *J. Am. Med. Assoc.* **76,** 1669–1671 (1921).
151. Advisory Commission on Narcotic and Drug Abuse, *Final Report,* Appendix I. US Govt. Printing Office, Washington, D.C., 1963.
152. U.S. Bureau of Narcotics, Concurring statement. Quoted in Eddy, N. B., "The National Research Council Involvement in the Opiate Problem," p. 145. Natl. Acad. Sci., Washington, D.C., 1973.
153. Committee on the Judiciary, U.S. Senate, 84th Congress, Treatment and rehabilitation of narcotic addicts. Quoted in *J. Am. Med. Assoc.* **165,** 1797 (1957).
154. No author (editorial), *J. Am. Med. Assoc.* **211,** 1847–1848 (1970).
155. Ausubel, D. P., The Dole-Nyswander treatment of heroin addiction. *J. Am. Med. Assoc.* **195,** 949–950 (1966).
156. Ausubel, D. P., Why compulsory closed-ward treatment of narcotic addicts? *Ill. Med. J.* **130,** 474–485 (1966).
157. Ausubel, D. P., "Why Compulsory Closed-Ward Treatment of Narcotic Addicts?," Spec. repr. N.Y. State Narcotic Addiction Control Commission, New York, 1968.
158. DiIenno, J., Methadone maintenance: Medicine or myth? *J. Albert Einstein Med. Cent.* **19,** 55–64 (1971).
159. Chein, I., Psychological functions of drug abuse. *In* "Scientific Basis of Drug Dependence, A Symposium" (H. Steinberg, ed.), p. 14. Churchill, London, 1969.
160. Meyer, R. E., On the nature of opiate reinforcement. *In* "Addiction" (P. Bourne, ed.), p. 26. Academic Press, New York, 1974.
161. Dole, V. P., and Nyswander, M. E., A medical treatment for diacetylmorphine (heroin) addiction. *J. Am. Med. Assoc.* **193,** 646–650 (1965).
162. Eddy, N. B., "The National Research Council Involvement in the Opiate Problem," p. 112. Natl. Acad. Sci., Washington, D.C., 1973.
163. World Health Organization Expert Committee on Drug Dependence, *W.H.O., Tech. Rep. Ser.* **460,** 22 (1970).
164. Goldstein, A., Blind dosage comparisons and other studies in a large methadone program. *J. Psychedelic Drugs,* **4,** 177 (1971).
165. Goldstein, A., Blind controlled dosage comparisons in 200 patients. *In* "Proceedings of the Third National Conference on Methadone Treatment," pp. 31–37. National Association for the Prevention of Addiction to Narcotics, New York, 1971.
166. Garbutt, G. D., and Goldstein, A., Blind comparisons of three methadone maintenance dosages in 180 patients. *In* "Proceedings of the Fourth National Conference on Methadone Treatment," pp. 411–414. National Association for the Prevention of Addiction to Narcotics, New York, 1972.
167. Goldstein, A., and Judson, B. A., Efficacy and side effects of three widely different methadone doses. *In* "Proceedings of the Fifth National Conference on Methadone Treatment," pp. 21–44. National Association for the Prevention of Addiction to Narcotics, New York, 1973.

168. Nelkin, D., "Methadone Maintenance: A Technological Fix," p. 128. Braziller, New York, 1973.
169. Danaceau, P., "Methadone Maintenance: The Experience of Four Programs," p. 60. Drug Abuse Council, Washington, D.C., 1973.
170. Goldstein, A., Hansteen, R. W., Horns, W. H., and Rado, M., Control of methadone dosage by patients. *In* "Developments in the Field of Drug Abuse" (E. Senay, V. Shorty, and H. Alksne, eds.), pp. 373–381. Schenkman, Cambridge, Massachusetts, 1975.
171. Department of Health, Education and Welfare, Listing of methadone with special requirements for use. *Fed. Regis.* **37**(242), Sect. 130.44 (d) (6) (c) (1), p. 26798 (1972).
172. Cohen, S., Methadone maintenance: A decade later. *J. Drug Issues* **4,** 327–331 (1974).
173. Department of Health, Education and Welfare, Listing of methadone with special requirements for use. *Fed. Regist.* **38**(90), 12211 (1973).
174. Department of Health, Education and Welfare, Listing of methadone with special requirements for use. *Fed. Regist.* **37**(242), 26791 (1972).
175. Department of Health, Education and Welfare, Listing of methadone with special requirements for use. *Fed. Regist.* **38**(90), 12211 (1973).
176. National Clearinghouse for Drug Abuse Information, "Special Bibliographies," No. 3, p. 5. Natl. Inst. Drug Abuse, Rockville, Maryland, 1975.
177. Bourne, P. G., "Methadone—Benefits and Shortcomings," p. 3. Drug Abuse Council, Washington, D.C., 1975.
178. DeLong, J. V., Treatment and rehabilitation. *In* "Dealing with Drug Abuse—A Report to the Ford Foundation," pp. 181 and 183. Praeger, New York, 1972.
179. Burt, M. R., and Pines, S., "Evaluation of the District of Columbia's Narcotic Treatment Administration Program, 1970–1973." Burt Associates; Bethesda, Maryland, 1975.
180. Hunt, G. H., and Odoroff, M. E., Followup study of narcotic drug addicts after hospitalization. *Public Health Rep.* **77,** 41–54 (1962).
181. Gay, G. R., Metzger, A. D., Bathurst, W., and Smith, D. E., Short-term detoxification on an outpatient basis. *Int. J. Addict.* **6,** 241–264 (1971).
182. Trussell, R. E., Drug abuse treatment programs. *Hospitals* **45,** 47–48 (1971).
183. Gudeman, J. E., Shader, R. F., and Hemenway, T. S., Methadone withdrawal in the treatment of heroin addiction. *Dis. Nerv. Syst.* **33,** 297–303 (1972).
184. Canada, A. T., Methadone in a thirty-day detoxification program for narcotic addicts: A critical review. *Int. J. Addict.* **7,** 613–617 (1972).
185. Moffett, A. D., Soloway, I. H., and Glick, M. X., Post-treatment behavior following ambulatory detoxification. *In* "Methadone—Experience and Issues" (C. D. Chambers and L. Brill, eds.), pp. 215–227. Behavioral Publications, New York, 1973.
186. Silsby, H., and Tennant, F. S., Short-term, ambulatory detoxification of opiate addicts using methadone. *Int. J. Addict.* **9,** 167–170 (1974).
187. Tennant, F. S., Russell, B. A., Casas, S. K., and Bleich, R. N., Heroin detoxification—a comparison of propoxyphene and methadone. *J. Am. Med. Assoc.* **232,** 1019–1022 (1975).
188. Wilson, B. K., Elms, R. R., and Thomson, C. P., Low-dosage use of methadone in expanded detoxification: An experimental comparison. *Arch. Gen. Psychiatry* **31,** 233–236 (1974).
189. Wilson, B. K., Elms, R. R., and Thomson, C. P., Outpatient versus hospital methadone detoxification. *Int. J. Addict.* **10,** 13–21 (1975).
190. Jonas, S., O'Dwyer, E., Zendel, J., and Sidel, V., Ambulatory heroin detoxification in a municipal hospital. *N.Y. State J. Med.* **72,** 2099–2105 (1972).
191. Isbell, H., and Vogel, V. H., The addiction liability of methadone and its uses in the treatment of the morphine abstinence syndrome. *Am. J. Psychiatry* **105,** 909–914 (1948–1949).

192. Newman, R. G., and Kagen, J. G., The New York City methadone maintenance treatment program after two years—an overview. *In* "Proceedings of the Fifth National Conference on Methadone Treatment," pp. 794–801. National Association for the Prevention of Addiction to Narcotics, New York, 1973.
193. Leslie, A. "A Benefit/Cost Analysis of New York City's Heroin Addiction Problems and Programs," Appendix A, p. 25. Office of Program Analysis, New York City Health Services Administration; 1971 (unpublished).
194. Chase, G., Memo to Mayor John Lindsay, March 12, 1971.
195. Richman, A., Utilization and review of methadone patient data. *In* "Proceedings of the Third National Conference on Methadone Treatment," pp. 22–27. National Association for the Prevention of Addiction to Narcotics, New York, 1971.
196. New York City Addiction Service Agency, Application to the Office of Economic Opportunity, Grant No. 2808, p. II-1 (1971).
197. New York City Addiction Services Agency, "Comprehensive Plan for the Control of Drug Abuse and Addiction," p. 4. 1971.
198. New York City Department of Health, "Ambulatory Detoxification Program Policy and Procedures Manual," p. 1. New York City Department of Health, New York, 1972 (unpublished).
199. Chatham, L., Letter to Commissioner Graham Finney, January 5, 1972.
200. Jonas, S. O'Dwyer, E., Zendel, J., and Sidel, V., Ambulatory heroin detoxification in a municipal hospital. *N.Y. State J. Med.* **72,** 2099–2105 (1972).
201. Department of Health, Education and Welfare, Listing of methadone with special requirements for use. *Fed. Regist.* **37**(242), Sect. 130.44 (d) (3) (ii), p. 26797 (1972).
202. New York City Health Code, Sect. 11.07, as amended April 10, 1973.
203. Kaveler, F., Densen, P. M., and Krug, B. C., The narcotics register project: Early Development. *Br. J. Addict.* **63,** 75–81 (1968).
204. Newman, R. G., and Cates, M. S., The New York City Narcotics Register: A case study. *Am. J. Public Health* **64,** suppl., 24–28 (1974).
205. Newman, R. G., Cates, M. S., Tytun, A., and Werbell, B., Narcotic addiction in New York City: Trends from 1968 to Mid-1973. *Am. J. Drug Alc. Abuse* **1,** 53–66 (1974).
206. Drug Abuse Council, "Survey of City/County Drug Abuse Activities," Publ. MS-8, p. 7. Drug Abuse Council, Washington, D.C., 1973.
207. Newman, R. G., Cates, M. S., Tytun, A., and Werbell, B., Narcotic addiction in New York City: Trends from 1968 to mid-1973. *Am. J. Drug Alc. Abuse* **1,** 53–66 (1974).
208. Department of Health, Education and Welfare, Listing of methadone with special requirements for use. *Fed. Regist.* **37**(242), 26798 (1972).
209. Renault, P. F., Methadone maintenance: The effect of knowledge of dosage. *Int. J. Addict.* **8,** 41–47 (1973).
210. Goldstein, A., Hansteen, R., Horns, W. H., and Rado, M., Control of methadone dosage by patients. *In* "Developments in the Field of Drug Abuse" (E. Senay, V. Shorty, and H. Alksne, eds.), pp. 373–381. Schenkman, Cambridge, Massachusetts, 1975.
211. Wikler, A., A psychodynamic study of a patient during experimental self-regulated readdiction to morphine. *Psychiatr. Q.* **26,** 270–293 (1952).
212. Aldrich, C. K., Experimental self-regulated readdiction to morphine. *Int. J. Addict.* **4,** 461–470 (1969).
213. Goldstein, A., Hansteen, R., Horns, W. H., and Rado, M., Control of methadone dosage by patients. *In* "Developments in the Field of Drug Abuse" (E. Senay, V. Shorty, and H. Alksne, eds.), p. 380. Schenkman, Cambridge, Massachusetts, 1975.
214. Gearing, F. R., Successes and failures in methadone maintenance treatment of heroin addiction in New York City. *In* "Proceedings of the Third National Conference on

Methadone Treatment," pp. 2–16. National Association for the Prevention of Addiction to Narcotics, New York, 1970.

215. Gearing, F. R., A road back from heroin addiction. *In* "Proceedings of the Fourth National Conference on Methadone Treatment," pp. 157–158. National Association for the Prevention of Addiction to Narcotics, New York, 1972.
216. Cutler, S. J., and Ederer, F., Maximum utilization of the life table method in analyzing survival. *J. Chronic Dis.* **8,** 699–712 (1958).
217. Greenwood, M., "The Errors of Sampling of the Survivorship Tables," Reports on Public Health and Medical Subjects, No. 33, Appendix I. Stationery Office, London, 1926.
218. Cushman, P., Arrests before and during methadone maintenance: Analysis of New York City police records. *In* "Proceedings of the Fourth National Conference on Methadone Treatment," pp. 487–488. National Association for the Prevention of Addiction to Narcotics, New York, 1972.
219. DeLong, G., Holland, S., and Rosenthal, M. S., Phoenix House—criminal activity of dropouts. *J. Am. Med. Assoc.* **222,** 687–689 (1972).
220. Gearing, F. R., A road back from heroin addiction. *In* "Procedures of the Fourth National Conference on Methadone Treatment," pp. 157–158. National Association for the Prevention of Addiction to Narcotics, New York. 1972.
221. Gearing, F. R., "Methadone Maintenance Treatment Program Report for 1973—The Year of Change," mimeo. Columbia University School of Public Health, New York, 1974.
222. Johnson, B., Corman, A. G., Khantzian, E. J., and Long, J., Clinical experiences with methadone maintenance in young adults. *In* "Proceedings of the Fifth National Conference on Methadone Treatment," pp. 601–609. National Association for the Prevention of Addiction to Narcotics, New York, 1973.
223. Newman, R. G., Bashkow, S., and Cates, M., Arrest histories before and after admission to a methadone maintenance treatment program. *Contemp. Drug Probl., pp. 417*–430 (1973).
224. Perkins, M. E., and Bloch, H. I., Survey of a methadone maintenance treatment program. *Am. J. Psychiatry* **126,** 1389–1396 (1970).
225. Bourne, P. G., "Methadone—Benefits and Shortcomings," p. 6. Drug Abuse Council, Washington, D.C., 1975.
226. World Health Organization, *W.H.O., Tech. Rep. Ser.* **407** (1969).
227. Methadone Maintenance Evaluation Committee, Progress report of evaluation of the methadone maintenance treatment program. *J. Am. Med. Assoc.* **206,** 2712–2714 (1968).
228. Joe, G. W., and Simpson, D. D., "Retention in Treatment of Drug Users Admitted to Treatment During 1971–1972," Rep. 74-15, p. 4. Texas Christian University Institute of Behavioral Research, Fort Worth, Texas, 1974.
229. Chambers, C. D., Babst, D. V., and Warner, A., Characteristics of patient retention and attrition. *In* "Methadone: Experiences and Issues" (C. D. Chambers, and L. Brill, eds.), pp. 109–119. Behavioral Publications, New York, 1973.
230. Bourne, P. G., "Methadone—Benefits and Shortcomings," p. 5. Drug Abuse Council, Washington, D.C., 1975.
231. Adams, R. G., Bloom, W. A., Capel, W. C., and Stewart, G. T., Heroin addicts on methadone replacement: A study of dropouts. *Int. J. Addict.* **6,** 269–277 (1971).
232. Babst, D. V., Chambers, C. D., and Warner, A., Patient characteristics associated with retention in a methadone maintenance program. *Br. J. Addict.* **66,** 195–204 (1971).
233. Gearing, F. R., Successes and failures in methadone maintenance treatment of heroin addiction in New York City. *In* "Proceedings of the Third National Conference on Methadone Treatment," pp. 2–16. National Association for the Prevention of Addiction to Narcotics, New York, 1970.

234. Quatrone, D., Profile of active and terminated patients in a methadone maintenance program. *In* "Proceedings of the Fifth National Conference on Methadone Treatment," pp. 760–766. National Association for the Prevention of Addiction to Narcotics, New York, 1973.
235. Rosenberg, O. M., and Patch, V. D., Methadone use in adolescent heroin addicts. *J. Am. Med. Assoc.* **220,** 991–993 (1972).
236. Sells, S. B., Person, P., and Joe, G. W., Comparison of behavioral indices of methadone maintenance patients who remain in treatment with those of patients who drop out early. *In* "Proceedings of the Fourth National Conference on Methadone Treatment," pp. 221–223. National Association for the Prevention of Addiction to Narcotics, New York, 1973.
237. Williams, H. R., and Johnston, W. E., Factors related to treatment retention in a methadone maintenance program. *In* "Proceedings of the Fourth National Conference on Methadone Treatment," pp. 439–442. National Association for the Prevention of Addiction to Narcotics, New York, 1973.
238. Bourne, P. G., "Methadone—Benefits and Shortcomings," pp. 3–4. Drug Abuse Council Washington, D.C., 1975.
239. Kreek, M. J., Pharmacological modalities of therapy: Methadone maintenance and the use of narcotic antagonists. *In* "Heroin Dependency" (B. Stimmel, ed.), p. 252. Stratton Intercontinental, New York, 1975.
240. Kaveler, F., Densen, P. M., and Krug, B. C., The narcotics register project: Early development. *Br. J. Addict.* **63,** 75–81 (1968).
241. Newman, R. G., and Cates, M. S., The New York City Narcotics Register: A case study. *Am. J. Public Health* **64,** Suppl., 24–28 (1974).
242. Newman, R. G., Cates, M. S., Tytun, A., and Werbell, B., Narcotic addiction in New York City: Trends from 1968 to Mid-1973. *Am. J. Drug Alc. Abuse* **1,** 53–66 (1974).
243. Maddux, J. F., and Bowden, C. L., Critique of success with methadone maintenance. *Am. J. Psychiatry* **129,** 440–446 (1972).
244. Lukoff, I. F., and Quatrone, D., "Heroin Use and Crime in a Methadone Maintenance treatment Program: A Two-year Followup of the Addiction Research and Treatment Corporation Program," p. 17. Columbia University, New York, 1973 (unpublished report).
245. Ellis, R., and Stephens, R. C., "The Arrest History of Narcotic Addicts Prior to Admission: A Methodological Note," p. 11. New York State Drug Abuse Control Commission, New York, 1976 (unpublished report).
246. Newman, R. G., Bashkow, S., and Cates, M. S., Arrest histories before and after admission to a methadone maintenance treatment program. *Contemp. Drug Probl.* **2,** 417–430 (1973).

Index

I

L

M

N

P

R

A B 7 C 8 D 9 E 0 F 1 G 2 H 3 I 4 J 5